Hibernate Recipes:

A Problem-Solution Approach

SRINIVAS GURUZU
GARY MAK

Apress®

Hibernate Recipes: A Problem-Solution Approach

ISBN-13 (pbk): 978-1-4302-2796-0

ISBN-13 (electronic): 978-1-4302-2797-7

Printed and bound in the United States of America 9 8 7 6 5 4 3 2 1

President and Publisher: Paul Manning
Lead Editor: Steve Anglin
Technical Reviewer: Sumit Pal and Dionysios G. Synodinos
Editorial Board: Clay Andres, Steve Anglin, Mark Beckner, Ewan Buckingham, Gary Cornell, Jonathan Gennick, Jonathan Hassell, Michelle Lowman, Matthew Moodie, Duncan Parkes, Jeffrey Pepper, Frank Pohlmann, Douglas Pundick, Ben Renow-Clarke, Dominic Shakeshaft, Matt Wade, Tom Welsh
Coordinating Editor: Anita Castro
Copy Editor: Tiffany Taylor
Compositor: Kimberly Burton
Indexer: BIM Indexing & Proofreading Services
Artist: April Milne
Cover Designer: Anna Ishchenko

Distributed to the book trade worldwide by Springer Science+Business Media, LLC., 233 Spring Street, 6th Floor, New York, NY 10013. Phone 1-800-SPRINGER, fax (201) 348-4505, e-mail orders-ny@springer-sbm.com, or visit www.springeronline.com.

For information on translations, please e-mail rights@apress.com, or visit www.apress.com.

Apress and friends of ED books may be purchased in bulk for academic, corporate, or promotional use. eBook versions and licenses are also available for most titles. For more information, reference our Special Bulk Sales–eBook Licensing web page at www.apress.com/info/bulksales.

The source code for this book is available to readers at www.apress.com. You will need to answer questions pertaining to this book in order to successfully download the code.

To my lovely wife, Usha

— Srinivas Guruzu

Contents at a Glance

About the Authors...xix

About the Technical Reviewer xx

Acknowledgements xxi

Chapter 1: Starting with Hibernate..1

Chapter 2: Basic Mapping and Object Identity 33

Chapter 3: Component Mapping 49

Chapter 4: Inheritance and Custom Mapping 69

Chapter 5: Many-to-One and One-to-One Mapping 95

Chapter 6: Collection Mapping 115

Chapter 7: Many-Valued Associations..137

Chapter 8: HQL and JPA Query Language...155

Chapter 9: Querying with Criteria and Example 167

Chapter 10: Working with Objects..179

Chapter 11: Batch Processing and Native SQL.....................................193

Chapter 12: Cashing in Hibernate..203

Chapter 13: Transactions and Concurrency 219

Chapter 14: Web Applications 237

 Index..265

Contents

■About the Authors.. xix

■About the Technical Reviewer xx

■Acknowledgements xxi

■Chapter 1: Starting with Hibernate.................................... 1

1.1 Setting Up Hibernate..3

    Problem 3

    Solution 3

    How It Works 4

        Installing the JDK 4

        Installing the Eclipse Web Tools Platform (WTP)..5

        Installing Derby 5

1.2 Programming with Basic JDBC...7

    Problem 7

    Solution 7

    How It Works 7

        Creating an Eclipse Project 7

        JDBC Initialization and Cleanup 8

        Using JDBC to Query a Database 8

        Using JDBC to Update a Database 8

        Creating the Domain Model..9

        Retrieving Object Graphs...10

        Persisting Object Graphs...11

        Problems with Using JDBC..12

1.3 Configuring Hibernate...12

Problem 12

Solution 12

How It Works 12

    Getting the Required Jars 13

    Creating Mapping Definitions 13

    Configuration 14

    Programmatic Configuration 14

    XML Configuration 15

    Opening and Closing Sessions 16

    Retrieving Objects 16

1.4 Configuring a JPA Project 17

Problem 17

Solution 17

How It Works 17

    Opening a Session 22

1.5 Using Entity Manager 23

Problem 23

Solution 23

How It Works 23

1.6 Enabling Logging in Hibernate 27

Problem 27

Solution 27

How It Works 28

    Inspecting the SQL Statements Issued by Hibernate 28

    Configuring Log4j 28

    Enabling Live Statistics 28

1.7 Generating a Database Schema Using Hibernate 29

Problem 29

Solution 29

How It Works 29

Creating an Ant Build File..29

Generating Database Schema Using SchemaExport...30

Updating a Database Schema Using SchemaUpdate..30

Specifying the Details of a Database Schema 30

Summary 31

Chapter 2: Basic Mapping and Object Identity 33

2.1 Providing an ID for Persistence 33

Problem 33

Solution 33

How It Works 33

2.2 Creating a Composite Key in Hibernate 38

Problem 38

Solution 39

How It Works 39

2.3 SaveOrUpdate in Hibernate 42

Problem 42

Solution 42

How It Works 43

2.4 Dynamic SQL Generation in Hibernate... 43

Problem 43

Solution 44

How It Works 44

2.5 Naming Entities in Hibernate.. 45

Problem 45

Solution 45

How It Works 46

Summary 48

Chapter 3: Component Mapping 49

3.1 Implementing a Value Type as a Component... 49

Problem 49

Solution 49

How It Works 49

Using JPA Annotations 52

3.2 Nesting Components 55

Problem 55

Solution 55

How It Works 56

3.3 Adding References in Components 58

Problem 58

Solution 58

How It Works 58

3.4 Mapping a Collection of Components 61

Problem 61

Solution 61

How It Works 61

3.5 Using Components as Keys to a Map 66

Problem 66

Solution 66

How It Works 66

Summary 67

■Chapter 4: Inheritance and Custom Mapping 69

4.1 Mapping Entities with Table per Class Hierarchy 70

Problem 70

Solution 70

How It Works 72

4.2 Mapping Entities with Table per Subclass 74

Problem 74

Solution 75

How It Works 75

4.3 Mapping Entities with Table per Concrete Class 78

Problem 78

Solution 78

How It Works 78

4.4 Custom Mappings 81

Problem 81

Solution 81

How It Works 81

4.5 CompositeUserType Mappings 87

Problem 87

Solution 87

How It Works 87

Summary 93

■Chapter 5: Many-to-One and One-to-One Mapping 95

5.1 Using Many-To-One Associations 95

Problem 95

Solution 96

How It Works 96

5.2 Using a Many-to-One Association with a Join Table 99

Problem 99

Solution 100

How It Works 100

5.3 Using Lazy Initialization on Many-to-One Associations 102

Problem 102

Solution 102

How It Works 103

5.4 Sharing Primary Key Associations 104

Problem 104

Solution 104

How It Works 104

5.5 Creating a One-to-One Association Using a Foreign Key 107

Problem 107

Solution 107

How It Works 107

5.6 Creating a One-to-One Association Using a Join Table 109

Problem 109

Solution 109

How It Works 109

Summary 113

■Chapter 6: Collection Mapping 115

6.1 Mapping a Set 115

Problem 115

Solution 115

How It Works 116

6.2 Mapping a Bag 118

Problem 118

Solution 118

How It Works 118

6.3 Mapping a List 122

Problem 122

Solution 122

How It Works 122

6.4 Mapping an Array 124

Problem 124

Solution 124

How It Works 124

6.5 Mapping a Map 126

Problem 126

Solution 126

How It Works 126

6.6 Sorting Collections 128

Problem 128

Solution 128

How It Works 129

Using the Natural Order 129

Writing Your Own Comparator 130

Sorting in the Database 132

6.6 Using Lazy Initialization 133

Problem 133

Solution 133

How It Works 134

Summary 135

Chapter 7: Many-Valued Associations 137

7.1 Mapping a One-to-Many Association with a Foreign Key 137

Problem 137

Solution 137

How It Works 138

7.2 Mapping a One-to-Many Bidirectional Association Using a Foreign Key 142

Problem 142

Solution 142

How It Works 143

7.3 Mapping a One-to-Many Bidirectional Association Using a Join Table 145

Problem 145

Solution 145

How It Works 145

7.4 Mapping a Many-to-Many Unidirectional Association with a Join Table 148

Problem 148

Solution 149

How It Works 149

7.5 Creating a Many-to-Many Bidirectional Association with a Join Table 150

Problem 150

Solution 150

How It Works 151

Summary 153

■Chapter 8: HQL and JPA Query Language 155

8.1 Using the Query Object 155

Problem 155

Solution 155

How It Works 156

Creating a Query Object 156

The from Clause 156

The where Clause 157

Pagination 157

Parameter Binding 158

Named Queries 160

8.2 Using the Select Clause 161

Problem 161

Solution 161

How It Works 161

8.3 Joining 163

Problem 163

Solution 163

How It Works 163

    Explicit Joins 163

    Implicit Joins 164

    Outer Joins 164

    Matching Text 164

    Fetching Associations 165

8.4 Creating Report Queries 165

Problem 165

Solution 165

How It Works 165

    Projection with Aggregation Functions 165

    Grouping Aggregated Results 166

Summary 166

■Chapter 9: Querying with Criteria and Example 167

9.1 Using Criteria 168

Problem 168

Solution 168

How It Works 168

9.2 Using Restrictions 169

Problem 169

Solution 169

How It Works 169

    Writing Subqueries 171

9.3 Using Criteria in Associations 172

Problem 172

Solution 172

How It Works 172

9.4 Using Projections 174

Problem 174

Solution 174

How It Works 174

    Aggregate Functions and Groupings with Projections 175

9.5 Querying by Example 176

Problem 176

Solution 176

How It Works 176

Summary 177

■ Chapter 10: Working with Objects 179

10.1 Identifying Persistent Object States 179

Problem 179

Solution 179

How It Works 179

    Transient Objects 179

    Persistent Objects 180

    Detached Objects 180

    Removed Objects 181

10.2 Working with Persistent Objects 182

Problem 182

Solution 182

How It Works 182

    Creating a Persistent Object 182

    Retrieving a Persistent Object 184

    Modifying a Persistent Object 185

    Deleting a Persistent Object 185

10.3 Persisting Detached Objects 186

Problem 186

Solution 186

How It Works 186

Reattaching a Detached Object 186

Merging a Detached Object 186

10.4 Using Data Filters 187

Problem 187

Solution 187

How It Works 188

10.5 Using Interceptors 190

Problem 190

Solution 190

How It Works 190

Summary 192

■Chapter 11: Batch Processing and Native SQL 193

11.1 Performing Batch Inserts 194

Problem 194

Solution 194

How It Works 194

11.2 Performing Batch Updates and Deletes 195

Problem 195

Solution 195

How It Works 195

11.3 Using Native SQL 197

Problem 197

Solution 197

How It Works 198

11.4 Using Named SQL Queries 199

Problem 199

Solution 199

How It Works 199

Summary 201

■**Chapter 12: Cashing in Hibernate** **203**

Using the Second-Level Cache in Hibernate...204

Concurrency Strategies 205

Cache Providers...205

What Are Cache Regions?..207

Caching Query Results...207

12.1 Using the First-Level Cache..207

    Problem 207

    Solution 208

    How It Works 208

12.2 Configuring the Second-Level Cache..209

    Problem 209

    Solution 209

    How It Works 209

12.3 Caching Associations..212

    Problem 212

    Solution 212

    How It Works 212

12.4 Caching Collections 213

    Problem 213

    Solution 213

    How It Works 213

12.5 Caching Queries..215

    Problem 215

    Solution 215

    How It Works 215

Summary 217

■**Chapter 13: Transactions and Concurrency** **219**

13.1 Using Programmatic Transactions in a Standalone Java Application 220

Problem 220

Solution 220

How It Works 221

13.2 Using Programmatic Transactions with JTA 223

Problem 223

Solution 223

How It Works 224

13.3 Enabling Optimistic Concurrency Control 228

Problem 228

Solution 228

How It Works 231

13.4 Using Pessimistic Concurrency Control 234

Problem 234

Solution 234

How It Works 234

Summary 236

■**Chapter 14: Web Applications** **237**

14.1 Creating a Controller for the Bookshop Web Application 238

Problem 238

Solution 238

How It Works 238

Creating a Dynamic Web Project 238

Configuring the Connection Pool 241

Developing an Online Bookshop 242

Creating a Global Session Factory 242

Listing Persistent Objects 242

Updating Persistent Objects 244

Creating Persistent Objects..249

Deleting Persistent Objects...252

14.2 Creating a Data-Access Layer 254

Problem 254

Solution 254

How It Works 255

Organizing Data Access in Data-Access Objects 255

Using Generic Data-Access Objects...257

Using a Factory to Centralize DAO Retrieval 259

Navigating Lazy Associations...261

Using the Open Session in View Pattern 262

Summary 264

■ Index..265

About the Authors

 **Srinivas Guruzu** is a Developer who has been coding for more than 8 years. After completing his MS in Mechanical Engineering, Srinivas worked on high traffic payment systems in the banking domain. He also has experience working in the insurance domain. Lately, he's been working with Spring and Hibernate building applications that integrate with other products as a part of large customer enrollment and file transmission system.

 **Gary Mak**, founder and chief consultant of Meta-Archit Software Technology Limited, has been a technical architect and application developer on the enterprise Java platform for over seven years. He is the author of the Apress books Spring Recipes: A Problem-Solution Approach and Pro SpringSource dm Server. In his career, Gary has developed a number of Java-based software projects, most of which are application frameworks, system infrastructures, and software tools. He enjoys designing and implementing the complex parts of software projects. Gary has a master's degree in computer science. His research interests include object-oriented technology, aspect-oriented technology, design patterns, software reuse, and domain-driven development.

Gary specializes in building enterprise applications on technologies including Spring, Hibernate, JPA, JSF, Portlet, AJAX, and OSGi. He has been using the Spring Framework in his projects for five years, since Spring version 1.0. Gary has been an instructor of courses on enterprise Java, Spring, Hibernate, Web Services, and agile development. He has written a series of Spring and Hibernate tutorials as course materials, parts of which are open to the public, and they're gaining popularity in the Java community. In his spare time, he enjoys playing tennis and watching tennis competitions.

About the Technical Reviewer

■ Sumit Pal has about 16 years of experience with Software Architecture, Design & Development on a variety of platforms including Java, J2EE. Sumit has worked in SQLServer Replication group, while with Microsoft for 2 years & with Oracle's OLAP Server group, while with Oracle for 7 years.

Apart from Certifications like IEEE-CSDP and J2EE Architect, Sumit also has an MS in Computer Science from the Asian Institute of Technology, Thailand.

Sumit has keen interest in Database Internals, Algorithms and Search Engine Technology Data Mining and Machine Learning. He has invented both basic generalized algorithms to find divisibility between numbers, as well as divisibility rules for prime numbers less than 100.

Sumit loves badminton and swimming, is an amateur astrophysicist, and is inculcating green habits into his daily life.

Sumit works as the Architect at Leapfrogrx.com

Acknowledgments

Would I do it again? Writing a book, I mean. Of course, Yes! However, anyone who believes a book project is a simple effort does not have any idea what goes into it. It takes a lot of commitment, focus, and support from family and friends.

Josh Long, thank you, thank you, thank you very much for introducing me to Apress; for believing in me and guiding me through everything that a new author like me needed to know. Gary Mak, thank you, for trusting me and letting me be a co-author for this book. Thank you, Apress and Steve Anglin for giving me the opportunity to write this book and trusting Josh Long's instincts. Tom Welsh, Sumit Pal, and Dionysios G. Synodinos, thank you, for reviewing and providing excellent suggestions. Being a first time author, the suggestions provided were of immense help in developing the book. Anita Castro answered the book and non-book related questions very patiently. Tiffany Taylor helped with grammer, spelling and consistency throughout the book. I am very grateful for support and help provided by the Apress team.

To my lovely wife, Usha, without whom I would not have been able to complete this book.

Srinivas Guruzu
Scottsdale, AZ

CHAPTER 1

■ ■ ■

Starting with Hibernate

An *object model* uses the principles of abstraction, encapsulation, modularity, hierarchy, typing, concurrency, polymorphism, and persistence. The object model enables you to create well-structured, complex systems. In an object model system, *objects* are the components of the system. Objects are instances of classes, and classes are related to other classes via inheritance relationships. An object has an identity, a state, and behavior. An object model helps you create reusable application frameworks and systems that can evolve over time. In addition, object-oriented systems are usually smaller than non-object-oriented implementations.

A *relational model* defines the structure of data, data manipulation, and data integrity. Data is organized in the form of tables, and different tables are associated by means of referential integrity (a foreign key). Integrity constraints such as a primary key, unique check constraints, and not null are used to maintain an entity's integrity in the relational model.

A relational data model isn't focused on supporting entity-type inheritance: entity-based polymorphic association from an object model can't be translated into similar entities in a relational model. In an object model, you use the state of the model to define equality between objects. But in a relational model, you use an entity's primary key to define equality of entities. Object references are used to associate different objects in an object model, whereas a foreign key is used to establish associations in a relational model. Object references in the object model facilitate easier navigation through the object graph.

Because these two models are distinctly different, you need a way to persist object entities (Java objects) into a relational database. Figures 1-1 and 1-2 provide a simple representation of the object model and the relational model.

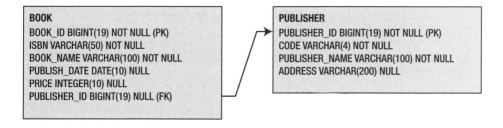

Figure 1-1. Entity-relationship (ER) diagram of Book and Publisher

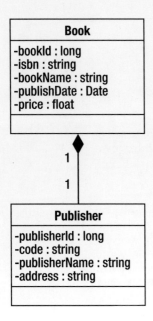

Figure 1-2. *Class diagram of Book and Publisher*

Object/relational mapping (ORM) frameworks help you take advantage of the features present in the object model (like Java) and the relational model (like database management systems [DBMS]). With the help of ORM frameworks, you can persist objects in Java to relational tables using metadata that describes the mapping between the objects and the database. The metadata shields the complexity of dealing directly with SQL and helps you develop solutions in terms of business objects.

An ORM solution can be implemented at various levels:

- *Pure relational:* An application is designed around the relational model.

- *Light object mapping:* Entities are represented as classes and are mapped manually to relational tables.

- *Medium object mapping:* An application is designed using an object model, and SQL is generated during build time using code-generation utilities.

- *Full object mapping:* This mapping supports sophisticated object modeling including composition, inheritance, polymorphism, and persistence by reachability.

The following are the benefits of using an ORM framework:

- *Productivity:* Because you use metadata to persist and query data, development time decreases and productivity increases.

- *Prototyping:* Using an ORM framework is extremely useful for quick prototyping.

- *Maintainability:* Because much of the work is done through configuration, your code has fewer lines and thus requires less maintenance.

- *Vendor independence:* An ORM abstracts an application from the underlying SQL database and SQL dialect. This gives you the portability to support multiple databases.

ORM frameworks also have some disadvantages:

- *Learning curve:* You may experience a steep learning curve as you learn how to map and, possibly, learn a new query language.

- *Overhead:* For simple applications that use a single database and data without many business requirements for complex querying, an ORM framework can be extra overhead.

- *Slower performance:* For large batch updates, performance is slower.

Hibernate is one of the most widely used ORM frameworks in the industry. It provides all the benefits of an ORM solution and implements the Java Persistence API (JPA) defined in the Enterprise JavaBeans (EJB) 3.0 specification.

Its main components are as follows:

- *Hibernate Core:* The Core generates SQL and relieves you from manually handling Java Database Connectivity (JDBC) result sets and object conversions. Metadata is defined in simple XML files. The Core offers various options for writing queries: plain SQL; Hibernate Query Language (HQL), which is specific to Hibernate; programmatic criteria, or Query by Example (QBE). It can optimize object loading with various fetching and caching options.

- *Hibernate Annotations:* With the introduction of Annotations in JDK 5.0, Hibernate provides the option of defining metadata using annotations. This reduces configuration using XML files and makes it simple to define required metadata directly in the Java source code.

- *Hibernate EntityManager:* The JPA specification defines programming interfaces, lifecycle rules for persistent objects, and query features. The Hibernate implementation for this part of the JPA is available as Hibernate EntityManager.

This book provides solutions using Hibernate Core and Annotations for each problem. The Hibernate version used is 3.3.2.

1.1 Setting Up Hibernate

Problem

What tools and libraries are required to set up Hibernate and get started?

Solution

You need JDK 1.5+, an IDE such as Eclipse, a database (this book uses Apache Derby), and SQL Squirrel to provide a GUI to use the database. You can also use Maven to configure your project. Maven is a software project-management and comprehension tool. Based on the concept of a project object model

3

(POM), Maven can manage a project's build, reporting, and documentation from a central piece of information. In Maven, the POM.XML is the central piece where all the information is stored.

The following libraries are required for the Hibernate 3.3.2 setup:

- `Hibernate3.jar`
- `Hibernate-commons-annotations.jar`
- `Hibernate-annotations.jar`
- `Hibernate-entitymanager.jar`
- `Antlr-2.7.6.jar`
- `Commons-collections-3.1.jar`
- `Dom4j-1.6.1.jar`
- `Javassist-3.9.0.GA.jar`
- `Jta-1.1.jar`
- `Slf4j-api-1.5.8.jar`
- `Ejb3-persistence.jar`
- `Slf4j-simple1.5.8.jar`

The following are required for the Derby setup :

- `Derby.jar`
- `Derbyclient.jar`
- `Derbynet.jar`
- `Derbytools.`

How It Works

The next few sections describe how to set up each of the required tools and then provide the solution to the problem. All the solutions are provided on a Windows platform. They can also be implemented on UNIX, provided you install and download the libraries and executables specific to the UNIX platform wherever applicable.

Installing the JDK

The JDK is an essential toolkit provided for Java application development. You can go to `http://java.sun.com/j2se/1.5.0/download.jsp` to download JDK 5.0. Install it into a folder such as `C:\jdk1.5.0`.

Installing the Eclipse Web Tools Platform (WTP)

Eclipse is an IDE for developing Java applications. The latest version is Galileo. You can install it from the following URL:
www.eclipse.org/downloads/download.php?file=/technology/epp/downloads/release/galileo/SR1/eclipse-jee-galileo-SR1-win32.zip.

Installing Derby

Derby is an open source SQL relational database engine written in Java. You can go to http://db.apache.org/derby/derby_downloads.html and download the latest version. Derby also provides plug-ins for Eclipse. The plug-in gives you the required jar files for development and also provides a command prompt (ij) in Eclipse to execute Data Definition Language (DDL) and Data Manipulation Language (DML) statements.

Creating a Derby Database Instance

To create a new Derby database called BookShopDB at the ij prompt, use the following command:

```
connect 'jdbc:derby://localhost:1527/BookShopDB;create=true;
user=book;password=book';
```

After the database is created, execute the SQL scripts in the next section to create the tables.

Creating the Tables (Relational Model)

These solutions use the example of a bookshop. Books are published by a publisher, and the contents of a book are defined by the chapters. The entities Book, Publisher, and Chapter are stored in the database; you can perform various operations such as reading, updating, and deleting.

Because an ORM is a mapping between an object model and a relational model, you first create the relational model by executing the DDL statements to create the tables/entities in the database. You later see the object model in Java and finally the mapping between the relational and the object models.

Create the tables for the online bookshop using the following SQL statements:

```
CREATE TABLE  PUBLISHER (
      CODE VARCHAR(4) NOT NULL ,
      PUBLISHER_NAME VARCHAR(100) NOT NULL,          ADDRESS VARCHAR(200),  PRIMARY KEY
(CODE)
);


CREATE TABLE  BOOK
   (ISBN VARCHAR(50) NOT NULL,
    BOOK_NAME VARCHAR(100) NOT NULL,
    PUBLISHER_CODE VARCHAR(4),      PUBLISH_DATE DATE,
    PRICE  integer,
    PRIMARY KEY (ISBN),     FOREIGN KEY (PUBLISHER_CODE)
    REFERENCES  PUBLISHER (CODE)
    );
```

```
CREATE TABLE  CHAPTER
  (BOOK_ISBN VARCHAR(50) NOT NULL,
   IDX integer NOT NULL,
   TITLE VARCHAR(100) NOT NULL,
   NUM_OF_PAGES integer,
   PRIMARY KEY (BOOK_ISBN, IDX),
   FOREIGN KEY (BOOK_ISBN)
   REFERENCES  BOOK (ISBN)
);
```

Figure 1-3 shows the entity model for the sample table structure.

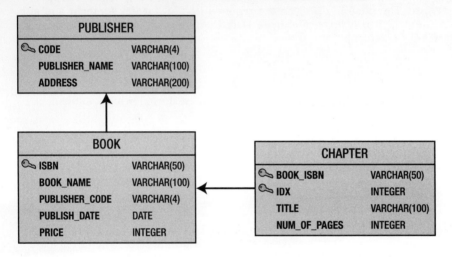

Figure 1-3. *Relational model diagram for the bookshop*

Next, let's input some data for these tables using |the following SQL statements:

```
insert into PUBLISHER(code, publisher_name, address)
values ('001', 'Apress', 'New York ,New York');
insert into PUBLISHER(code, publisher_name, address)
values ('002', 'Manning', 'San Francisco', 'CA')
insert into book(isbn, book_name, publisher_code, publish_date, price)
values ('PBN123', 'Spring Recipes', '001', DATE('2008-02-02'), 30)
insert into book(isbn, book_name, publisher_code, publish_date, price)
values ('PBN456', 'Hibernate Recipes', '002', DATE('2008-11-02'), 40)
```

1.2 Programming with Basic JDBC

Problem

The traditional way to access a relational database is to use Java Database Connectivity (JDBC). Some common problems with using JDBC directly are as follows:

- You must manually handle database connections. There is always the risk that connections aren't closed, which can lead to other problems.

- You have to write a lot of bulky code, because all the fields required for inserts, updates, and queries must be explicitly mentioned.

- You have to manually handle associations. For complex data, this can be a major issue.

- The code isn't portable to other databases.

Solution

This section shows how you perform basic Create, Read, Update, and Delete (CRUD) operations using JDBC and describes the problems with using basic JDBC. You see how the object model is translated into the relational data model.

How It Works

To Start, you will need to create an eclipse project. You will need to install Derby jars and configure

Creating an Eclipse Project

To begin developing your Java application, you create a bookshop project in Eclipse. To set up the Derby database, you can install the core and UI plug-ins or download the Derby jar files and add them to your Eclipse project classpath.

To install the Derby plug-ins for Eclipse, do the following:

1. Download the plug-ins from `http://db.apache.org/derby/releases/release-10.5.3.0.cgi`.

2. Extract the zip files to your Eclipse home. If Eclipse is located at `C:\eclipse`, extract the zips to the same location.

3. Restart Eclipse. You should see the Derby jar files—`derby.jar`, `derbyclient.jar`, `derbynet.jar`, and `derbytools.jar`—added to your project's classpath.

4. Select your project, and right-click. Select Apache Derby, and then select Add Network Server.

5. Click the "Start Derby Network Server" button.

6. After the server starts, select the ij option. The SQL prompt appears in the console window.

7. At the prompt, execute the SQL statements from the previous recipe's "Creating the Tables (Relational Model)" section.

JDBC Initialization and Cleanup

You must load the JDBC driver and create a connection to that database before you can execute any SQL statements. The JDBC driver for Derby is in the derby.jar file that was added to your project's build path during Derby's installation. Be careful: you must remember to close that connection (whether an exception is raised or not). Connections are a costly resource—if they aren't closed after use, the application will run out of them and stop working:

```
Class.forName("org.apache.derby.jdbc.EmbeddedDriver");
Connection connection = DriverManager.getConnection(
"jdbc:derby://localhost:1527/BookShopDB", "book", "book");
try {
// Using the connection to query or update database
} finally {
connection.close();
}
```

Using JDBC to Query a Database

For demonstration purpose, let's query for a book whose ISBN is 1932394419. Here's the JDBC code for this task:

```
PreparedStatement stmt = connection.prepareStatement
("SELECT * FROM BOOK WHERE ISBN = ?");
stmt.setString(1, "1932394419");
ResultSet rs = stmt.executeQuery();
while (rs.next())
{
      System.out.println("ISBN : " + rs.getString("ISBN"));
      System.out.println("Book Name : " + rs.getString("BOOK_NAME"));
      System.out.println("Publisher Code : " +
rs.getString("PUBLISHER_CODE"));
      System.out.println("Publish Date : " +         rs.getDate("PUBLISH_DATE"));
      System.out.println("Price : " + rs.getInt("PRICE"));
      System.out.println();
}
rs.close();
stmt.close();
```

Using JDBC to Update a Database

Let's update the title of the book whose ISBN is 1932394419. Here's the JDBC code:

```
PreparedStatement stmt = connection.prepareStatement(
"UPDATE BOOK SET BOOK_NAME = ? WHERE ISBN = ?");
stmt.setString(1, "Hibernate Quickly 2nd Edition");
stmt.setString(2, "1932394419");
int count = stmt.executeUpdate();
System.out.println("Updated count : " + count);
stmt.close();
```

Creating the Domain Model

You use normal JavaBeans to build your object/domain model. These JavaBeans are called Plain Old Java Objects (POJOs). This term is used to distinguish them from Enterprise JavaBeans (EJBs). EJBs are Java objects that implement one of the javax.ejb interfaces and that need to be deployed in an EJB container. Note that each of these POJOs must have a no-argument constructor:

```
public class Publisher {
      private String code;
      private String name;
      private String address;
      // Getters and Setters
}
public class Book {
      private String isbn;
      private String name;
      private Publisher publisher;
      private Date publishDate;
      private int price;
      private List chapters;
      // Getters and Setters
}
public class Chapter {
      private int index;
      private String title;
      private int numOfPages;
      // Getters and Setters
}
```

You use a foreign key to reference PUBLISHER from the BOOK table, but it's a many-to-one association represented with a list of chapters in the Book class. You use a foreign key to reference BOOK from the CHAPTER table, but there's nothing referencing the Book class from the Chapter class. In contrast, a Book object has a list of Chapter objects (one-to-many association). This is a case of an *object-relational mismatch*, which focuses on the association between two classes or tables in their corresponding model. To handle the incompatibility of these models, you need to do some conversion/translation when you retrieve and save your object model. This is called object/relational mapping (O/R Mapping or ORM).

Let's say your Bookshop sells audio and video discs. In the object-oriented model, this can be represented by using a Disc superclass and two subclasses called AudioDisc and VideoDisc (see Figure 1-4). On the relational database side, you don't have a way to map this inheritance relationship. This is a major object-relational system mismatch.

You may also want to use a *polymorphic query* that refers to the `Disc` class and have the query return its subclasses. SQL doesn't support this kind of requirement—this is another object-relational system mismatch.

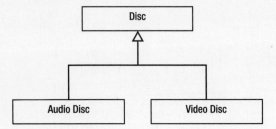

Figure 1-4. Inheritance in the object model

You can see that there are differences between an object model and a relational model. The object model is based on the analysis of the business domain, and therefore this forms the domain model. The relational model or tables are defined based on how the data is organized in rows and columns. ORM frameworks like Hibernate provide strategies to overcome the association mismatch, inheritance mismatch, and the polymorphic mismatch.

Retrieving Object Graphs

Suppose you have a web page in your application that shows a book's details (including ISBN, book name, publisher name, publisher address, publish date, and all the chapters in the book). You can use the following JDBC code fragment to get the result set:

```
PreparedStatement stmt = connection.prepareStatement(
"SELECT * FROM BOOK, PUBLISHER WHERE BOOK.PUBLISHER_CODE = PUBLISHER.CODE
AND BOOK.ISBN = ?");
stmt.setString(1, isbn);
ResultSet rs = stmt.executeQuery();
Book book = new Book();
if (rs.next())
{
      book.setIsbn(rs.getString("ISBN"));
      book.setName(rs.getString("BOOK_NAME"));
      book.setPublishDate(rs.getDate("PUBLISH_DATE"));
      book.setPrice(rs.getInt("PRICE"));

      Publisher publisher = new Publisher();
      publisher.setCode(rs.getString("PUBLISHER_CODE"));
      publisher.setName(rs.getString("PUBLISHER_NAME"));
      publisher.setAddress(rs.getString("ADDRESS"));
      book.setPublisher(publisher);
}
rs.close();
stmt.close();
```

```
List chapters = new ArrayList();
stmt = connection.prepareStatement("SELECT * FROM CHAPTER WHERE BOOK_ISBN = ?");
stmt.setString(1, isbn);
rs = stmt.executeQuery();
while (rs.next()) {
        Chapter chapter = new Chapter();
        chapter.setIndex(rs.getInt("IDX"));
        chapter.setTitle(rs.getString("TITLE"));
        chapter.setNumOfPages(rs.getInt("NUM_OF_PAGES"));
        chapters.add(chapter);
}
book.setChapters(chapters);
rs.close();
stmt.close();
return book;
```

The result set must be iterated through to create **book** and **publisher** objects. To retrieve the chapters, you have to execute another SQL statement based on the book's **ISBN** property. A group of objects with such an association is called an *object graph*.

Persisting Object Graphs

Suppose you want to provide a web page where users can input a book's information, including the publisher and chapters. When the user is finished, the entire object graph is saved to the database:

```
PreparedStatement stmt = connection.prepareStatement(
"INSERT INTO PUBLISHER (CODE, PUBLISHER_NAME, ADDRESS) VALUES (?, ?, ?)");
stmt.setString(1, book.getPublisher().getCode());
stmt.setString(2, book.getPublisher().getName());
stmt.setString(3, book.getPublisher().getAddress());
stmt.executeUpdate();
stmt.close();

stmt = connection.prepareStatement(
"INSERT INTO BOOK (ISBN, BOOK_NAME, PUBLISHER_CODE, PUBLISH_DATE, PRICE)
VALUES (?, ?, ?, ?, ?)");
stmt.setString(1, book.getIsbn());
stmt.setString(2, book.getName());
stmt.setString(3, book.getPublisher().getCode());

stmt.setDate(4, new java.sql.Date(book.getPublishDate().getTime()));
stmt.setInt(5, book.getPrice());
stmt.executeUpdate();
stmt.close();

stmt = connection.prepareStatement(
"INSERT INTO CHAPTER (BOOK_ISBN, IDX, TITLE, NUM_OF_PAGES) VALUES (?, ?, ?, ?)");
for (Iterator iter = book.getChapters().iterator(); iter.hasNext();)
{
        Chapter chapter = (Chapter) iter.next();
```

```
        stmt.setString(1, book.getIsbn());
        stmt.setInt(2, chapter.getIndex());
        stmt.setString(3, chapter.getTitle());
        stmt.setInt(4, chapter.getNumOfPages());
        stmt.executeUpdate();
    }
    stmt.close();
```

Problems with Using JDBC

Using JDBC means you can execute any kind of SQL statements. For a simple task, you have to code many SELECT, INSERT, UPDATE, and DELETE statements repeatedly. This results in the following issues:

- *Too much copy code:* When you perform object retrieval, you need to copy the fields in a ResultSet to the properties of an object. When you perform object persistence, you need to copy the properties of an object to the parameters in PreparedStatement.

- *Manually handled associations:* When you perform object retrieval, you have to perform a table join or read from several tables to get an object graph. When you perform object persistence, you must update several tables accordingly.

- *Database dependent:* The SQL statements you wrote for one database may not work with another brand of database. Although the chance is very small, you may have to migrate to another database.

1.3 Configuring Hibernate

Problem

How do you configure a Java project that uses an object/relational framework like Hibernate as a persistence framework? How do you configure Hibernate programmatically?

Solution

Hibernate is a powerful ORM framework for developing Java applications. You need to import the required jars into your project's classpath and create mapping files that map the state of a Java entity to the columns of its corresponding table. From your Java application, you execute CRUD operations on the object entities. Hibernate takes care of translating the object state from the object model to the relational model.

How It Works

To configure a Java project to use Hibernate framework, you need to start with downloading the required jars and configuring them in the build path.

Getting the Required Jars

You can go to `www.hibernate.org/` and download Hibernate Core 3.3.2. After you download the compressed Hibernate distribution, extract it to a directory such as `C:\hibernate`. In Eclipse, go to Windows ▶ Preferences ▶ Java ▶ Build Path ▶ User Libraries, add a custom library named `Hibernate`, and add the following jars to it:

```
${Hibernate_Install_Dir}/hibernate3.jar
${Hibernate_Install_Dir}/lib/antlr.jar
${Hibernate_Install_Dir}/lib/asm.jar
${Hibernate_Install_Dir}/lib/asm-attrs.jars
${Hibernate_Install_Dir}/lib/cglib.jar
${Hibernate_Install_Dir}/lib/commons-collections.jar
${Hibernate_Install_Dir}/lib/commons-logging.jar
${Hibernate_Install_Dir}/lib/dom4j.jar
${Hibernate_Install_Dir}/lib/ehcache.jar
${Hibernate_Install_Dir}/lib/jta.jar
${Hibernate_Install_Dir}/lib/log4j.jar
```

Defining a custom library this way makes it easy to reuse in another project. If you have another project that uses Hibernate, you can import this user library into that project. Follow these steps to add this user library to a project's build path:

1. Right-click your project in Eclipse.

2. Select BuildPath ▶ Configure Build Path ▶ Libraries tab.

3. Click the Add Library button.

4. Select User Library, and click Next.

5. Select Hibernate, and click Finish.

The custom library is now configured to your project's build path.

Creating Mapping Definitions

First, you ask Hibernate to retrieve and persist the book objects for you. For simplicity, let's ignore the publisher and chapters at this moment. You create an XML file `Book.hbm.xml` in the same package as the `Book` class. This file is called the *mapping definition* for the `Book` class. The `Book` objects are called *persistent objects* or *entities* because they can be persisted in a database and represent the real-world entities:

```xml
<?xml version="1.0" encoding="UTF-8"?>
<!DOCTYPE hibernate-mapping PUBLIC
"-//Hibernate/Hibernate Mapping DTD 3.0//EN"
"http://hibernate.sourceforge.net/hibernate-mapping-3.0.dtd">
<hibernate-mapping package="com.metaarchit.bookshop">
    <class name="Book" table="BOOK">
    <id name="isbn" type="string" column="ISBN" />
    <property name="name" type="string" column="BOOK_NAME" />
    <property name="publishDate" type="date" column="PUBLISH_DATE"/>
```

```
        <property name="price" type="int" column="PRICE" />
      </class>
</hibernate-mapping>
```

Each persistent object must have an identifier. It's used by Hibernate to identify that object uniquely. Here, you use the ISBN as the identifier for a Book object.

Configuration

Before Hibernate can retrieve and persist objects for you, you need to tell it your application's settings. For example, which kind of objects are persistent objects? What kind of database are you using? How do you connect to the database? You can configure Hibernate three ways:

- *Programmatic configuration:* Use the API to load the hbm file, load the database driver, and specify the database connection details.

- *XML configuration:* Specify the database connection details in an XML file that's loaded along with the hbm file. The default file name is hibernate.cfg.xml. You can use another name by specifying the name explicitly.

- *Properties file configuration:* This is similar to the XML configuration but uses a .properties file. The default name is hibernate.properties.

This solution introduces only the first two approaches (programmatic and XML configuration). The properties file configuration is much like XML configuration.

Programmatic Configuration

The following code loads the configuration programmatically. The Configuration class provides the API to load the hbm files, to specify the driver to be used for the database connection, and to provide other connection details:

```
Configuration configuration = new Configuration()
.addResource("com/metaarchit/bookshop/Book.hbm.xml")
.setProperty("hibernate.dialect", "org.hibernate.dialect.DerbyDialect")
.setProperty("hibernate.connection.driver_class", "org.apache.derby.jdbc.EmbeddedDriver")
.setProperty("hibernate.connection.url", "jdbc:derby://localhost:1527/BookShopDB")
.setProperty("hibernate.connection.username", "book")
.setProperty("hibernate.connection.password", "book");
SessionFactory factory = configuration.buildSessionFactory();
```

Instead of using addResource() to add the mapping files, you can also use addClass() to add a persistent class and let Hibernate load the mapping definition for this class:

```
Configuration configuration = new Configuration()
.addClass(com.metaarchit.bookshop.Book.class)
.setProperty("hibernate.dialect", "org.hibernate.dialect.DerbyDialect")
.setProperty("hibernate.connection.driver_class", "org.apache.derby.jdbc.EmbeddedDriver")
.setProperty("hibernate.connection.url", "jdbc:derby://localhost:1527/BookShopDB")
.setProperty("hibernate.connection.username", "book")
```

```
.setProperty("hibernate.connection.password", "book");
SessionFactory factory = configuration.buildSessionFactory();
```

If your application has hundreds of mapping definitions, you can pack it in a jar file and add it to the Hibernate configuration. This jar file must be found in your application's classpath:

```
Configuration configuration = new Configuration()
.addJar(new File("mapping.jar"))
.setProperty("hibernate.dialect", "org.hibernate.dialect.DerbyDialect")
.setProperty("hibernate.connection.driver_class", "org.apache.derby.jdbc.EmbeddedDriver")
.setProperty("hibernate.connection.url", "jdbc:derby://localhost:1527/BookShopDB")
.setProperty("hibernate.connection.username", "book")
.setProperty("hibernate.connection.password", "book");
SessionFactory factory = configuration.buildSessionFactory();
```

SessionFactory

The following statement creates a Hibernate `SessionFactory`:

```
SessionFactory factory = configuration.buildSessionFactory();
```

A *session factory* is a global object for maintaining `org.hibernate.Session` objects. It's instantiated once, and it's thread-safe. You can look up the `SessionFactory` from a Java Naming and Directory Interface (JNDI) context in an `ApplicationServer` or any other location.

XML Configuration

Another way to configure Hibernate is to use an XML file. You create the file `hibernate.cfg.xml` in the source directory, so Eclipse copies it to the root of your classpath:

```
<?xml version="1.0" encoding="UTF-8"?>
<!DOCTYPE hibernate-configuration PUBLIC
"-//Hibernate/Hibernate Configuration DTD 3.0//EN"
"http://hibernate.sourceforge.net/hibernate-configuration-3.0.dtd">
<hibernate-configuration>
<session-factory>
<property name="connection.driver_class">
   org.apache.derby.jdbc.EmbeddedDriver
</property>
<property name="connection.url">jdbc:derby://localhost:1527/BookShopDB</property>
<property name="connection.username">book</property>
<property name="connection.password">book</property>
<property name="dialect">org.hibernate.dialect.DerbyDialect</property>
<mapping resource="com/metaarchit/bookshop/Book.hbm.xml" />
</session-factory>
</hibernate-configuration>
```

Now, the code fragment to build up a session factory can be simplified. The configuration loads your `hibernate.cfg.xml` file from the root of the classpath:

```
Configuration configuration = new Configuration().configure();
```

This method loads the default hibernate.cfg.xml from the root class path. The new Configuration() loads the hibernate.properties file, and the configure() method loads hibernate.cfg.xml if hibernate.properties isn't found. If you need to load another configuration file located elsewhere (not in the root classpath), you can use the following code:

```
new Configuration().configure("/config/recipes.cfg.xml")
```

This code looks for recipes.cfg.xml in the config subdirectory of your classpath.

Opening and Closing Sessions

A Hibernate Session object represent a unit of work and is bound to the current thread. It represents a transaction in a database. A session begins when getCurrentSession() is first called on the current thread. The Session object is then bound to the current thread. When the transaction ends with a commit or rollback, Hibernate unbinds the session from the thread and closes it.

Just as when you use JDBC, you need to do some initial cleanup for Hibernate. First, you ask the session factory to open a new session for you. After you finishing your work, you must remember to close the session:

```
Session session = factory.openSession();
try {
        // Using the session to retrieve objects
}catch(Exception e)
{
        e.printStackTrace();
} finally {
        session.close();
}
```

Retrieving Objects

Given the ID (an ISBN, in this case) of a book, you can retrieve the unique Book object from the database. There are two ways to do that:

```
Book book = (Book) session.load(Book.class, isbn);
```

and

```
Book book = (Book) session.get(Book.class, isbn);
```

What's the difference between load() and get()? First, when the given ID can't be found, load() throws an exception org.hibernate.ObjectNotFoundException, whereas get() returns a null object. Second, load() just returns a proxy by default; the database isn't hit until the proxy is first invoked. get() hits the database immediately. The load method is useful when you only need a proxy and don't need to make a database call. You just need a proxy, when in a given session you need to associate an entity before persisting.

Just as you can use SQL to query a database, you can use Hibernate to query objects, using Hibernate Query Language (HQL). For example, the following codes queries for all the **Book** objects:

```
Query query = session.createQuery("from Book");
List books = query.list();
```

If you're sure only one object will match, you can use the **uniqueResult()** method to retrieve the unique result object:

```
Query query = session.createQuery("from Book where isbn = ?");
query.setString(0, isbn);
Book book = (Book) query.uniqueResult();
```

1.4 Configuring a JPA Project

Problem

How do you manage the metadata required for ORM? Can you use any mechanism other than specifying the metadata in XML files? How do you configure a JPA project?

Solution

The EJB3.0 specification defines the Java Persistence API, which provides ORM using a Java domain model to manage a relational database. Different providers implement this API:

- *TopLink:* This is a Java ORM solution currently owned by Oracle. Here's the URL for more details about TopLink:
  www.oracle.com/technology/products/ias/toplink/index.html.

- *JDO:* The JDO API is a standard interface-based Java model abstraction of persistence developed by the Java Community Process. The current JDO 2.0 is Java Specification Request 243. Beginning with JDO 2.0, the development of the API is taking place within Apache JDO open source.

- *Hibernate:* This is a very popular ORM framework. Hibernate provides Hibernate Annotations, which implement JPA standard and also provide more advanced mapping features. We will be demonstrating configuring a JPA project that uses Hibernate Annotations.

How It Works

To use Hibernate Annotations, download the **HibernateAnnotation** package from the Hibernate site: www.hibernate.org/6.html. The following jars need to be in your Eclipse project build path in addition to the Hibernate core jar files:

- `hibernate-annotations.jar`
- `lib/hibernate-comons-annotations.jar`
- `lib/ejb3-persistence.jar`

Configure the session factory in `hibernate.cfg.xml`. (Note that if you change the name of this file to anything other than `hibernate.cfg.xml`, you must upload the file programmatically.) The **dialect** property is used to define the name of the database. This enables Hibernate to generate SQL optimized for a particular relational database. You use Derby as a database in this case, so you use `org.hibernate.dialect.DerbyDialect`. Also, if you change the database—say, from Derby to Oracle—you must change the value from `org.hibernate.dialect.DerbyDialect` to `org.hibernate.dialect.Oracle9Dialect`. This is how portability is achieved using Hibernate. Some of the common dialects that Hibernate supports are as follows

- DB2Dialect (supports DB2)
- FrontBaseDialect
- HSQLDialect
- InformixDialect
- IngresDialect
- InterbaseDialect
- MySQLDialect
- Oracle8Dialect
- Oracle9Dialect
- Oracle10Dialect
- PointbaseDialect
- PostgreSQLDialect
- ProgressDialect
- ProgressDialect
- SybaseDialect

Here's a sample configuration for the database BookShopDB:

```xml
<?xml version='1.0' encoding='utf-8'?>
<!DOCTYPE hibernate-configuration PUBLIC
        "-//Hibernate/Hibernate Configuration DTD 3.0//EN"
        "http://hibernate.sourceforge.net/hibernate-configuration-3.0.dtd">
<hibernate-configuration>
    <session-factory>
        <!-- Database connection settings -->
        <property name="connection.driver_class">
           org.apache.derby.jdbc.EmbeddedDriver
```

```
        </property>
        <property name="connection.url">
          jdbc:derby://localhost:1527/BookShopDB
        </property>
        <property name="connection.username">book</property>
        <property name="connection.password">book</property>
        <!-- JDBC connection pool (use the built-in) -->
        <property name="connection.pool_size">1</property>

              <!-- SQL dialect -->
        <property name="dialect">
         org.hibernate.dialect.DerbyDialect
        </property>

        <!-- Enable Hibernate's automatic session context management -->
        <property name="current_session_context_class">thread</property>
         <!-- Disable the second-level cache  -->
        <property name="cache.provider_class">
         org.hibernate.cache.NoCacheProvider
        </property>
        <!-- Echo all executed SQL to stdout -->
        <property name="show_sql">true</property>
        <!-- Drop and re-create the database schema on startup -->
        <!-- property name="hbm2ddl.auto">update</property> -->
        <mapping class="com.hibernaterecipes.annotations.domain.Book"/>
    </session-factory>
</hibernate-configuration>
```

When you use annotations, you don't need the additional mapping file (`*.hbm.xml`). The metadata for the ORM is specified in the individual classes. You only need to add the class mapping in `hibernate.cfg.xml`. In the previous example, the line

```
<mapping class="com.hibernaterecipes.annotations.domain.Book"/>
```

takes care of the class mapping. Next, let's look at `Book.java` with annotations for the table name, column names, and other attributes:

```
package com.hibernaterecipes.annotations.domain;

import java.util.Date;
import javax.persistence.Column;
import javax.persistence.*;
import javax.persistence.Entity;
import javax.persistence.Table;

/**
 * @author Guruzu
 *
 */
@Entity
@Table (name="BOOK")
```

```java
public class Book {

    @Column (name="isbn")
    @Id
    String isbn;

    @Column (name="book_Name")
    String bookName;

    @Column (name="publisher_code")
    String publisherCode;

    @Column (name="publish_date")
    Date publishDate;

    @Column (name="price")
    Long price;

    /**
     * @return the isbn
     */
    public String getIsbn() {
        return isbn;
    }
    /**
     * @param isbn the isbn to set
     */
    public void setIsbn(String isbn) {
        this.isbn = isbn;          }
    /**
     * @return the bookName
     */
    public String getBookName() {
        return bookName;
    }
    /**
     * @param bookName the bookName to set
     */
    public void setBookName(String bookName) {
    this.bookName = bookName;
    }
    /**
     * @return the publisherCode
     */
    public String getPublisherCode() {
        return publisherCode;
    }
    /**
     * @param publisherCode the publisherCode to set
     */
    public void setPublisherCode(String publisherCode) {
        this.publisherCode = publisherCode;
```

```
}
/**
* @return the publishDate
*/        public Date getPublishDate() {
return publishDate;
}
/**
* @param publishDate the publishDate to set
*/
public void setPublishDate(Date publishDate) {
        this.publishDate = publishDate;
}
/**
* @return the price
*/
public Long getPrice() {
        return price;
}
/**
* @param price the price to set
*/
public void setPrice(Long price) {
        this.price = price;
}
```

}

@Entity is defined by the EJB3.0 specification to annotate an entity bean. An entity represents a lightweight persistent domain object.

An entity class must have a public or protected no-arg constructor. It may have other constructors as well. It should be a top level class and must not be final. If the entity is to be passed by value (that is, through a remote interface) it must implement Serializable.

The state of the entity is represented by the entity's instance variables. The instance variables must be accessed only from within the entity class. The client of the entity shouldn't be able to access the state of the entity directly. The instance variables must have private, protected, or package visibility.

Every entity must have a primary key. The primary key must be declared only once in the entity hierarchy.

You can generate the set and get methods using the Eclipse IDE. Select the instance variables for which you need to generate the methods, right-click the selection, and select Source ▶ Generate Getters and Setters. Doing so displays all the variables for which the methods must be generated. Select the required variables, and click OK. The getter and setter are generated in your source code.

In the previous class, the name of the table BOOK is specified with the name attribute of the Table annotation. The variable isbn is the primary key, which is specified by the @Id tag. The rest of the columns are specified by the @column annotation. If the @column annotation isn't specified, the names of the instance variables are considered column names. Every nonstatic and nontransient properties of an entity bean are considered persistent unless you specify @Transient. @Transient properties are ignored by the EntityManager when you map persistent properties.

Opening a Session

Opening a session is similar to doing so in Hibernate in general, except you use
`AnnotationConfiguration` to build the session factory:

```
public class SessionManager {

        private static final SessionFactory sessionFactory = buildSessionFactory();

        private static SessionFactory buildSessionFactory() {
                try {
                        // Create the SessionFactory from hibernate.cfg.xml
                        return new                                      AnnotationConfiguration()
        .configure().buildSessionFactory();
                }
                catch (Throwable ex) {
                        // Make sure you log the exception, as it might be swallowed
ex.printStackTrace();

                        throw new ExceptionInInitializerError(ex);
                }
        }

        public static SessionFactory getSessionFactory() {
            return sessionFactory;
        }
}
```

If the configuration file name isn't `hibernate.cfg.xml` (in this case, it's named `annotation.cfg.xml`),
build the session factory the using the following statement:

```
new  AnnotationConfiguration()
.configure("annotation.cfg.xml")
.buildSessionFactory();
```

There are other overloaded `configure()` methods that you can use appropriately.

This section uses a Data Access Object (DAO) for database operations. The DAO is a design pattern
used to abstract and encapsulate all access to the data source. For this example, it contains code to
create the `SessionFactory` and a `Session` object and to fetch and update data in the database:

```
public class BookDAO {

        /**
         * To query all details of a book
         * @return
         */
        public List<Book> readAll() {

                Session session = SessionManager.getSessionFactory().getCurrentSession();
                 session.beginTransaction();
                 List<Book> booksList = session.createQuery("from Book").list();
```

```java
        session.getTransaction().commit();
        return booksList;
}

/**
 * To create a book
 * @return
 */
public void create(Book bookObj) {

        Session session=SessionManager.getSessionFactory().getCurrentSession();
        session.beginTransaction();
        session.saveOrUpdate(bookObj);
        session.getTransaction().commit();

}

}
```

The `readAll` method queries all data from the BOOK table that's mapped in `hibernate.cfg.xml`. The `create` method inserts a new row into the BOOK table.

1.5 Using Entity Manager

Problem

Is there a generalized mechanism to configure ORM with less dependency on individual providers like Hibernate, TopLink, and so on?

Solution

A *persistence context* is defined by the JPA specification as a set of managed entity instances where the entity instances and their lifecycles are managed by an entity manager. Each ORM vendors provides its own entity manager, which is a wrapper around the core API and thus supports the JPA programming interfaces, JPA entity instance lifecycles, and the query language. This provides a generalized mechanism for object/relational development and configuration.

How It Works

You obtain the Hibernate EntityManager from an entity manager factory. When container-managed entity managers are used, the application doesn't interact directly with the entity manager factory. Such entity managers are obtained mostly through JNDI lookup. In the case of application-managed entity managers, the application must use the entity manager factory to manage the entity manager and the persistence context lifecycle. This example uses the application-managed entity manager.

`EntityManagerFactory` has the same role as the `SessionFactory` in Hibernate. It acts a factory class that provides the `EntityManager` class to the application. It can be configured either programmatically or using XML. When you use XML to configure it, the file must be named `persistence.xml` and must be located in your classpath.

Here's the `persistence.xml` file for the `Book` example:

```xml
<?xml version="1.0" encoding="UTF-8"?>
<persistence xmlns="http://java.sun.com/xml/ns/persistence"
   xmlns:xsi="http://www.w3.org/2001/XMLSchema-instance"
   xsi:schemaLocation=
   "http://java.sun.com/xml/ns/persistence
http://java.sun.com/xml/ns/persistence/persistence_1_0.xsd"
   version="1.0">

   <persistence-unit name="book" transaction-type="RESOURCE_LOCAL">
                        <provider>org.hibernate.ejb.HibernatePersistence</provider>
      <class>com.hibernaterecipes.annotations.domain.Book</class>

      <properties>
         <property name="hibernate.connection.driver_class"
            value="org.apache.derby.jdbc.EmbeddedDriver"/>
         <property name="hibernate.connection.username"
            value="book"/>
         <property name="hibernate.connection.password"
            value="book"/>
         <property name="hibernate.connection.url"
            value="jdbc:derby://localhost:1527/BookShopDB"/>
         <property name="hibernate.dialect"
            value="org.hibernate.dialect.DerbyDialect"/>
      </properties>
   </persistence-unit>
</persistence>
```

In this `persistence.xml` file, the complete unit is defined by `<persistence-unit>`. This name should match the name used when you create a `EntityManagerFactory`.

The transaction-type `RESOURCE_LOCAL` is used here. Two transaction types define transactional behavior: JTA and `RESOURCE_LOCAL`. JTA is used in J2EE managed applications where the container is responsible for transaction propagation. For application-managed transactions, you can use `RESOURCE_LOCAL`.

The `<provider>` tag specifies the third-party ORM implementation you use. In this case, it's configured to use the Hibernate Persistence provider.

The entity instances are configured with the `<class>` tag.

The rest of the properties are similar to what you configured in `hibernate.cfg.xml`, including the driver class of the database you're connecting to, the connection URL, a username, a password, and the dialect.

Here's the code to create the `EntityManagerFactory` (EMF) from the configuration and to obtain the `EntityManager` from the EMF:

```java
package com.hibernaterecipes.annotations.dao;

import javax.persistence.EntityManager;
import javax.persistence.EntityManagerFactory;
import javax.persistence.Persistence;
```

```
public class SessionManager {

        public static EntityManager getEntityManager() {
            EntityManagerFactory managerFactory =
Persistence.createEntityManagerFactory("book");
            EntityManager manager = managerFactory.createEntityManager();

            return manager;
        }
}
```

`Persistence.createEntityManagerFactory` creates the EMF. The parameter that it takes is the name of the persistence unit—in this case, "book". This should be the same as the name specified in the persistence.xml file's `persistence-unit` tag:

```
<persistence-unit name="book" transaction-type="RESOURCE_LOCAL">
```

The entity instance Book remains the same as defined in JPA:

```
package com.hibernaterecipes.annotations.domain;

import java.util.Date;

import javax.persistence.Column;
import javax.persistence.Id;
import javax.persistence.Entity;
import javax.persistence.Table;

@Entity
@Table (name="BOOK")
public class Book {
        @Column (name="isbn")
        @Id
        String isbn;

        @Column (name="book_Name")
        String bookName;

        @Column (name="publisher_code")
        String publisherCode;

        @Column (name="publish_date")
        Date publishDate;

        @Column (name="price")
        Long price;

        /**
         * @return the isbn
         */
```

```java
    public String getIsbn() {
            return isbn;
    }
    /**
     * @param isbn the isbn to set
     */
    public void setIsbn(String isbn) {
            this.isbn = isbn;
    }
    /**
     * @return the bookName
     */
    public String getBookName() {
            return bookName;
    }
    /**
     * @param bookName the bookName to set
     */
    public void setBookName(String bookName) {
            this.bookName = bookName;
    }
    /**
     * @return the publisherCode
     */
    public String getPublisherCode() {
            return publisherCode;
    }
    /**
     * @param publisherCode the publisherCode to set
     */
    public void setPublisherCode(String publisherCode) {
            this.publisherCode = publisherCode;
    }
    /**
     * @return the publishDate
     */
    public Date getPublishDate() {
            return publishDate;
    }
    /**
     * @param publishDate the publishDate to set
     */
    public void setPublishDate(Date publishDate) {
            this.publishDate = publishDate;
    }
    /**
     * @return the price
     */
    public Long getPrice() {
            return price;
    }
    /**
```

```
        * @param price the price to set
        */
      public void setPrice(Long price) {
            this.price = price;
      }
}
```

The following is the DAO call to fetch the **Book** details:

```
public List<Book> readFromManager() {

            EntityManager manager = SessionManager.getEntityManager();
            EntityTransaction tran = manager.getTransaction();
            tran.begin();
            Query query = manager.createQuery("select b from Book b");
            List<Book> list = query.getResultList();
            tran.commit();
            manager.close();
            return list;
      }
```

From the main method, you invoke the DAO method to list the **Book** details:

```
List<Book> list = bookDAO.readFromManager();
                  System.out.println("List of Books - " + list.size());
```

1.6 Enabling Logging in Hibernate

Problem

How do you determine what SQL query is being executed by Hibernate? How do you see Hibernate's internal workings?. How do you enable logging to troubleshoot complex issues related to Hibernate?

Solution

Hibernate utilizes Simple Logging Facade for Java (SLF4J) to log various system events. SLF4J is distributed as a free software license. It abstracts the actual logging framework that an application uses. SLF4J can direct your logging output to several logging frameworks:

- *NOP:* Null logger implementation

- *Simple:* A logging antiframework that is very simple to use and that attempts to solve every logging problem in one package

- *Log4j version 1.2:* A widely used open source logging framework

- *JDK 1.4 logging:* A logging API provided by Java

- *JCL:* An open source Commons logging framework that provides an interface with thin wrapper implementations for other logging tools

- *Logback:* A serializable logger that, when used, logs after its deserialization depending on your chosen binding

To set up logging, you need `slf4j-api.jar` in your classpath together with the jar file for your preferred binding—`slf4j-log4j12.jar` in the case of log4j. You can also enable a property called `showsql` to see the exact query being executed. You can configure a logging layer like Apache log4j to enable Hibernate class- or package-level logging. And you can use the Statistics Interface provided by Hibernate to obtain some detailed information.

How It Works

You will have to configure the Hibernate property show_sql and log4J to enable logging.

Inspecting the SQL Statements Issued by Hibernate

Hibernate generates SQL statements that let you access the database behind the scene. You can set the `show_sql` property to true in the `hibernate.cfg.xml` XML configuration file to print the SQL statements to stdout:

```
<property name="show_sql">true</property>
```

Configuring Log4j

Hibernate can also use the log4j logging library to log SQL statements and parameters. Make sure the `log4j.jar` file is included in your project's classpath. Create a properties file named `log4j.properties` in the source root folder; this file is used to configure the log4j library:

```
### direct log messages to stdout ###
log4j.appender.stdout=org.apache.log4j.ConsoleAppender
log4j.appender.stdout.Target=System.out
log4j.appender.stdout.layout=org.apache.log4j.PatternLayout
log4j.appender.stdout.layout.ConversionPattern=%d{yyyy-MM-dd HH:mm:ss} %5p %c{1}:%L - %m%n
### direct messages to file hibernate.log ###
#log4j.appender.file=org.apache.log4j.FileAppender
#log4j.appender.file.File=hibernate.log
#log4j.appender.file.layout=org.apache.log4j.PatternLayout
#log4j.appender.file.layout.ConversionPattern=%d{yyyy-MM-dd HH:mm:ss} %5p %c{1}:%L - %m%n
log4j.rootLogger=error, stdout
log4j.logger.org.hibernate.SQL=debug
log4j.logger.org.hibernate.type=debug
```

Enabling Live Statistics

You can enable live statistics by setting the property `hibernate.generate_statistics` in the configuration file:

```
<property name="hibernate.generate_statistics">true</property>
```

You can also enable live statistics programmatically by using the Statistics Interface:

```
Statistics stats = sessionFactory.getStatistics();
stats.setStatisticsEnabled(true);
Transaction tx = session.beginTransaction();
List<Book> books = session.createQuery("from Book").list();
for(Book bo : books)
{
        System.out.println(bo);
}
stats.getSessionOpenCount();
stats.logSummary();
session.close();
```

1.7 Generating a Database Schema Using Hibernate

Problem

How can Hibernate help you generate or update a schema?

Solution

Hibernate uses apache Ant task definitions to create and update database schema.

How It Works

Creating an Ant Build File

You use Apache Ant to define the building process. (For more information about Ant, see http://ant.apache.org/.) Create the following build.xml file in the project root:

```
<project name="BookShop" default="schemaexport">
<property name="build.dir" value="bin" />
<property name="hibernate.home" value="c:/hibernate-3.1" />
<property name="derby.home" value="c:/derby" />
<path id="hibernate-Classpath">
<fileset dir="${hibernate.home}">
<include name="**/*.jar" />
</fileset>
<fileset dir="${derby.home}">
<include name="lib/*.jar" />
</fileset>
```

```
<pathelement path="${build.dir}" />
</path>
<!-- Defining Ant targets -->
</project>
```

Generating Database Schema Using SchemaExport

You use the `schemaexport` task provided by Hibernate to generate the SQL statements to create a database schema. It reads the `dialect` property from the Hibernate configuration file (`hibernate.cfg.xml`) to determine which brand of database you're using:

```
<target name="schemaexport">
<taskdef name="schemaexport"
classname="org.hibernate.tool.hbm2ddl.SchemaExportTask"
Classpathref="hibernate-Classpath" />
<schemaexport config="${build.dir}/hibernate.cfg.xml"
output="BookShop.sql" />
</target>
```

Updating a Database Schema Using SchemaUpdate

During the development cycle, you may change your object model frequently. It isn't efficient to destroy and rebuild the schema every time. The `schemaupdate` task updates an existing database schema:

```
<target name="schemaupdate">
<taskdef name="schemaupdate"
classname="org.hibernate.tool.hbm2ddl.SchemaUpdateTask"
Classpathref="hibernate-Classpath" />
<schemaupdate config="${build.dir}/hibernate.cfg.xml" text="no"/>
</target>
```

Specifying the Details of a Database Schema

In the previous mapping example, you discarded some table details, such as column length and the not-null constraint. If you generate a database schema from this mapping, you must provide these kinds of details:

```
<hibernate-mapping package="com.hibernaterecipes.bookshop">
<class name="Book" table="BOOK">
<id name="isbn" type="string">
<column name="ISBN" length="50" />
</id>
<property name="name" type="string">
<column name="BOOK_NAME" length="100" not-null="true" />
</property>
<property name="publishDate" type="date" column="PUBLISH_DATE" />
<property name="price" type="int" column="PRICE" />
```

```
</class>
</hibernate-mapping>
```

Summary

In this chapter, you've learned what object/relational mapping is and what its benefits are over JDBC. Hibernate is one of the most widely used ORM frameworks in the industry. Using JDBC directly has many disadvantages, including complicated handling of the `ResultSet` and the fact that it isn't portable against different databases. To overcome these issues, you can use ORM for ease of development and to maintain software efficiently.

To configure Hibernate, you need various third-party jars that must be specified in the classpath. The `.hbm` and `.hibernate.cfg.cml` XML files are required in order to configure the objects that are mapped to tables; they also contain the database connection details. You use `org.hibernate.SessionFactory` to create `org.hibernate.Session` objects that represent units of work. Other database operations are performed using the `Session` object.

You can also perform Hibernate configuration and database operations with annotations. These are Hibernate Annotations which implement the Java Persistence standards defined by the EJB3.0 specification, and thus all details can be specified through annotations.

CHAPTER 2

■ ■ ■

Basic Mapping and Object Identity

A primary key in a database table is used to uniquely identify a record in that table. The primary key value can't be null and is unique within a table. The primary key is also used to establish a relationship between two tables—it's defined as a foreign key in the associated table. Because the primary key is used to identify a particular record, it can also be called the *database identifier*. The database identifier is exposed to the application by Hibernate through an identifier property of the persistent entity. This chapter discusses the various ways to generate an identifier (primary key) for a database record. You learn about metadata configurations and their effect on the persistence mechanism.

2.1 Providing an ID for Persistence

Problem

How do you generate an identifier for a database entity? What are the possible strategies?

Solution

An id element (`<id>`) is used to create a mapping in the Hibernate XML file. The id element has attributes such as `column`, `type`, and `generator` that you use to generate the identifier. The JPA specification requires that every entity must have a primary key. From JPA's perspective, an `@id` is used to define how an identifier is generated.

When you use inheritance mapping, more than one class can be mapped to a table. These classes (subclass and superclass) are said to be in an *entity hierarchy*. The primary key must be defined exactly once in an entity hierarchy, either on the entity that is the root of the entity hierarchy or on a mapped superclass of the entity hierarchy. Attributes such as `@GeneratedValue` and `@column` are used to define column mapping and strategy.

How It Works

You need to ask Hibernate to generate this ID for you before persisting to the database. Hibernate provides many built-in strategies for ID generation:

- Database sequence

- Native generator

- Increment generator

- Hilo generator

Some of them are available only for specified databases; for instance, the sequence strategy isn't supported in MYSQL but is provided by Oracle.

JPA also provides a way to generate identifiers.

Hibernate XML Mapping

We'll look at each of these strategies in turn, starting with the database sequence. For this section, we'll insert three books into the database. Below is the Launch class used to insert records into the Book table:

```java
package com.hibernaterecipes.chapter2;

import java.util.Date;
import java.util.List;

import org.hibernate.Session;
import org.hibernate.SessionFactory;
import org.hibernate.Transaction;
import org.hibernate.cfg.Configuration;
import org.hibernate.stat.Statistics;


/**
 * @author Guruzu
 *
 */
public class Launch_2_1 {
  private static SessionFactory sessionFactory;

  public static Session getSession() {
    if(sessionFactory == null)
    {
      sessionFactory = new Configuration().configure()
      .buildSessionFactory();
    }
    Session hibernateSession = sessionFactory.openSession();
    return hibernateSession;
  }

  public static void main(String[] args) {
    Session session = getSession();
    Statistics stats = sessionFactory.getStatistics();
    stats.setStatisticsEnabled(true);
    Transaction tx = session.beginTransaction();
```

```
      for(int i =0;i<3;i++)
      {
        BookCh2 book = new BookCh2();
        book.setName("Book Name "+(i+1));
        book.setPrice(39);
        book.setPublishDate(new Date());
        session.save(book);
      }
      tx.commit();
      stats.getSessionOpenCount();
      stats.logSummary();
      session.close();
  }
}
```

Using the Database Sequence

The most common way to generate an ID uses an auto-incremented sequence number. For some kinds of databases, including Hyper Structured Query Language Database (HSQLDB), you can use a sequence/generator to generate this sequence number. HSQLDB is a relational database management system written in Java; it supports a large subset of SQL-92 and SQL-2003 standards. This strategy is called *sequence*.

Let's use the book shop as an example again. Because a single persistent object can't have more than one ID, you need to change the ISBN to a simple property and add a not-null and unique constraint on it.

```
<?xml version="1.0" encoding="UTF-8"?>
<!DOCTYPE hibernate-mapping PUBLIC
"-//Hibernate/Hibernate Mapping DTD 3.0//EN"
"http://hibernate.sourceforge.net/hibernate-mapping-3.0.dtd">
<hibernate-mapping package="com.hibernaterecipes.chapter2" auto-import="false" >
  <import class="BookCh2" rename="bkch2"/>
  <class name="BookCh2" table="BOOK" dynamic-insert="true" dynamic-update="true">
    <id name="isbn"  column="isbn" type="long">
      <generator class="sequence">
        <param name="sequence">BOOK_SEQUENCE</param>
      </generator>
    </id>
    <property name="name" type="string" column="BOOK_NAME" />
    <property name="publishDate" type="date" column="PUBLISH_DATE" />
    <property name="price" type="int" column="PRICE" />
  </class>
</hibernate-mapping>
```

Using a Native Generator

Native generators provide portability, because Hibernate can determine the generator method supported by the underlying database. Generators using the native class use identity or sequence columns depending on the available database support. If neither method is supported, the native generator falls back to a hi/lo generator method to create unique primary key values.

Let's see how this works. In the BookCh2.java class, change the isbn property from type String to long, as shown here:

```java
public class BookCh2 {
  private long isbn;

  private String name;
  private Date publishDate;
  private int price;
  private Publisher publisher;
  private List chapters;

  // getters and setters
}
```

And edit the Book.xml mapping file to contain the id element:

```xml
<?xml version="1.0" encoding="UTF-8"?>
<!DOCTYPE hibernate-mapping PUBLIC
"-//Hibernate/Hibernate Mapping DTD 3.0//EN"
"http://hibernate.sourceforge.net/hibernate-mapping-3.0.dtd">
<hibernate-mapping package="com.hibernaterecipes.chapter2" auto-import="false">
  <class name="BookCh2" table="BOOK">
    <id column="ISBN" type="long">
      <generator class="native">
      </generator>
    </id>
    <property name="name" type="string" column="BOOK_NAME" />
    <property name="publishDate" type="date" column="PUBLISH_DATE" />
    <property name="price" type="int" column="PRICE" />
  </class>
</hibernate-mapping>
```

The native generator that you use here uses other identity generators such as identity, sequence, hilo, and increment. The choice of which generator to use depends on the underlying database. The Identifier type is of type long, short, or int.

Using an Increment Generator

The increment generator reads the maximum primary key column value from the table and increments the value by one. It isn't advisable to use this when the application is deployed in a cluster of servers because each server generates an ID and it may conflict with the generation on the other server. The increment generator isn't available in JPA.

Edit the Book.xml Hibernate mapping file as follows:

```xml
<?xml version="1.0" encoding="UTF-8"?>
<!DOCTYPE hibernate-mapping PUBLIC
"-//Hibernate/Hibernate Mapping DTD 3.0//EN"
"http://hibernate.sourceforge.net/hibernate-mapping-3.0.dtd">
<hibernate-mapping package="com.hibernaterecipes.chapter2" auto-import="false">
  <class name="BookCh2" table="BOOK">
```

```
  <id column="ISBN" type="long">
    <generator class="increment">
    </generator>
  </id>
  <property name="name" type="string" column="BOOK_NAME" />
  <property name="publishDate" type="date" column="PUBLISH_DATE" />
  <property name="price" type="int" column="PRICE" />
  </class>
</hibernate-mapping>
```

The Identifier is of type long, short, or int.

Using the increment generator, the primary key of the table in which the record is created is incremented. And using the sequence generator, the database sequence is incremented. You can also use a sequence to generate a primary key for multiple tables, whereas an increment generator can only be used to create a primary key for its own table.

Using the Hilo Generator

The hilo generator uses the hi/lo algorithm to generate the identifiers that are unique to a particular database. It retrieves the high value from a global source (by default, the hibernate_unique_key table and next_hi column) and the low value from a local source. The max_lo value option is provided to define how many low values are added before a high value is fetched. The two values are added to generate a unique identifier.

Edit the Book.xml mapping file as shown here:

```
<?xml version="1.0" encoding="UTF-8"?>
<!DOCTYPE hibernate-mapping PUBLIC
"-//Hibernate/Hibernate Mapping DTD 3.0//EN"
"http://hibernate.sourceforge.net/hibernate-mapping-3.0.dtd">
<hibernate-mapping package="com.hibernaterecipes.chapter2" auto-import="false">
  <class name="BookCh2" table="BOOK">
    <id column="ISBN" type="long">
      <generator class="hilo">
      </generator>
    </id>
    <property name="name" type="string" column="BOOK_NAME" />
    <property name="publishDate" type="date" column="PUBLISH_DATE" />
    <property name="price" type="int" column="PRICE" />
  </class>
</hibernate-mapping>
```

The hilo generator is of type long.

This generator should *not* be used with a user-supplied connection. The high value *must* be fetched in a separate transaction from the Session transaction, so the generator must be able to obtain a new connection and commit it. Hence this implementation may not be used when the user is supplying connections. In that case, a SequenceHiLoGenerator is a better choice (where supported).

The hilo generator is used for batch operations. When Hibernate is using an application server data source to obtain connections enlisted with JTA, you must properly configure the hibernate.transaction.manager_lookup_property. The hibernate.transaction.manager_lookup is the classname of a TransactionManagerLookup.

Using JPA to Generate Identifiers

For the entity class using JPA annotations, update the **Book** class to add the **@id**, **@GeneratedValue**, and **@column** annotations, as shown next. The **strategy** value for **GeneratedValue** is **GenerationType.AUTO**, which translates into the native option in Hibernate XML mapping:

```java
package com.hibernaterecipes.annotations.domain;

import java.util.Date;
import javax.persistence.Column;
import javax.persistence.Entity;
import javax.persistence.GeneratedValue;
import javax.persistence.GenerationType;
import javax.persistence.Id;
import javax.persistence.Table;

@Entity
@Table (name="BOOK")
public class BookCh2 {

    @Id
    @GeneratedValue (strategy=GenerationType.AUTO)
    @Column (name="ISBN")
    private long isbn;

    @Column (name="book_Name")
    private String bookName;

    /*@Column (name="publisher_code")
    String publisherCode;*/

    @Column (name="publish_date")
    private Date publishDate;

    @Column (name="price")
    private Long price;

    // getters and setters
}
```

2.2 Creating a Composite Key in Hibernate

Problem

How do you create a composite key in Hibernate?

Solution

A table with a composite key can be mapped with multiple properties of the class as identifier properties. The `<composite-id>` element accepts `<key-property>` property mappings and `<key-many-to-one>` mappings as child elements. The persistent class must override `equals()` and `hashCode()` to implement composite identifier equality. It must also implement `Serializable`.

How It Works

In some cases, you can use Hibernate to access a legacy database that includes tables using a *composite key* (a primary key composed of multiple columns). With this kind of legacy table, it isn't easy to add an ID column for use as primary key. Suppose you have a legacy `CUSTOMER` table that was created using the following SQL statement:

```
CREATE TABLE CUSTOMER (
COUNTRY_CODE VARCHAR(2) NOT NULL,
ID_CARD_NO VARCHAR(30) NOT NULL,
FIRST_NAME VARCHAR(30) NOT NULL,
LAST_NAME VARCHAR(30) NOT NULL,
ADDRESS VARCHAR(100),
EMAIL VARCHAR(30),
PRIMARY KEY (COUNTRY_CODE, ID_CARD_NO)
);
```

You input some data for this table using the following SQL statements:

```
INSERT INTO CUSTOMER (COUNTRY_CODE, ID_CARD_NO, FIRST_NAME, LAST_NAME, ADDRESS, EMAIL)
VALUES ('mo', '1234567(8)', 'Gary', 'Mak', 'Address for Gary', 'gary@mak.com');
```

For the object model, you develop the following persistent class for the `CUSTOMER` table. Each column is mapped to a `String`-type property:

```java
public class Customer {
  private String countryCode;
  private String idCardNo;
  private String firstName;
  private String lastName;
  private String address;
  private String email;
  // Getters and Setters
}
```

Then, you create a mapping definition for the `Customer` class. You use `<composite-id>` to define the object ID, which consists of two properties, `countryCode` and `idCardNo`:

```xml
<hibernate-mapping>
  <class name="Customer" table="CUSTOMER">
    <composite-id>
      <key-property name="countryCode" type="string" column="COUNTRY_CODE" />
```

```xml
        <key-property name="idCardNo" type="string" column="ID_CARD_NO"/>
    </composite-id>
    <property name="firstName" type="string" column="FIRST_NAME" />
    <property name="lastName" type="string" column="LAST_NAME" />
    <property name="address" type="string" column="ADDRESS" />
    <property name="email" type="string" column="EMAIL" />
  </class>
</hibernate-mapping>
```

When a new persistent object is added to your application, you need to define it in the hibernate.cfg.xml configuration file:

```xml
<mapping resource="com/metaarchit/bookshop/Customer.hbm.xml" />
```

When you use load() or get() to retrieve a specified object from the database, you need to provide that object's ID. Which type of object should be passed as the ID? At the moment, you can pass a newly created Customer object with countryCode and idCardNo set. Note that Hibernate requires that any ID class must implement the java.io.Serializable interface:

```java
public class Customer implements Serializable {
  ...
}
Customer customerId = new Customer();
customerId.setCountryCode("mo");
customerId.setIdCardNo("1234567(8)");
Customer customer = (Customer) session.get(Customer.class, customerId);
```

It doesn't make sense to pass a whole persistent object as the ID. A better way is to extract the fields that form the ID as a separate class:

```java
public class CustomerId implements Serializable {
  private String countryCode;
  private String idCardNo;
  public CustomerId(String countryCode, String idCardNo) {
    this.countryCode = countryCode;
    this.idCardNo = idCardNo;
  }
}
```

Then, modify the Customer persistent class to use this new ID class:

```java
public class Customer implements Serializable {
  private CustomerId id;
  private String firstName;
  private String lastName;
  private String address;
  private String email;
  // Getters and Setters
}
```

The mapping definition should also be modified to use the ID class:

```xml
<hibernate-mapping>
  <class name="Customer" table="CUSTOMER">
    <composite-id name="id" class="CustomerId">
      <key-property name="countryCode" type="string" column="COUNTRY_CODE" />
      <key-property name="idCardNo" type="string" column="ID_CARD_NO"/>
    </composite-id>
    <property name="firstName" type="string" column="FIRST_NAME" />
    <property name="lastName" type="string" column="LAST_NAME" />
    <property name="address" type="string" column="ADDRESS" />
    <property name="email" type="string" column="EMAIL" />
  </class>
</hibernate-mapping>
```

To retrieve a Customer object, you need to specify the ID. This time, you pass in an instance of CustomerId type:

```java
CustomerId customerId = new CustomerId("mo", "1234567(8)");
Customer customer = (Customer) session.get(Customer.class, customerId);
```

To persist a Customer object, you use an instance of CustomerId type as its ID:

```java
Customer customer = new Customer();
customer.setId(new CustomerId("mo", "9876543(2)"));
customer.setFirstName("Peter");
customer.setLastName("Lou");
customer.setAddress("Address for Peter");
customer.setEmail("peter@lou.com");
session.save(customer);
```

For Hibernate caching to work correctly, you need to override the equals() and hashCode() methods of the custom ID class. The equals() method is used to compare two objects for equality, and the hashCode() method provides an object's hash code. You use EqualsBuilder and HashCodeBuilder to simplify the equals() and hashCode() implementations. These classes are the provided by Jakarta Commons Lang library; you can download it from http://jakarta.apache.org/site/downloads/downloads_commons-lang.cgi. After you download the library, include the commons-lang-2.1.jar in your project's Java build path:

```java
public class CustomerId implements Serializable {
  ...
  public boolean equals(Object obj) {
    if (!(obj instanceof CustomerId)) return false;
    CustomerId other = (CustomerId) obj;
    return new EqualsBuilder().append(countryCode, other.countryCode)
      .append(idCardNo, other.idCardNo)
      .isEquals();
  }

  public int hashCode() {
    return new HashCodeBuilder().append(countryCode)
      .append(idCardNo)
```

```
      .toHashCode();
  }
}
```

However, if this `Customer` persistent class is designed from scratch, you should provide it with an auto-generated primary ID. Define the business keys `countryCode` and `idCardNo` as not-null, and add a multicolumn unique constraint. The `<properties>` tag can be used to group several properties:

```
public class Customer {
  private Long id;
  private String countryCode;
  private String idCardNo;
  private String firstName;
  private String lastName;
  private String address;
  private String email;
  // Getters and Setters
}
```

```
<hibernate-mapping>
  <class name="Customer" table="CUSTOMER">
    <id name="id" type="long" column="ID">
      <generator class="native"/>
    </id>
    <properties name="customerKey" unique="true">
      <property name="countryCode" type="string" column="COUNTRY_CODE" not-null="true" />
      <property name="idCardNo" type="string" column="ID_CARD_NO" not-null="true" />
    </properties>
    ...
  </class>
</hibernate-mapping>
```

2.3 SaveOrUpdate in Hibernate

Problem

How does save and update work for the `saveOrUpdate()` method in Hibernate?

Solution

Hibernate provides a method `saveOrUpdate()` for persisting objects. It determines whether an object should be saved or updated. This method is very useful for transitive object persistence.

```
session.saveOrUpdate(book);
```

How It Works

If a persistent object using an autogenerated ID type is passed to the `saveOrUpdate()` method with an empty ID value, it's treated as a new object that should be inserted into the database. Hibernate first generates an ID for this object and then issues an `INSERT` statement. Otherwise, if the ID value isn't empty, Hibernate treats it as an existing object and issues an `UPDATE` statement for it.

How does Hibernate treat an ID as empty? For the `Book` class, the `isbn` type is a primitive `long`. You should assign a number as the unsaved value. Typically, you choose "0" as unsaved, because it's the default value for the `long` data type. But it's a problem that you can't have an object whose ID value is really "0":

```
<id name="isbn" type="long" column="ISBN" unsaved-value="0">
  <generator class="native"/>
</id>
```

The solution to this problem is to use a primitive wrapper class as your ID type (`java.lang.Long` in this case). Then, null is treated as the unsaved value. You can use any number within the range of the `long` data type as the ID value:

```
public class Book {
  private Long isbn;
  private String name;
  private Publisher publisher;
  private Date publishDate;
  private int price;
  private List chapters;
  // Getters and Setters
}
```

This is also the case for other persistent properties, such as the `price` property in the `Book` class. When the price of a book is unknown, which value should be assigned to this field? Should it be "0" or a negative number? Neither seems suitable. Instead, you can change the type to a primitive wrapper class (`java.lang.Integer` in this case) and use null to represent an unknown value:

```
public class Book {
  private Long isbn;
  private String name;
  private Publisher publisher;
  private Date publishDate;
  private Integer price;
  private List chapters;
  // Getters and Setters
}
```

2.4 Dynamic SQL Generation in Hibernate

Problem

What does dynamic SQL generation mean? Why do you need to enable it, and how do you do so?

Solution

On application startup, Hibernate creates SQL statements for each of its persistent classes. That means Hibernate creates SQL statements for the Create, Read, Update, and Delete (CRUD) operations but doesn't execute these statements. So, on application startup, an insert statement (create), a delete, a read, and an update are created. The update statement is created to update each and every field. At runtime, if the value isn't changed, it's updated with the old value. The CRUD statements are cached in memory by Hibernate.

Dynamic SQL generation means turning off this Hibernate feature. You may want to do so because the feature can mean a longer startup time for the application. The amount of time depends on the number of entity classes in the application. Caching these SQL statements in memory can impact the performance of sensitive application more in terms of unnecessary memory.

How It Works

For the class element, add the attributes `dynamic-insert` and `dynamic-update` and set them to true. The `Book.xml` mapping file becomes the following:

```xml
<?xml version="1.0" encoding="UTF-8"?>
<!DOCTYPE hibernate-mapping PUBLIC
"-//Hibernate/Hibernate Mapping DTD 3.0//EN"
"http://hibernate.sourceforge.net/hibernate-mapping-3.0.dtd">
<hibernate-mapping package="com.hibernaterecipes.chapter2" auto-import="false">
  <class name="BookCh2" table="BOOK" dynamic-insert="true" dynamic-update="true">
    <id column="isbn" type="long">
      <generator class="native">
      </generator>
    </id>
    <property name="name" type="string" column="BOOK_NAME" />
    <property name="publishDate" type="date" column="PUBLISH_DATE" />
    <property name="price" type="int" column="PRICE" />
  </class>
</hibernate-mapping>
```

The annotation mapping is as follows:

```java
package com.hibernaterecipes.annotations.domain;

import java.util.Date;

import javax.persistence.Column;
import javax.persistence.Entity;
import javax.persistence.GeneratedValue;
import javax.persistence.GenerationType;
import javax.persistence.Id;
import javax.persistence.Table;

import org.hibernate.annotations.AccessType;

/**
```

```
 * @author Guruzu
 *
 */
@Entity
@org.hibernate.annotations.Entity(dynamicInsert = true, dynamicUpdate = true)
@Table (name="BOOK")
public class BookCh2 {

  @Id
  @GeneratedValue (strategy=GenerationType.TABLE)
  @Column (name="ISBN")
  private long isbn;

  @Column (name="book_Name")
  private String bookName;


  @Column (name="publish_date")
  private Date publishDate;

  @Column (name="price")
  private Long price;

  // getters and setters
}
```

With the `dynamic-insert` property set to `true`, Hibernate does *not* include null values for properties (for properties that aren't set by the application) during an `INSERT` operation. With the `dynamic-update` property set to true, Hibernate does *not* include unmodified properties in the `UPDATE` operation.

2.5 Naming Entities in Hibernate

Problem

How do you distinguish one entity from another when they have the same name? What are the uses of the `Package` attribute in the `hibernate-mapping` element?

Solution

Turning off the `auto-import` option prevents Hibernate from loading class names at startup. You can use the `import` element, a child element of `hibernate-mapping`, to rename the entity into something more distinct. The `package` option lets you skip entering the full package name every time the entity is accessed.

How It Works

In the Book.xml mapping file, set auto-import to false, provide the package, and add the import element as shown here:

```xml
<?xml version="1.0" encoding="UTF-8"?>
<!DOCTYPE hibernate-mapping PUBLIC
"-//Hibernate/Hibernate Mapping DTD 3.0//EN"
"http://hibernate.sourceforge.net/hibernate-mapping-3.0.dtd">
<hibernate-mapping package="com.hibernaterecipes.chapter2" auto-import="false" >
  <import class="BookCh2" rename="bkch2"/>
  <class name="BookCh2" table="BOOK" dynamic-insert="true" dynamic-update="true">
    <id name="isbn"  column="isbn" type="long">
      <generator class="native">
      </generator>
    </id>
    <property name="name" type="string" column="BOOK_NAME" />
    <property name="publishDate" type="date" column="PUBLISH_DATE" />
    <property name="price" type="int" column="PRICE" />
  </class>
</hibernate-mapping>
```

Now, you can access the entity as follows:

```java
package com.hibernaterecipes.chapter2;

import java.util.List;

import org.hibernate.Session;
import org.hibernate.SessionFactory;
import org.hibernate.Transaction;
import org.hibernate.cfg.Configuration;

public class Launch_2_4 {
  private static SessionFactory sessionFactory;

  public static Session getSession() {
    if(sessionFactory == null)
    {
      sessionFactory = new Configuration().configure()
      .buildSessionFactory();
    }
    Session hibernateSession = sessionFactory.openSession();
    return hibernateSession;
  }

  public static void main(String[] args) {
    Session session = getSession();
    List<BookCh2> booksList = session.createQuery("from bkch2").list();
    for(BookCh2 bo : booksList)
    {
```

```
      System.out.println(bo);
    }
    session.close();

  }

}
```

In the JPA entity, you need to add the following:

```
@Entity (name="bkch2")
@org.hibernate.annotations.Entity(dynamicInsert = true, dynamicUpdate = true)
@Table   (name="BOOK")
public class BookCh2 {
  //All the usual fields
}
```

And the BookDAO class can use the entity name to access it:

```
/**
 * Book DAO
 */
package com.hibernaterecipes.annotations.dao.ch2;

import java.util.List;

import javax.persistence.Query;
import javax.persistence.EntityManager;
import javax.persistence.EntityTransaction;
import org.hibernate.Session;
import com.hibernaterecipes.annotations.dao.SessionManager;
import com.hibernaterecipes.annotations.domain.BookCh2;


/**
 * @author Guruzu
 *
 */
public class BookDAO {

  /**
   * To query all details of a book
   * @return
   */
  public List<BookCh2> readAll() {

    Session session = SessionManager.getSessionFactory().getCurrentSession();

    session.beginTransaction();

    List<BookCh2> booksList = session.createQuery("from bkch2").list();
```

```
        session.getTransaction().commit();

        return booksList;
    }

    public List<BookCh2> readFromManager() {

        EntityManager manager = SessionManager.getEntityManager();
        EntityTransaction tran = manager.getTransaction();
        tran.begin();
        Query query = manager.createQuery("select b from bkch2 b");
        List<BookCh2> list = query.getResultList();
        return list;
    }
}
```

Summary

In this chapter, you learned how and when to use various identity generators. The chapter also demonstrated the implementation of composite keys. You've seen how Hibernate saves persistent entities and creates new records in a database. And you've learned how to use metadata like dynamic-insert and dynamic-update to configure your persistence mechanism.

CHAPTER 3

Component Mapping

Hibernate makes it easy to employ a fine-grained domain model. That means you can have more classes than tables. In other words, you can map a single record in a table to more than one class. You do so by having one class of type Entity and the others of Value types.

Hibernate classifies objects as either entity type or value type. An object of entity type is an independent entity and has its own lifecycle. It has its own primary key and hence its own database identity. A value type doesn't have an identifier. A value type belongs to an entity. Value type objects are bound by the lifecycle of the owning entity instance. When a value type is persisted, the value type's state is persisted in the owning entity's table row. Hibernate uses the component element, and JPA has the @Embeddable and @Embedded annotations to achieve the fine-grained model. This chapter goes through the implementation details.

3.1 Implementing a Value Type as a Component

Problem

How do you create a component? How do you create a fine-grained object model to map to a single row in a relational model?

Solution

A component element (<Component>) is used to map the value type object. You get the name component from the word *Composition* because the component is contained within an entity. In the case of JPA, embeddable and embedded annotations are used.

How It Works

We'll look at how Hibernate and JPA solves this problem in the sections below. Both solutions, however, need a new orders table. Use the following CREATE statement to create a new table called ORDERS:

```
CREATE TABLE ORDERS (id bigint NOT NULL, WEEKDAY_RECIPIENT varchar(100),WEEKDAY_PHONE
varchar(100),WEEKDAY_ADDRESS varchar(100), HOLIDAY_RECIPIENT varchar(100),HOLIDAY_PHONE
varchar(100),HOLIDAY_ADDRESS varchar(100),PRIMARY KEY (id));
```

Using Hibernate XML Mapping

In the online bookshop application, a customer can place an order to purchase some books. Your staff processes the order and delivers the books. The customer can specify different recipients and contact details for different periods (weekdays and holidays).

First, you add a new persistent class `Orders` to the application:

```
package com.hibernaterecipes.chapter3;

import com.hibernaterecipes.bookstore.Book;

/**
 * @author Guruzu
 *
 */
public class Orders {

  private Long id;
  private BookCh2 book;
  private String weekdayRecipient;
  private String weekdayPhone;
  private String weekdayAddress;
  private String holidayRecipient;
  private String holidayPhone;
  private String holidayAddress;

  //getters and setters
}
```

Then, you create a mapping definition for this persistent class. You map the properties of this class as usual:

```
<?xml version="1.0" encoding="UTF-8"?>
<!DOCTYPE hibernate-mapping PUBLIC
"-//Hibernate/Hibernate Mapping DTD 3.0//EN"
"http://hibernate.sourceforge.net/hibernate-mapping-3.0.dtd">
<hibernate-mapping package="com.hibernaterecipes.chapter3">
  <class name="Orders" table="ORDERS">
    <id name="id" type="long" column="ID">
      <generator class="native" />
    </id>
    <property name="weekdayRecipient" type="string" column="WEEKDAY_RECIPIENT" />
    <property name="weekdayPhone" type="string" column="WEEKDAY_PHONE" />
    <property name="weekdayAddress" type="string" column="WEEKDAY_ADDRESS" />
    <property name="holidayRecipient" type="string" column="HOLIDAY_RECIPIENT" />
    <property name="holidayPhone" type="string" column="HOLIDAY_PHONE" />
    <property name="holidayAddress" type="string" column="HOLIDAY_ADDRESS" />
    <many-to-one name="book" class="com.hibernaterecipes.chapter2.BookCh2"
                 column="isbn" cascade="save-update"/>
  </class>
</hibernate-mapping>
```

You may feel that the `Orders` class isn't well designed because the `recipient`, `phone`, and `address` properties are duplicated for weekdays and holidays. From the object-oriented perspective, you should create a class (called, say, `Contact`) to encapsulate them:

```
package com.hibernaterecipes.chapter3;

public class Contact {
  private long id;
  private String recipient;
  private String phone;
  private String address;

  // getters and setters
}

package com.hibernaterecipes.chapter3;

import com.hibernaterecipes.bookstore.Book;

public class Orders {

  private Long id;
  private Book book;
        private Contact weekdayContact;
        private Contact holidayContact;

        // getters and setters
}
```

Now the changes are finished for Java. But how can you modify the Hibernate mapping definition to reflect the changes? According to the techniques you've learned, you can specify `Contact` as a new persistent class and use a one-to-one association (the simplest way is to use a `<many-to-one>` association with `unique="true"`) to associate `Orders` and `Contact`:

```
<hibernate-mapping package=" com.hibernaterecipes.chapter3">
  <class name="Contact" table="CONTACT">
    <id name="id" type="long" column="ID">
      <generator class="native" />
    </id>
    <property name="recipient" type="string" column="RECIPIENT" />
    <property name="phone" type="string" column="PHONE" />
    <property name="address" type="string" column="ADDRESS" />
  </class>
</hibernate-mapping>

<hibernate-mapping package="com.hibernaterecipes.chapter3">
  <class name="Orders" table="ORDERS">

    ...
    <many-to-one name="weekdayContact" class="Contact" column="CONTACT_ID"
                 unique="true" />
    <many-to-one name="holidayContact" class="Contact" column="CONTACT_ID"
```

```
                    unique="true" />
  </class>
</hibernate-mapping>
```

In this case, modeling the Contact class as a standalone persistent class seems unnecessary. This is because a Contact object is meaningless when it's separated from an order object. The function of the Contact class is to provide some kind of logical grouping. The contact details are completely dependent on the Orders class. For a bookshop application, it doesn't make much sense to hold contact information as separate entities (entities that have a database identity or primary key). For this kind of requirement, where you can associate an object with a dependent object, you use what Hibernate calls *components*:

```
<?xml version="1.0" encoding="UTF-8"?>
<!DOCTYPE hibernate-mapping PUBLIC
"-//Hibernate/Hibernate Mapping DTD 3.0//EN"
"http://hibernate.sourceforge.net/hibernate-mapping-3.0.dtd">
<hibernate-mapping package="com.hibernaterecipes.chapter3">
  <class name="Orders" table="ORDERS">
    <id name="id" type="long" column="ID">
      <generator class="native" />
    </id>
    <component name="weekdayContact" class="Contact">
      <property name="recipient" type="string" column="WEEKDAY_RECIPIENT" />
      <property name="phone" type="string" column="WEEKDAY_PHONE" />
      <property name="address" type="string" column="WEEKDAY_ADDRESS" />
    </component>
    <component name="holidayContact" class="Contact">
      <property name="recipient" type="string" column="HOLIDAY_RECIPIENT" />
      <property name="phone" type="string" column="HOLIDAY_PHONE" />
      <property name="address" type="string" column="HOLIDAY_ADDRESS" />
    </component>
  </class>
</hibernate-mapping>
```

No new persistent object is introduced. All the columns mapped for these components are in the same table as their parent object. Components don't have an identity, and they exist only if their parent does. They're most suitable for grouping several properties as a single object.

Using JPA Annotations

When you're using JPA annotations, for the Contact class, you need to annotate the class as Embeddable. You also map the columns to the regular default database columns:

```
package com.hibernaterecipes.annotations.domain;

import javax.persistence.Column;
import javax.persistence.Embeddable;
import javax.persistence.Entity;

@Embeddable
public class Contact {
```

```java
  private String recipient;
  private String phone;
  private String address;
  /**
   * @return the recipient
   */
  @Column (name = "WEEKDAY_RECIPIENT")
  public String getRecipient() {
    return recipient;
  }
  /**
   * @param recipient the recipient to set
   */
  public void setRecipient(String recipient) {
    this.recipient = recipient;
  }
  /**
   * @return the phone
   */
  @Column (name = "WEEKDAY_PHONE")
  public String getPhone() {
    return phone;
  }
  /**
   * @param phone the phone to set
   */
  public void setPhone(String phone) {
    this.phone = phone;
  }
  /**
   * @return the address
   */
  @Column (name = "WEEKDAY_ADDRESS")
  public String getAddress() {
    return address;
  }
  /**
   * @param address the address to set
   */
  public void setAddress(String address) {
    this.address = address;
  }
  /* (non-Javadoc)
   * @see java.lang.Object#toString()
   */
  @Override
  public String toString() {
    return "Contact [address=" + address + ", phone=" + phone
        + ", recipient=" + recipient + "]";
```

```
    }

}
```

For the Orders class, you annotate the weekday contact as embedded. For the holiday contact, you annotate the access as embedded and override the values provided in the Contact class as follows:

```
package com.hibernaterecipes.annotations.domain;

import javax.persistence.AttributeOverride;
import javax.persistence.AttributeOverrides;
import javax.persistence.Column;
import javax.persistence.Embedded;
import javax.persistence.Entity;
import javax.persistence.GeneratedValue;
import javax.persistence.GenerationType;
import javax.persistence.Id;
import javax.persistence.Table;

@Entity
@org.hibernate.annotations.Entity(dynamicInsert = true, dynamicUpdate = true)
@Table (name="ORDERS")
public class Orders {

  private Long id;
  private Contact weekdayContact;
  private Contact holidayContact;
  /**
   * @return the id
   */
  @Id
  @GeneratedValue (strategy=GenerationType.AUTO)
  @Column (name="ID")
  public Long getId() {
    return id;
  }
  /**
   * @param id the id to set
   */
  public void setId(Long id) {
    this.id = id;
  }

  /**
   * @return the weekdayContact
   */
  @Embedded
  public Contact getWeekdayContact() {
    return weekdayContact;
  }
  /**
```

```
 * @param weekdayContact the weekdayContact to set
 */
public void setWeekdayContact(Contact weekdayContact) {
  this.weekdayContact = weekdayContact;
}
/**
 * @return the holidayContact
 */
@Embedded
@AttributeOverrides({@AttributeOverride(name="recipient",
              column=@Column(name="HOLIDAY_RECIPIENT")),
@AttributeOverride(name="phone",
              column=@Column(name="HOLIDAY_PHONE")),
@AttributeOverride(name="address",
              column=@Column(name="HOLIDAY_ADDRESS"))})

public Contact getHolidayContact() {
  return holidayContact;
}
/**
 * @param holidayContact the holidayContact to set
 */
public void setHolidayContact(Contact holidayContact) {
  this.holidayContact = holidayContact;
}
/* (non-Javadoc)
 * @see java.lang.Object#toString()
 */
@Override
public String toString() {
  return "Orders [holidayContact=" + holidayContact + ", id=" + id
      + ", weekdayContact=" + weekdayContact + "]";
}

}
```

3.2 Nesting Components

Problem

How do you nest a component within a component?

Solution

Components can be defined to be *nested*—that is, embedded within other components. As per the JPA specification, support for only one level of embedding is required.

How It Works

You can define the Phone property as a component and embed it in the contact component:

```
package com.hibernaterecipes.chapter3;

public class Phone {

  private String areaCode;
  private String telNo;

  // getters and setters
}
```

Change the phone from type String to type Phone.

```
package com.hibernaterecipes.chapter3;

public class Contact {
  private String recipient;
  private Phone phone;
  private String address;

  // getters and setters
}
```

Also create a new XML file names Orders.xml, and add the nested component as show here:

```
<?xml version="1.0" encoding="UTF-8"?>
<!DOCTYPE hibernate-mapping PUBLIC
"-//Hibernate/Hibernate Mapping DTD 3.0//EN"
"http://hibernate.sourceforge.net/hibernate-mapping-3.0.dtd">
<hibernate-mapping package="com.hibernaterecipes.chapter3">
  <class name="Orders" table="BOOK_ORDERS">
    <id name="id" type="long" column="ID">
      <generator class="native" />
    </id>
    <component name="weekdayContact" class="Contact">
      <property name="recipient" type="string" column="WEEKDAY_RECIPIENT" />
      <component name="phone" class="Phone">
        <property name="areaCode" type="string" column="WEEKDAY_AREACODE" />
        <property name="telNo" type="string" column="WEEKDAY_TELEPHONE" />
      </component>
      <property name="address" type="string" column="WEEKDAY_ADDRESS" />
    </component>
    <component name="holidayContact" class="Contact">
      <property name="recipient" type="string" column="HOLIDAY_RECIPIENT" />
      <component name="phone" class="Phone">
        <property name="areaCode" type="string" column="HOLIDAY_AREACODE" />
        <property name="telNo" type="string" column="HOLIDAY_TELEPHONE" />
      </component>
```

```
        <property name="address" type="string" column="HOLIDAY_ADDRESS" />
      </component>
    </class>
</hibernate-mapping>
```

And now, add this new XML to the Hibernate XML mapping file. You can use the nested components as shown here in the main method:

```java
package com.hibernaterecipes.chapter3;

import org.hibernate.Session;
import org.hibernate.SessionFactory;
import org.hibernate.Transaction;
import org.hibernate.cfg.Configuration;
import org.hibernate.stat.Statistics;

public class Launch {
  private static SessionFactory sessionFactory;

  public static Session getSession() {
    if(sessionFactory == null)
    {
      sessionFactory = new Configuration().configure()
      .buildSessionFactory();
    }
    Session hibernateSession = sessionFactory.openSession();
    return hibernateSession;
  }
  public static void main(String[] args) {
    Session session = getSession();
    Statistics stats = sessionFactory.getStatistics();
    stats.setStatisticsEnabled(true);
    Transaction tx = session.beginTransaction();
    Orders ord = new Orders();
    Phone wdPhn = new Phone();
    Phone hlPhn = new Phone();
    wdPhn.setAreaCode("480");
    wdPhn.setTelNo("5463152");
    hlPhn.setAreaCode("702");
    hlPhn.setTelNo("5643569");
    Contact cnt = new Contact();
    Contact weekDayCnt = new Contact();
    cnt.setAddress("132,vacation street, Miami, Fl - 23232");
    cnt.setPhone(wdPhn);
    cnt.setRecipient("John Doe 1");
    weekDayCnt.setRecipient("John Doe");
    weekDayCnt.setAddress("512364, Permanent home, Scottsdale, AZ - 85254");
    weekDayCnt.setPhone(hlPhn);
    ord.setWeekdayContact(weekDayCnt);
    ord.setHolidayContact(cnt);
    session.save(ord);
    tx.commit();
```

```
        stats.getSessionOpenCount();
        stats.logSummary();
        session.close();

    }

}
```

3.3 Adding References in Components

Problem

How do you add a reference to a component's parent object? How do you provide associations within a component?

Solution

You can add a reference to the parent object by using the `<parent>` tag. The component tag allows for many-to-one and one-to-one associations with other tables.

How It Works

A component can have a reference to its parent object through a `<parent>` mapping:

```
public class Contact {
  private Orders order;
  private String recipient;
  private Phone phone;
  private String address;
  // Getters and Setters
}
```

```
<?xml version="1.0" encoding="UTF-8"?>
<!DOCTYPE hibernate-mapping PUBLIC
"-//Hibernate/Hibernate Mapping DTD 3.0//EN"
"http://hibernate.sourceforge.net/hibernate-mapping-3.0.dtd">
<hibernate-mapping package="com.hibernaterecipes.chapter3">
  <class name="Orders" table="ORDERS">
    <id name="id" type="long" column="ID">
      <generator class="native" />
    </id>
    <component name="weekdayContact" class="Contact">
      <parent name="order" />
      <property name="recipient" type="string" column="WEEKDAY_RECIPIENT" />
      <property name="phone" type="string" column="WEEKDAY_PHONE" />
      <property name="address" type="string" column="WEEKDAY_ADDRESS" />
    </component>
```

```xml
      <component name="holidayContact" class="Contact">
        <parent name="order" />
        <property name="recipient" type="string" column="HOLIDAY_RECIPIENT" />
        <property name="phone" type="string" column="HOLIDAY_PHONE" />
        <property name="address" type="string" column="HOLIDAY_ADDRESS" />
      </component>
   </class>
</hibernate-mapping>
```

In JPA, you add the reference to the parent entity and annotate the accessor method with @Parent:

```java
package com.hibernaterecipes.annotations.domain;

import javax.persistence.Column;
import javax.persistence.Embeddable;
import javax.persistence.Entity;

import org.hibernate.annotations.Parent;

@Embeddable
public class Contact {

  private String recipient;
  private String phone;
  private String address;
  private Orders order;

  @Parent
  public Orders getOrder() {
    return order;
  }

  // other getters and setters
}
```

A component can be used to group not only normal properties, but also many-to-one and one-to-one associations. Suppose you want to associate the address of an order to the address in your customer database. To do this, create an address table using the following query:

```sql
CREATE TABLE ADDRESS (id bigint NOT NULL,STREET_ADDRESS_1 varchar(100),STREET_ADDRESS_2
varchar(100),CITY varchar(100),STATE varchar(2),ZIP_CODE INT,PRIMARY KEY (id))
```

Now, create the entity class and the Hibernate mapping XML file:

```java
package com.hibernaterecipes.chapter3;

public class Address {
  private Long id;
  private String address1;
  private String address2;
  private String city;
```

```
  private String state;
  private Integer zipCode;

  // getters and setters
}
```

```xml
<?xml version="1.0" encoding="UTF-8"?>
<!DOCTYPE hibernate-mapping PUBLIC
"-//Hibernate/Hibernate Mapping DTD 3.0//EN"
"http://hibernate.sourceforge.net/hibernate-mapping-3.0.dtd">
<hibernate-mapping package="com.hibernaterecipes.chapter3">
  <class name="Address" table="ADDRESS">
    <id name="id" type="long" column="ID">
      <generator class="native" />
    </id>
    <property name="address1" type="string" column="STREET_ADDRESS_1" />
    <property name="address2" type="string" column="STREET_ADDRESS_2" />
    <property name="city" type="string" column="CITY" />
    <property name="state" type="string" column="STATE" />
    <property name="zipCode" type="integer" column="ZIP_CODE" />
  </class>
</hibernate-mapping>
```

And now, edit the Contact class as follows:

```java
package com.hibernaterecipes.chapter3;

public class Contact {
  private String recipient;
  private Phone phone;
  private Address address;

        // getters and setters
}
```

Change the Orders XML mapping file to include the association:

```xml
<?xml version="1.0" encoding="UTF-8"?>
<!DOCTYPE hibernate-mapping PUBLIC
"-//Hibernate/Hibernate Mapping DTD 3.0//EN"
"http://hibernate.sourceforge.net/hibernate-mapping-3.0.dtd">
<hibernate-mapping package="com.hibernaterecipes.chapter3">
  <class name="Orders" table="ORDERS">
    <id name="id" type="long" column="ID">
      <generator class="native" />
    </id>
    <component name="weekdayContact" class="Contact">
      <property name="recipient" type="string" column="WEEKDAY_RECIPIENT" />
      <component name="phone" class="Phone">
        <property name="areaCode" type="string" column="WEEKDAY_AREACODE" />
```

```
      <property name="telNo" type="string" column="WEEKDAY_TELEPHONE" />
    </component>
    <many-to-one name="address" class="Address" column="WEEKDAY_ADDRESS_ID" />
  </component>
  <component name="holidayContact" class="Contact">
    <property name="recipient" type="string" column="HOLIDAY_RECIPIENT" />
    <component name="phone" class="Phone">
      <property name="areaCode" type="string" column="HOLIDAY_AREACODE" />
      <property name="telNo" type="string" column="HOLIDAY_TELEPHONE" />
    </component>
    <many-to-one name="address" class="Address" column="HOLIDAY_ADDRESS_ID" />
  </component>
  </class>
</hibernate-mapping>
```

3.4 Mapping a Collection of Components

Problem

Does Hibernate support mapping a collection of dependent objects? How do you map a collection of components?

Solution

Hibernate provides `<composite-element>` for mapping a collection of components. The collection elements/tags `<set>`, `<list>`, `<map>`, `<bag>`, and `<idbag>` can accommodate the `<composite-element>` to map a collection of dependent objects.

How It Works

Suppose you need to support a more flexible contact mechanism for book orders. A customer can specify several contact points for a book delivery, because they may not sure which one is most suitable for a specified time period. Your staff tries these contact points one by one when they deliver books. You can use a `java.util.Set` to hold all the contact points for an order:

```
public class Orders {
private Contact weekdayContact;
private Contact holidayContact;
private Set contacts;
// Getters and Setters
}
```

You need to create a separate table as follows:

```
CREATE TABLE ORDERS_CONTACT (ORDER_ID bigint NOT NULL, RECIPIENT varchar(100),AREACODE
varchar(100),TELEPHONE varchar(100),ADDRESS varchar(100))
```

To map many contact points for an order in Hibernate, you can use a collection of components. You use `<composite-element>` to define the components in a collection. For simplicity, you first roll back your Contact class to its original form:

```java
public class Contact {
  private String recipient;
  private String phone;
  private String address;
  // Getters and Setters
  // equals and hashCode implementation
}
```

```xml
<?xml version="1.0" encoding="UTF-8"?>
<!DOCTYPE hibernate-mapping PUBLIC
"-//Hibernate/Hibernate Mapping DTD 3.0//EN"
"http://hibernate.sourceforge.net/hibernate-mapping-3.0.dtd">
<hibernate-mapping package="com.hibernaterecipes.chapter3">
  <class name="Orders" table="ORDERS">
    <id name="id" type="long" column="ID">
      <generator class="native" />
    </id>
    <set name="contacts" table="ORDERS_CONTACT">
      <key column="ORDER_ID" />
      <composite-element class="Contact">
        <property name="recipient" type="string" column="RECIPIENT" />
        <property name="phone" type="string" column="TELEPHONE" />
        <property name="address" type="string" column="ADDRESS" />
      </composite-element>
    </set>
  </class>
</hibernate-mapping>
```

In this implementation, you use the `<set>` tag. Because `java.util.Set` doesn't allow for duplicate elements, you need to implement the `equals()` and `hashCode()` methods. The database's primary key shouldn't be the only property used for comparison in the implementation of `equals()` and `hashCode()`. If the database primary key is the only property used in the implementation of `equals()` and `hashCode()`, then users can't add multiple `contacts` to the `set`, because the primary key will be `null` before it's persisted. It's recommended that you use other properties as well to obtain uniqueness among objects. Hence, proper implementation of `equals()` and `hashCode()` is required to ensure that duplicate elements aren't added. Note that `<composite-element>` doesn't allow null values when the enclosing collection tag is a `<set>` because for delete operations, Hibernate needs to identify each composite element to be able to delete that particular element.

In additional to normal properties, you can define nested components and associations in a collection. You use `<nested-composite-element>` to define nested components in a collection. Let's perform the necessary changes to the `Contact` class first:

```java
public class Contact {
  private String recipient;
  private Phone phone;
  private Address address;
```

```
  // Getters and Setters
}
<hibernate-mapping package=" com.hibernaterecipes.chapter3">
  <class name="Orders" table="ORDERS">
    <set name="contacts" table="ORDERS_CONTACT">
      <key column="ORDER_ID" />
      <composite-element class="Contact">
        <property name="recipient" type="string" column="RECIPIENT" />
        <property name="phone" type="string" column="PHONE" />
        <nested-composite-element name="phone" class="Phone">
          <property name="areaCode" type="string" column="PHONE_AREA_CODE" />
          <property name="telNo" type="string" column="PHONE_TEL_NO" />
        </nested-composite-element>
        <property name="address" type="string" column="ADDRESS" />
        <many-to-one name="address" class="Address" column="ADDRESS_ID" />
      </composite-element>
    </set>
  </class>
</hibernate-mapping>
```

In JPA, change the Orders class as shown here:

```
package com.hibernaterecipes.annotations.domain;

import java.io.Serializable;
import java.util.Set;
import javax.persistence.CascadeType;
import javax.persistence.Column;
import javax.persistence.Entity;
import javax.persistence.FetchType;
import javax.persistence.GeneratedValue;
import javax.persistence.GenerationType;
import javax.persistence.Id;
import javax.persistence.JoinColumn;
import javax.persistence.JoinTable;
import javax.persistence.OneToMany;
import javax.persistence.Table;
import org.hibernate.annotations.CollectionOfElements;
import org.hibernate.annotations.Target;

@Entity
@org.hibernate.annotations.Entity(dynamicInsert = true, dynamicUpdate = true)
@Table (name="ORDERS")
public class Orders implements Serializable{

  private Long id;
  private Set<Contact> contacts;

  /**
   * @return the id
   */
```

```java
@Id
@GeneratedValue (strategy=GenerationType.AUTO)
@Column (name="ID")
public Long getId() {
   return id;
}

public void setId(Long id) {
   this.id = id;
}
/**
 * @return the contacts
 */
@CollectionOfElements (targetElement=Contact.class,fetch=FetchType.EAGER)
@JoinTable (name = "ORDERS_CONTACT" ,
    joinColumns = @JoinColumn(name="ORDER_ID"))
public Set<Contact> getContacts() {
   return contacts;
}

public void setContacts(Set<Contact> contacts) {
   this.contacts = contacts;
}
/* (non-Javadoc)
 * @see java.lang.Object#toString()
 */
@Override
public String toString() {
   return "Orders [contacts=" + contacts + ", id=" + id + "]";
}
}
```

The Contact table must be provided with the new table name. Also note that you still don't have a primary key for the new table ORDERS_CONTACT:

```java
package com.hibernaterecipes.annotations.domain;

import java.io.Serializable;
import javax.persistence.Column;
import javax.persistence.Embeddable;
import javax.persistence.Table;
import org.hibernate.annotations.Parent;

@Embeddable
@Table (name="ORDERS_CONTACT")
public class Contact implements Serializable{

   private String recipient;
   private String phone;
   private String address;
   private Orders order;
```

```java
/**
 * @return the recipient
 */
@Column (name = "RECIPIENT")
public String getRecipient() {
  return recipient;
}
/**
 * @param recipient the recipient to set
 */
public void setRecipient(String recipient) {
  this.recipient = recipient;
}
/**
 * @return the phone
 */
@Column (name = "TELEPHONE")
public String getPhone() {
  return phone;
}
/**
 * @param phone the phone to set
 */
public void setPhone(String phone) {
  this.phone = phone;
}
/**
 * @return the address
 */
@Column (name = "ADDRESS")
public String getAddress() {
  return address;
}
/**
 * @param address the address to set
 */
public void setAddress(String address) {
  this.address = address;
}

/**
 * @return the order
 */
@Parent
public Orders getOrder() {
  return order;
}
/**
 * @param order the order to set
 */
public void setOrder(Orders order) {
  this.order = order;
```

```
    }
    /* (non-Javadoc)
     * @see java.lang.Object#toString()
     */
    @Override
    public String toString() {
      return "Contact [address=" + address + ", phone=" + phone
          + ", recipient=" + recipient + "]";
    }
}
```

3.5 Using Components as Keys to a Map

Problem

Normally, the key to a map can be a `String`, a `Long`, an `Integer`, and so on. But what if you need to implement your own map key? Does Hibernate allow you to map a component class as a key to a map? If so, how do you map components as keys to a map?

Solution

Hibernate provides `<composite-map-key>`, which lets you use components as map keys.

How It Works

Suppose you want to extend your collection of contact points to be of `java.util.Map` type. You can use date periods as the keys of the map. You create a class `Period` to encapsulate the start date and end date of a period, and you use that as your map's key type. You then define this period as a component in the `Orders` class. The customer can now specify the most suitable contact point for a particular date period:

```
public class Period {
  private Date startDate;
  private Date endDate;
  // Getters and Setters
}
<hibernate-mapping package="com.metaarchit.bookshop">
  <class name="Orders" table="ORDERS">
...
    <map name="contacts" table="ORDERS_CONTACT">
      <key column="ORDER_ID" />
      <composite-map-key class="Period">
        <key-property name="startDate" type="date" column="START_DATE" />
        <key-property name="endDate" type="date" column="END_DATE" />
      </composite-map-key>
      <composite-element class="Contact">
        <property name="recipient" type="string" column="RECIPIENT" />
```

```
        <nested-composite-element name="phone" class="Phone">
          <property name="areaCode" type="string" column="PHONE_AREA_CODE" />
          <property name="telNo" type="string" column="PHONE_TEL_NO" />
        </nested-composite-element>
        <many-to-one name="address" class="Address" column="ADDRESS_ID" />
      </composite-element>
    </map>
  </class>
</hibernate-mapping>
```

For the map-key component to work properly, you need to override the `equals()` and `hashCode()` methods of the component class:

```
public class Period {
  ...
  public boolean equals(Object obj) {
    if (!(obj instanceof Period)) return false;
    Period other = (Period) obj;
    return new EqualsBuilder().append(startDate, other.startDate)
      .append(endDate, other.endDate)
      .isEquals();
  }
  public int hashCode() {
    return new HashCodeBuilder().append(startDate)
      .append(endDate)
      .toHashCode();
  }
}
```

Summary

In this chapter, you've learned a way to achieve a finer-grained object model by using value types as components. You've effectively created an object graph for use in an application, but it's represented in the database as a single record in a table. You've also seen a way to bridge the gap between relational model and object model by using simple `value` types. You've learned how to nest components within other components and how to add the parent reference in a component. And you've seen how to map a collection of components in an entity and use components as key to a `java.util.Map`.

CHAPTER 4

■ ■ ■

Inheritance and Custom Mapping

Inheritance, polymorphic associations, and polymorphic queries are supported by entities. The JPA specification says that both concrete and abstract classes can be entities and can be mapped with the `Entity` annotation. Non-entity classes and entity classes can extend each other. Hibernate provides the `MappedSuperClass` annotation (`@MappedSuperclass`) to enable inheritance mapping and to let you map abstract or concrete entity subclasses. The mapped superclass doesn't have its own separate table.

Hibernate provides four strategies for mapping an inheritance hierarchy:

- *Table per class hierarchy:* The class hierarchy is represented in one table. A discriminator column identifies the type and the subclass.

- *Table per subclass:* The superclass has a table and each subclass has a table that contains only un-inherited properties: the subclass tables have a primary key that is a foreign key of the superclass.

- *Table per concrete class with unions:* the superclass can be an abstract class or even an interface. If the superclass is concrete, an additional table is required to map the properties of that class.

- *Table per concrete class with implicit polymorphism:* each table contains all the properties of the concrete class and the properties that are inherited from its superclasses. Here, all the subclasses are mapped as separate entities.

This chapter discusses these strategies in detail and shows how to implement them.

The properties of all persistent entities are of certain types, such as `String`. Some of the important basic types supported by Hibernate are as follows:

- `integer`, `long`, `short`, `float`, `double`, `character`, `byte`, `boolean`, `yes_no`, and `true_false`. Type mappings for Java primitives and wrapper classes.

- `string`. Type mappings from `java.lang.String` to something like a `VARCHAR`.

- `date`, `time`, and `timestamp`. Type mapping from `java.util.Date` and its subclasses to their appropriate SQL types.

Other basic mappings supported by Hibernate include `calendar`, `calendar_date`, `big_decimal`, `big_integer`, `locale`, `timezone`, `currency`, `class`, `binary`, `text`, and `serializable`. Hibernate also provides an API to implement your own custom types. You can use two packages, `org.hibernate.type` and `org.hibernate.userType`, to define object types. You can define your own custom types either by implementing `org.hibernate.type.Type` directly or by extending one of the abstract classes provided in the `org.hibernate.type` package; or you can implement one of the interfaces in the `org.hibernate.userType` package. This chapter discusses the custom mapping types available in Hibernate's `org.hibernate.userType` package. You go through the implementation details of the `userType` and `CompositeUserType` extensions.

4.1 Mapping Entities with Table per Class Hierarchy

Problem

How do you map entities using the table per class hierarchy strategy? And when should you use it?

Solution

To use the table per class hierarchy strategy, you need to create a single table that contains the state of the complete class hierarchy. The key is that the subclass state can't have not-null constraints. This is a disadvantage, because data integrity is compromised. Because all the state is in the same table, it's a denormalized model.

With this strategy, you get the advantage of good performance for both polymorphic and nonpolymorphic queries. The denormalization of the class hierarchy in the relational model can cause data stability and maintainability issues, so it's a good idea to run this by your DBA.

You use the audio and video section of your bookshop to learn about inheritance mapping. Suppose that your bookshop also sells CDs and DVDs. Figure 4-1 shows the class diagram of the object model you map as table per class hierarchy.

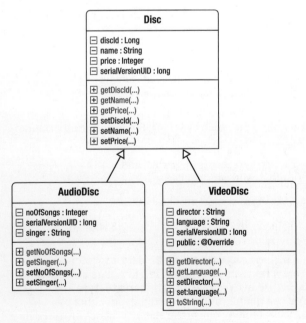

Figure 4-1. Class diagram of the object model

You first create a class `Disc` and provide a mapping definition for it:

```
public class Disc {
  private Long id;
  private String name;
  private Integer price;
  // Getters and Setters
}
```

```xml
<hibernate-mapping package="com.hibernaterecipes.chapter4.tablePerClassHierarchy">
  <class name="Disc" table="Disc_1">
    <id name="discId" type="long" column="DISC_ID">
      <generator class="native"/>
    </id>
    <discriminator column="DISC_TYPE" type="string" />
    <property name="name" type="java.lang.String" column="NAME" />
    <property name="price" type="java.lang.Integer" column="PRICE" />

  </class>
</hibernate-mapping>
```

You primarily sell two kinds of discs: audio discs and video discs. Each kind has different properties. From an object-oriented perspective, you should model these two kinds of discs, **AudioDisc** and **VideoDisc**, as *subclasses* of **Disc** to represent an "is-a" relationship. In Java, you use the **extends** keyword to define a subclass of a class. Conversely the class **Disc** is called the *superclass* or *parent class* of **AudioDisc** and **VideoDisc**:

```
public class AudioDisc extends Disc {
  private String singer;
  private Integer numOfSongs;
  // Getters and Setters
}
```

```
public class VideoDisc extends Disc {
  private String director;
  private String language;
  // Getters and Setters
}
```

The relationship between a subclass (such as **AudioDisc** or **VideoDisc**) to its parent class (**Disc**) is called *inheritance*. All the subclasses and their parents make up a *class hierarchy*. A relational model has no concept of inheritance—that means you must define a mapping mechanism to persist the inheritance relationships of your object model.

For the disc hierarchy, you can use the following query to find all the discs in your system, both audio and video. This kind of query is called a *polymorphic query*.

```
Session session = factory.openSession();
try {
  Query query = session.createQuery("from Disc");
  List discs = query.list();
  return discs;
```

```
} finally {
  session.close();
}
```

Suppose you want to support disc reservation for your online bookshop. You can create a class Reservation and define a many-to-one association to the Disc class. Because the concrete class of the disc may be AudioDisc or VideoDisc, and this can only be determined at runtime, this kind of association is called *polymorphic association*:

```
public class Reservation {
  private Long id;
  private Disc disc;
  private Customer customer;
  private int quantity;
}
```

How It Works

In Hibernate, the subclass element is used to create a table per class hierarchy mapping. The discriminator element is used to associate the subclasses with the superclass. The following query creates the table:

```
CREATE TABLE "BOOK"."DISC_1"
  (    "DISC_ID" BIGINT NOT NULL ,
        "NAME" VARCHAR(250 ) NOT NULL ,
    "PRICE" BIGINT,
    "DISC_TYPE" VARCHAR(50),
        "SINGER" VARCHAR(50),
        "NO_OF_SONGS" BIGINT,
        "DIRECTOR" VARCHAR(50),
        "LANGUAGE" VARCHAR(50),
    CONSTRAINT "DISC_1_PK" PRIMARY KEY ("DISC_ID") );
```

The Hibernate mapping file looks like this:

```
<hibernate-mapping package="com.hibernaterecipes.chapter4.tablePerClassHierarchy">
  <class name="Disc" table="Disc_1">
    <id name="discId" type="long" column="DISC_ID">
      <generator class="native"/>
    </id>
    <discriminator column="DISC_TYPE" type="string" />
    <property name="name" type="java.lang.String" column="NAME" />
    <property name="price" type="java.lang.Integer" column="PRICE" />
    <subclass name="AudioDisc" discriminator-value="AUDIO">
      <property name="singer" type="java.lang.String" column="SINGER" />
      <property name="noOfSongs" type="java.lang.Integer" column="NO_OF_SONGS" />
    </subclass>
    <subclass name="VideoDisc" discriminator-value="VIDEO">
      <property name="director" type="java.lang.String" column="DIRECTOR" />
      <property name="language" type="java.lang.String" column="LANGUAGE" />
```

```
        </subclass>
    </class>
</hibernate-mapping>
```

The class is mapped to the top-level class, which is `Disc`. The persistent classes `AudioDisc` and `VideoDisc` are distinguished from each other by the `discriminator`, which is mapped to a column `DISC_TYPE`. The other properties of the superclass are mapped using the `property` element.

The persistent classes are mapped with the `subclass` element, which has a `discriminator-value` attribute that differentiates if from other persistent classes. So, when an `AudioDisc` is saved, the `DISC_TYPE` column for that record has the value `AUDIO`. Similarly, for `VideoDisc` records, the `DISC_TYPE` column holds the value `VIDEO`. The subclass element contains properties of the persistent class. It can also contain nested subclass elements; collection elements like `list`, `map`, and `set`; and a `one-to-one` or `many-to-one` element.

To implement this in JPA, you have the `Disc` class use the `Inheritance` and `DiscriminatorColumn` annotations as shown here:

```
@Entity
@Inheritance (strategy=InheritanceType.SINGLE_TABLE)
@DiscriminatorColumn(name="DISC_TYPE",
    discriminatorType=DiscriminatorType.STRING)
public class Disc_1 implements Serializable {

    @Id
    @GeneratedValue (strategy=GenerationType.AUTO)
    @Column (name="DISC_ID")
    private Long discId;

    @Column (name="NAME")
    private String name;

    @Column (name="PRICE")
    private Integer price;

    //Getters  and Setters
}
```

This inheritance strategy is described by an inheritance type of `SINGLE_TABLE`; the discriminator column name and type are also defined in the parent class. Subclasses like `AudioDisc` use the `Discriminator` annotation to describe the value to be used:

```
@Entity
@DiscriminatorValue ("AUDIO")
public class AudioDisc_1 extends Disc_1 implements Serializable {

    private static final long serialVersionUID = 8510682776718466795L;

    @Column (name="NO_OF_SONGS")
    private Integer noOfSongs;

    @Column (name="SINGER")
    private String singer;
```

```
//Getters  and Setters
}
```

Similarly, the **VideoDisc** class is as follows:

```
@Entity
@DiscriminatorValue ("VIDEO")
public class VideoDisc_1 extends Disc_1 implements Serializable {

    private static final long serialVersionUID = -3637473456207740684L;

    @Column (name="DIRECTOR")
    private String director;
    @Column (name="LANGUAGE")
    private String language;

    //Getters  and Setters
}
```

To save an audio disc record, Hibernate executes a SQL that looks like this:

```
insert into Disc_1 (NAME, PRICE, SINGER, NO_OF_SONGS, DISC_TYPE, DISC_ID)
values (?, ?, ?, ?, 'AUDIO', ?)
```

If you query for audio discs, you use a query something like **session.createQuery("from AudioDisc").list();**. Hibernate converts this into a query like the following:

```
select a.DISC_ID, a.NAME , a.PRICE , a.SINGER , a.NO_OF_SONGS from Disc_1 a where
a.DISC_TYPE='AUDIO'
```

If you query for the superclass **Disc** using **session.createQuery("from Disc").list();**, the query that Hibernate executes is

```
select a.DISC_ID , a.NAME, a.PRICE , a.SINGER , a.NO_OF_SONGS , a.DIRECTOR, a.LANGUAGE ,
a.DISC_TYPE from Disc_1 a _
```

You can see that polymorphic queries are easy with this strategy. This approach should be your default choice for all simple problems. Also use this strategy when subclasses have few properties and inherit most of the properties. The idea is to keep the nullable columns from all the subclasses at a minimum.

4.2 Mapping Entities with Table per Subclass

Problem

How do you map entities using the table per subclass strategy? And when should you use it?

Solution

To use the table per subclass strategy, you need to create a superclass **Disc** (and a corresponding table) and create a table per subclass that contains only un-inherited properties. The two tables are associated with a foreign key: the subclass tables have a primary key that is a foreign key of the superclass. The advantage of this strategy is that the model is normalized.

How It Works

Begin by creating the tables using the following queries:

```
CREATE TABLE "BOOK"."DISC_2"
   ( "DISC_ID" BIGINT NOT NULL ,
 "NAME" VARCHAR(250 ) NOT NULL ,
 "PRICE" BIGINT,
  CONSTRAINT "DISC_2_PK" PRIMARY KEY ("DISC_ID") )

CREATE TABLE "BOOK"."AUDIO_DISC_2"
   ( "DISC_ID" BIGINT NOT NULL ,
 "SINGER" VARCHAR(50),"NO_OF_SONGS" BIGINT,
  CONSTRAINT "DISC_2_FK" FOREIGN KEY ("DISC_ID") REFERENCES DISC_2(DISC_ID))

CREATE TABLE "BOOK"."VIDEO_DISC_2"
   ( "DISC_ID" BIGINT NOT NULL ,
 "DIRECTOR" VARCHAR(50),"LANGUAGE" VARCHAR(50),
  CONSTRAINT "DISC_2_1_FK" FOREIGN KEY ("DISC_ID") REFERENCES DISC_2(DISC_ID))
```

In Hibernate, the superclass element is as follows:

```
public class Disc_2 implements Serializable {


  private static final long serialVersionUID = -5119119376751110049L;

  private Long discId;
  private String name;
  private Integer price;

  // getters and setters
}
```

And the audio and video subclasses look like this:

```
public class AudioDisc_2 extends Disc_2 implements Serializable {

  private static final long serialVersionUID = 1542177945025584005L;
  private Integer noOfSongs;
  private String singer;
  // getters and setters
```

```
}

public class VideoDisc_2 extends Disc_2 implements Serializable {

  private static final long serialVersionUID = 3052184294723526581L;
  private String director;
  private String language;
  // getters and setters
}
```

The mapping file is as follows:

```
<hibernate-mapping package="com.hibernaterecipes.chapter4.tablePerSubClass">
  <class name="Disc_2" table="Disc_2">
    <id name="discId" type="long" column="DISC_ID">
      <generator class="native"/>
    </id>
    <property name="name" type="java.lang.String" column="NAME" />
    <property name="price" type="java.lang.Integer" column="PRICE" />
    <joined-subclass name="AudioDisc_2" table="AUDIO_DISC_2">
      <key column="DISC_ID"></key>
      <property name="singer" type="java.lang.String" column="SINGER" />
      <property name="noOfSongs" type="java.lang.Integer" column="NO_OF_SONGS" />
    </joined-subclass>
    <joined-subclass name="VideoDisc_2" table="VIDEO_DISC_2">
      <key column="DISC_ID"></key>
      <property name="director" type="java.lang.String" column="DIRECTOR" />
      <property name="language" type="java.lang.String" column="LANGUAGE" />
    </joined-subclass>
  </class>
</hibernate-mapping>
```

The superclass Disc is defined as the root class and has a primary key of DISC_ID. The subclass is mapped using the joined-subclass element, and the joined-subclass element defines the subclass table with the attribute table. The joined-subclass classes like the AudioDisc class have a key element that provides for the association between itself and its parent.

Using JPA annotation, the superclass (Disc in this case) uses the Inheritance annotation with the inheritance strategy type of JOINED:

```
@Entity
@Inheritance (strategy=InheritanceType.JOINED)
public abstract class Disc_2 implements Serializable {

  private static final long serialVersionUID = 3087285416805917315L;
  @Id
  @GeneratedValue (strategy=GenerationType.AUTO)
  @Column (name="DISC_ID")
  private Long discId;
  @Column (name="NAME")
```

```
    private String name;
    @Column (name="PRICE")
    private Integer price;

    //getters and settes
}
```

The audio and video subclasses are annotated like regular entity classes and are associated with the parent class with the **PrimaryKeyJoinColumn** annotation. **PrimaryKeyJoinColumn** is required only when the name of the column in the subclass is different from that of the superclass. When the name of the primary column is the same in both classes, Hibernate inherits the property and column from the superclass:

```
@Entity
@Table (name="AUDIO_DISC_2")
@PrimaryKeyJoinColumn (name="DISC_ID")
public class AudioDisc_2 extends Disc_2 implements Serializable {

    private static final long serialVersionUID = 8510682776718466795L;

    @Column (name="NO_OF_SONGS")
    private Integer noOfSongs;
    @Column (name="SINGER")
    private String singer;
        // getter and setters
}

@Entity
@Table (name="VIDEO_DISC_2")
@PrimaryKeyJoinColumn (name="DISC_ID")
public class VideoDisc_2 extends Disc_2 implements Serializable {

    private static final long serialVersionUID = -3637473456207740684L;

    @Column (name="DIRECTOR")
    private String director;
    @Column (name="LANGUAGE")
    private String language;

        // getter and setters
}
```

If you query for a disc, Hibernate uses an outer join to determine the associated subclasses. The query that is used is as follows; as you can see, it may not be simple—at least, not as simple as it looks from the mapping you gave Hibernate:

```
select a.DISC_ID , a.NAME , a.PRICE , b.SINGER , b.NO_OF_SONGS , c.DIRECTOR , c.LANGUAGE ,
case when b.DISC_ID is not null then 1
    when c.DISC_ID is not null then 2
    when a.DISC_ID is not null then 0 else -1 end as clazz_
from Disc_2 a
```

```
left outer join AUDIO_DISC_2 b on a.DISC_ID=b.DISC_ID
left outer join VIDEO_DISC_2 c on a.DISC_ID=c.DISC_ID
```

To query the subclasses, Hibernate uses the following inner join:

```
select b.DISC_ID , a.NAME , a.PRICE , b.SINGER  b.NO_OF_SONGS
from AUDIO_DISC_2 b inner join Disc_2 a
on b.DISC_ID=a.DISC_ID
```

You should use this strategy when there is a requirement to use polymorphic associations and polymorphic queries. The subclasses' state varies a great deal: that is, the properties that one subclass holds are very different from the properties that other subclasses hold. Also, when the class hierarchy is spread across many classes (depth of inheritance), this strategy can have an impact on performance.

4.3 Mapping Entities with Table per Concrete Class

Problem

How do you map entities using the table per concrete class strategy? And when should you use it?

Solution

You can use the table per concrete class strategy two ways:

- Table per concrete class with implicit polymorphism

- Table per concrete class with unions

Using table per concrete class with implicit polymorphism, the table contains all the properties of the concrete class and the properties that are inherited from its superclasses. All subclasses are mapped as separate entities. You should use this strategy when the requirement for polymorphic association or polymorphic query is minimal. Another issue with this strategy is that columns are duplicated; this can cause maintenance problems because a change to the superclass requires you to change multiple tables. The mapping is similar to a regular entity, so you don't work through an example of it.

Using table per concrete class with unions, the superclass can be an abstract class or even an interface. The subclasses are mapped using the **union-subclass** element. If the superclass is concrete, an additional table is required to map the properties of that class.

How It Works

You begin by creating the tables using the following Data Definition Language (DDL):

```
CREATE TABLE "BOOK"."AUDIO_DISC_3"
   ( "DISC_ID" BIGINT NOT NULL ,
 "NAME" VARCHAR(250 ) NOT NULL ,
 "PRICE" BIGINT,
 "SINGER" VARCHAR(50),"NO_OF_SONGS" BIGINT,
```

```
    CONSTRAINT "DISC_3_0_PK" PRIMARY KEY ("DISC_ID") )

CREATE TABLE "BOOK"."VIDEO_DISC_3"
   ( "DISC_ID" BIGINT NOT NULL ,
 "NAME" VARCHAR(250 ) NOT NULL ,
 "PRICE" BIGINT,
 "DIRECTOR" VARCHAR(50),"LANGUAGE" VARCHAR(50),
   CONSTRAINT "DISC_3_1_PK" PRIMARY KEY ("DISC_ID") )
```

The Disc, AudioDisc, and VideoDisc classes are as follows:

```
public abstract class Disc_3 implements Serializable {
    private static final long serialVersionUID = -5119119376751110049L;
    private Long discId;
    private String name;
    private Integer price;
    //getters and setters
}

public class AudioDisc3 extends Disc_3 implements Serializable {
    private static final long serialVersionUID = -8314602929677976050L;
    private Integer noOfSongs;
    private String singer;
    //getters and setters
}

public class VideoDisc_3 extends Disc_3 implements Serializable {
    private static final long serialVersionUID = -6857479057343664829L;
    private String director;
    private String language;
    //getters and setters
}
```

Note that the Disc_3 class is an abstract class. The Hibernate mapping file is as follows:

```
<hibernate-mapping package="com.hibernaterecipes.chapter4.tablePerClassHierarchy">
  <class name="Disc_3" abstract="true">
    <id name="discId" type="long" column="DISC_ID">
      <generator class="native"/>
    </id>
    <property name="name" type="java.lang.String" column="NAME" />
    <property name="price" type="java.lang.Integer" column="PRICE" />
    <union-subclass name="AudioDisc_3" table="AUDIO_DISC_3">
      <property name="singer" type="java.lang.String" column="SINGER" />
      <property name="noOfSongs" type="java.lang.Integer" column="NO_OF_SONGS" />
    </union-subclass>
    <union-subclass name="VideoDisc_3" table="VIDEO_DISC_3">
      <property name="director" type="java.lang.String" column="DIRECTOR" />
      <property name="language" type="java.lang.String" column="LANGUAGE" />
    </union-subclass>
  </class>
```

```
</hibernate-mapping>
```

The superclass **Disc_3** must be declared **abstract="true"**. If you choose not to have an abstract superclass, then you need a separate table for the superclass properties. The primary key is shared among all the concrete classes in the hierarchy. The primary key and inherited properties are mapped with the root class element. This way, duplication of inherited properties in each subclass isn't required. The concrete class is mapped to a single table the way **AudioDisc_3** is mapped to the **AUDIO_DISC_3** table; it inherits the superclass properties and the identifier. The concrete class is mapped using the **union-subclass** element.

The JPA specifications state that the table per concrete class is optional. However, Hibernate provides the implementation. In JPA annotations, you have the superclass **Disc** (**Disc_4** in the following case) use the **Inheritance** annotation and the **TABLE_PER_CLASS** inheritance type strategy:

```
@Entity
@Inheritance (strategy=InheritanceType.TABLE_PER_CLASS)
public abstract class Disc_4 implements Serializable {

    private static final long serialVersionUID = 3087285416805917315L;

    @Id
    @GeneratedValue (strategy=GenerationType.AUTO)
    @Column (name="DISC_ID")
    private Long discId;
    @Column (name="NAME")
    private String name;
    @Column (name="PRICE")
    private Integer price;

    //getters and setters
}
```

All the concrete class has to do is to declare itself as an **Entity** with the **Entity** annotation:

```
@Entity
@Table (name="AUDIO_DISC_4")
public class AudioDisc_4 extends Disc_4 implements Serializable {

    private static final long serialVersionUID = 8510682776718466795L;

    @Column (name="NO_OF_SONGS")
    private Integer noOfSongs;
    @Column (name="SINGER")
    private String singer;
    //getters and setters
}
```

Because the mapping is table per concrete class, the query created is for direct concrete class. If you need a polymorphic querying capability, you must make the superclass a persistent class (have a table of its own).

4.4 Custom Mappings

Problem

What are the various extensions that Hibernate provides to implement custom mapping types? How do you create UserType custom mapping?

Solution

Hibernate provides an interface that you can implement to define your own custom mapping types. The extensions are listed in the org.hibernate.usertype package and are as follows:

- **CompositeUserType**: This user type exposes the internals of the value type to Hibernate, which allows you to query for specific internal properties.

- **EnhancedUserType**: This is used when marshalling of value types to and from XML is required. It lets you use the custom type in identifier and discriminator mappings.

- **LoggableUserType**: This type is used when you want custom logging of the corresponding value types.

- **ParameterizedType**: You can set parameters for a type by using a nested type element for the **property** element in the mapping file or by defining a typedef.

- **UserCollectionType**: Use this type when you want to implement a custom collection mapping type and when you have to persist a non-JDK type collection.

- **UserType**: This is a basic extension point. It provides a basic framework to implement custom loading and storing of **value** type instances.

- **UserVersionType**: This type is used for a version property.

How It Works

Let's say your object model has a phone object. The phone object has two properties: **areaCode** and **telNo**. The database has a single column for this phone object, of the format **areaCode-telNo**. It's recommended by Hibernate that the **phone** class be immutable, which means you need to make the properties final and have a constructor that sets these properties on initialization. Using an immutable class makes the implementation easier.

The following example demonstrates the implementation for a mutable class:

```
public class PhoneCh4_4 {

  private String areaCode;
  private String telNo;
  // getters and setters
}
```

You can write your own phone type that implements the **UserType** interface. The implementation, shown in a moment, uses the following methods:

- **Assemble**: Reconstructs an object from the cacheable representation. If the object is immutable, then you can return the cached object. Mutable objects are expected to at least perform a deep copy.

- **Disassemble**: Called when Hibernate is storing the object as a serialized object in second-level memory or cache. (Caching in discussed further in Chapter 12.) For immutable objects, you typecast the object as serializable and return it. For mutable objects, you should return a deep copy. Also, it may not as simple if the mutable object has other associations. Associations should be cached as identifier values.

- **deepCopy**: Returns the persistent state of the object. For immutable objects, it can return the object itself.

- **Equals**: Checks the equality of two instances for persistent state.

- **hashCode**: Performs a hash-code implementation for the instance.

- **isMutable**: Specifies whether objects of this type are immutable.

- **nullSafeGet**: Retrieves the object from the JDBC resultset.

- **nullSafeSet**: Writes the object property value to the JDBC prepared statement.

- **replace**: Used when you're merging with a detached instance. For immutable objects, you can return the first parameter (original). For mutable objects, you return a copy of the first parameter. A recursive copy should be performed if the mutable objects have component fields.

- returnedClass: Specifies the class returned by the nullSafeGet method.

- sqlTypes: Returns the SQL types for the columns mapped by this type. The types are indentified as codes, and codes are defined in **java.sql.Types**.

The implementation is as follows:

```
package com.hibernaterecipes.chapter4.custommappings;

import java.io.Serializable;
import java.sql.PreparedStatement;
import java.sql.ResultSet;
import java.sql.SQLException;
import java.util.StringTokenizer;

import org.hibernate.Hibernate;
import org.hibernate.HibernateException;
import org.hibernate.type.SerializationException;
import org.hibernate.usertype.UserType;

import com.hibernaterecipes.chapter4.custommappings.PhoneCh4_4;

/**
```

```java
 * @author Guruzu
 *
 */
public class PhoneUserType implements UserType {

  /* (non-Javadoc)
   * @see org.hibernate.usertype.UserType#assemble(java.io.Serializable, java.lang.Object)
   */
  @Override
  public Object assemble(Serializable cached, Object owner)
      throws HibernateException {
    return deepCopy(cached);
  }

  /* (non-Javadoc)
   * @see org.hibernate.usertype.UserType#deepCopy(java.lang.Object)
   */
  @Override
  public Object deepCopy(Object value) throws HibernateException {
    if(value==null)
      return null;
    PhoneCh4_4 phoneValue = (PhoneCh4_4)value;
    PhoneCh4_4 phoneCopied = new PhoneCh4_4();
    phoneCopied.setAreaCode(phoneValue.getAreaCode());
    phoneCopied.setTelNo(phoneValue.getTelNo());
    return phoneCopied;
  }

  /* (non-Javadoc)
   * @see org.hibernate.usertype.UserType#disassemble(java.lang.Object)
   */
  @Override
  public Serializable disassemble(Object value) throws HibernateException {
    Object deepCopy = deepCopy(value);

    if (!(deepCopy instanceof Serializable)) {
      throw new SerializationException(value.getClass().getName()
          + " is not serializable ",null);
    }

    return (Serializable) deepCopy;
  }

  /* (non-Javadoc)
   * @see org.hibernate.usertype.UserType#equals(java.lang.Object, java.lang.Object)
   */
  @Override
  public boolean equals(Object x, Object y) throws HibernateException {
    if(x == y)
      return true;
```

83

```java
  if(x ==null || y == null)
    return false;

  return x.equals(y);
}

/* (non-Javadoc)
 * @see org.hibernate.usertype.UserType#hashCode(java.lang.Object)
 */
@Override
public int hashCode(Object PhoneCh4_4) throws HibernateException {
  assert (PhoneCh4_4 != null);

  return PhoneCh4_4.hashCode();
}

/* (non-Javadoc)
 * @see org.hibernate.usertype.UserType#isMutable()
 */
@Override
public boolean isMutable() {

  return true;
}

/* (non-Javadoc)
 * @see org.hibernate.usertype.UserType#nullSafeGet(java.sql.ResultSet,
java.lang.String[], java.lang.Object)
 */
@Override
public Object nullSafeGet(ResultSet resultSet, String[] names, Object owner)
    throws HibernateException, SQLException {
  String completeTelNo = resultSet.getString(names[0]);

  if(resultSet.wasNull()) {
    return null;
  }
  String areaCode = null;
  String telNo = null;
  StringTokenizer st = new StringTokenizer(completeTelNo,"-");
   while (st.hasMoreTokens()) {
     if(areaCode == null)
     {
       areaCode = st.nextToken();
     }else
     {
       telNo = st.nextToken();
     }
   }
  PhoneCh4_4 phn = new PhoneCh4_4();
  phn.setAreaCode(areaCode);
```

```java
    phn.setTelNo(telNo);
    return phn;

  }

  /* (non-Javadoc)
   * @see org.hibernate.usertype.UserType#nullSafeSet(java.sql.PreparedStatement,
java.lang.Object, int)
   */
  @Override
  public void nullSafeSet(PreparedStatement statement, Object value, int index)
      throws HibernateException, SQLException {

    if(value == null) {
      statement.setNull(index, Hibernate.STRING.sqlType());
    } else {
      PhoneCh4_4 phone = (PhoneCh4_4)value;

      statement.setString(index, phone.convertToCompleteTelNum());
    }

  }

  /* (non-Javadoc)
   * @see org.hibernate.usertype.UserType#replace(java.lang.Object, java.lang.Object,
java.lang.Object)
   */
  @Override
  public Object replace(Object original, Object target, Object owner)
      throws HibernateException {

    return deepCopy(original);
  }

  /* (non-Javadoc)
   * @see org.hibernate.usertype.UserType#returnedClass()
   */
  @Override
  public Class returnedClass() {

    return com.hibernaterecipes.chapter4.custommappings.PhoneCh4_4.class;
  }

  /* (non-Javadoc)
   * @see org.hibernate.usertype.UserType#sqlTypes()
   */
  @Override
  public int[] sqlTypes() {

    return new int [] {java.sql.Types.VARCHAR};
```

```
    }

}
```

Now that you've completed the implementation of the **UserType** interface, the Hibernate mapping file for the order class is as follows:

```
<hibernate-mapping package="com.hibernaterecipes.chapter4.custommappings">
  <class name="OrdersCh4_4" table="ORDERS">
    <id name="id" type="long" column="ID">
      <generator class="native" />
    </id>
    <property name="weekdayRecipient" type="string" column="WEEKDAY_RECIPIENT" />
    <property name="weekdayPhone"
              type="com.hibernaterecipes.chapter4.custommappings.PhoneUserType"
              column="WEEKDAY_PHONE" />
    <property name="weekdayAddress" type="string" column="WEEKDAY_ADDRESS" />
    <property name="holidayRecipient" type="string" column="HOLIDAY_RECIPIENT" />
    <property name="holidayPhone" type="string" column="HOLIDAY_PHONE" />
    <property name="holidayAddress" type="string" column="HOLIDAY_ADDRESS" />
  </class>
</hibernate-mapping>
```

In JPA annotations, the order class uses the annotation **org.hibernate.annotations.Type** and defines the type to be PhoneUserType:

```
@Entity (name="OrderCh4_4")
@Table (name="ORDERS")
public class OrdersCh4_4 {

  @Id
  @GeneratedValue (strategy=GenerationType.AUTO)
  @Column (name="ID")
  private Long id;
  //private Book book;
  @Column (name="WEEKDAY_RECIPIENT")
  private String weekdayRecipient;

  @org.hibernate.annotations.Type
  (type = "com.hibernaterecipes.annotations.custommapping.PhoneUserType")
  @Column (name="WEEKDAY_PHONE")
  private PhoneCh4_4 weekdayPhone;

  @Column (name="WEEKDAY_ADDRESS")
  private String weekdayAddress;
  @Column (name="HOLIDAY_RECIPIENT")
  private String holidayRecipient;
  @org.hibernate.annotations.Type
  (type = "com.hibernaterecipes.annotations.custommapping.PhoneUserType")
  @Column (name="HOLIDAY_PHONE")
  private PhoneCh4_4 holidayPhone;
```

```
@Column (name="HOLIDAY_ADDRESS")
private String holidayAddress;

// getters and setters
}
```

You can use this **UserType** to handle issues that accompany legacy databases. It can also perform validation or talk to an LDAP directory. The implementation doesn't support proper querying, which means you can't create a criteria object and search for all orders that have a specific area code. In addition, to cache an object of type **UserType**, the object must be serializable.

4.5 CompositeUserType Mappings

Problem

What if you want to query for just a telephone number or get all phone numbers that are within a single area code? You implemented the **UserType** interface to map to a single database column, which makes it less flexible to query in such scenarios. The **CompositeUserType** interface lets you map properties to multiple columns. How do you create the **CompositeUserType** custom mapping?

Solution

You need to implement the **CompositeUserType** interface to get the power of Hibernate queries. By implementing the **CompositeUserType** interface, the properties of the **UserType** are exposed to Hibernate queries. Here, you map the properties of the phone object to two separate columns: one for the area code and one for the telephone number.

How It Works

The implementation of **CompositeUserType** has methods very similar to those of **UserType**. It doesn't have the **sqlTypes()** method. The implementation is as follows:

```
package com.hibernaterecipes.chapter4.custommappings;

import java.io.Serializable;
import java.sql.PreparedStatement;
import java.sql.ResultSet;
import java.sql.SQLException;

import org.hibernate.Hibernate;
import org.hibernate.HibernateException;
import org.hibernate.engine.SessionImplementor;
import org.hibernate.type.SerializationException;
import org.hibernate.type.Type;
import org.hibernate.usertype.CompositeUserType;
```

```java
import com.hibernaterecipes.chapter4.custommappings.PhoneCh4_4;

/**
 * @author Guruzu
 *
 */
public class PhoneCompositeUserType implements CompositeUserType {

  /* (non-Javadoc)
   * @see org.hibernate.usertype.CompositeUserType#assemble(java.io.Serializable,
org.hibernate.engine.SessionImplementor, java.lang.Object)
   */
  @Override
  public Object assemble(Serializable cached, SessionImplementor implementor,
      Object obj) throws HibernateException {
    return deepCopy(cached);
  }

  /* (non-Javadoc)
   * @see org.hibernate.usertype.CompositeUserType#deepCopy(java.lang.Object)
   */
  @Override
  public Object deepCopy(Object value) throws HibernateException {
    if(value==null)
      return null;
    PhoneCh4_4 phoneValue = (PhoneCh4_4)value;
    PhoneCh4_4 phoneCopied = new PhoneCh4_4();
    phoneCopied.setAreaCode(phoneValue.getAreaCode());
    phoneCopied.setTelNo(phoneValue.getTelNo());
    return phoneCopied;
  }

  /* (non-Javadoc)
   * @see org.hibernate.usertype.CompositeUserType#disassemble(java.lang.Object,
org.hibernate.engine.SessionImplementor)
   */
  @Override
  public Serializable disassemble(Object value, SessionImplementor implementor)
      throws HibernateException {
    Object deepCopy = deepCopy(value);

    if (!(deepCopy instanceof Serializable)) {
      throw new SerializationException(value.getClass().getName()
        + " is not serializable ",null);
    }

    return (Serializable) deepCopy;
  }

  /* (non-Javadoc)
```

```
 * @see org.hibernate.usertype.CompositeUserType#equals(java.lang.Object,
java.lang.Object)
 */
@Override
public boolean equals(Object x, Object y) throws HibernateException {
  if(x == y)
    return true;

  if(x ==null || y == null)
    return false;

  return x.equals(y);
}

/* (non-Javadoc)
 * @see org.hibernate.usertype.CompositeUserType#getPropertyNames()
 */
@Override
public String[] getPropertyNames() {
  return new String[]{"areaCode", "telNo"};
}

/* (non-Javadoc)
 * @see org.hibernate.usertype.CompositeUserType#getPropertyTypes()
 */
@Override
public Type[] getPropertyTypes() {
  return new Type[] {Hibernate.STRING, Hibernate.STRING};
}

/* (non-Javadoc)
 * @see org.hibernate.usertype.CompositeUserType#getPropertyValue(java.lang.Object, int)
 */
@Override
public Object getPropertyValue(Object component, int property)
    throws HibernateException {
  PhoneCh4_4 phone = (PhoneCh4_4)component;
  if(property == 0)
    return phone.getAreaCode();
  else
    return phone.getTelNo();
}

/* (non-Javadoc)
 * @see org.hibernate.usertype.CompositeUserType#hashCode(java.lang.Object)
 */
@Override
public int hashCode(Object phone) throws HibernateException {
  assert (phone != null);

  return phone.hashCode();
```

```java
  }

  /* (non-Javadoc)
   * @see org.hibernate.usertype.CompositeUserType#isMutable()
   */
  @Override
  public boolean isMutable() {
    return true;
  }

  /* (non-Javadoc)
   * @see org.hibernate.usertype.CompositeUserType#nullSafeGet(java.sql.ResultSet,
java.lang.String[], org.hibernate.engine.SessionImplementor, java.lang.Object)
   */
  @Override
  public Object nullSafeGet(ResultSet resultSet, String[] names,
      SessionImplementor session, Object owner) throws HibernateException,
      SQLException {
    String areaCode = resultSet.getString(names[0]);
    if(resultSet.wasNull()) {
      return null;
    }
    String telNo = resultSet.getString(names[1]);


    return new PhoneCh4_4(areaCode, telNo);
  }

  /* (non-Javadoc)
   * @see org.hibernate.usertype.CompositeUserType#nullSafeSet(java.sql.PreparedStatement,
java.lang.Object, int, org.hibernate.engine.SessionImplementor)
   */
  @Override
  public void nullSafeSet(PreparedStatement statement, Object value, int index,
      SessionImplementor session) throws HibernateException, SQLException {
    if(value == null) {
      statement.setNull(index, Hibernate.STRING.sqlType());
      statement.setNull(index+1, Hibernate.STRING.sqlType());
    } else {
      PhoneCh4_4 phone = (PhoneCh4_4)value;
      statement.setString(index, phone.getAreaCode());
      statement.setString(index+1, phone.getTelNo());
    }

  }

  /* (non-Javadoc)
   * @see org.hibernate.usertype.CompositeUserType#replace(java.lang.Object,
java.lang.Object, org.hibernate.engine.SessionImplementor, java.lang.Object)
   */
  @Override
```

```java
public Object replace(Object original, Object target, SessionImplementor owner,
    Object arg3) throws HibernateException {

  return deepCopy(original);
}

/* (non-Javadoc)
 * @see org.hibernate.usertype.CompositeUserType#returnedClass()
 */
@Override
public Class returnedClass() {
  return com.hibernaterecipes.chapter4.custommappings.PhoneCh4_4.class;
}

/* (non-Javadoc)
 * @see org.hibernate.usertype.CompositeUserType#setPropertyValue(java.lang.Object, int,
java.lang.Object)
 */
@Override
public void setPropertyValue(Object component, int index, Object value)
    throws HibernateException {
  String columnValue = (String) value;

  PhoneCh4_4 phone = (PhoneCh4_4)component;
  if(index == 0)
  {
    phone.setAreaCode(columnValue);
  }else if (index == 1)
  {
    phone.setTelNo(columnValue);
  }else
  {
    throw new IllegalArgumentException("Unknown Property - "+index);
  }
}
}
```

The nullSafetGet and nullSafetSet methods are updated to handle two properties. The following methods are new:

- getPropertyNames: Specifies the property names to use in a query. Obviously, they have to match the name of the object property.

- getPropertyValue: Gets the property value.

- setPropertyValue: Sets the property value.

The Hibernate mapping for the order class is now as follows:

```xml
<hibernate-mapping package="com.hibernaterecipes.chapter4.custommappings">
  <class name="OrdersCh4_5" table="BOOK_ORDERS_2">
    <id name="id" type="long" column="ID">
      <generator class="native" />
```

```xml
    </id>
    <component name="weekdayContact" class="ContactCh4_5">
      <property name="recipient" type="string" column="WEEKDAY_RECIPIENT" />
      <property name="phone"
                type="com.hibernaterecipes.chapter4.custommappings.PhoneCompositeUserType">
        <column name="WEEKDAY_AREACODE"></column>
        <column name="WEEKDAY_TELEPHONE"></column>
      </property>
      <many-to-one name="address" class="com.hibernaterecipes.chapter3.Address"
                   column="WEEKDAY_ADDRESS_ID" />
    </component>
    <component name="holidayContact" class="ContactCh4_5">
      <property name="recipient" type="string" column="HOLIDAY_RECIPIENT" />
      <property name="phone"
                type="com.hibernaterecipes.chapter4.custommappings.PhoneCompositeUserType">
        <column name="HOLIDAY_AREACODE"></column>
        <column name="HOLIDAY_TELEPHONE"></column>
      </property>
      <many-to-one name="address" class="com.hibernaterecipes.chapter3.Address"
                   column="HOLIDAY_ADDRESS_ID" />
    </component>
  </class>
</hibernate-mapping>
```

The phone object now maps to two columns: one to store the area code and the second to store the telephone number.

Using JPA annotations, the orders class is as follows:

```java
@Entity
@org.hibernate.annotations.Entity(dynamicInsert = true, dynamicUpdate = true)
@Table (name="BOOK_ORDERS_2")
public class OrdersCh4_5 {

  private Long id;
  private ContactCh4_5 weekdayContact;
  private ContactCh4_5 holidayContact;

  @Id
  @GeneratedValue (strategy=GenerationType.AUTO)
  @Column (name="ID")
  public Long getId() {
    return id;
  }

  public void setId(Long id) {
    this.id = id;
  }


  @Embedded
  @AttributeOverrides (
```

```
  {@AttributeOverride(name="recipient",column=@Column(name="WEEKDAY_RECIPIENT")),
  @AttributeOverride(name="phone.areaCode",column=@Column(name="WEEKDAY_AREACODE")),
  @AttributeOverride(name="phone.telNo",column=@Column(name="WEEKDAY_TELEPHONE")),
  @AttributeOverride(name="address",column=@Column(name="ADDRESS"))}
)
public ContactCh4_5 getWeekdayContact() {
  return weekdayContact;
}

public void setWeekdayContact(ContactCh4_5 weekdayContact) {
  this.weekdayContact = weekdayContact;
}

@Embedded
@AttributeOverrides (
 {@AttributeOverride(name="recipient",column=@Column(name="HOLIDAY_RECIPIENT")),
  @AttributeOverride(name="phone.areaCode",column=@Column(name="HOLIDAY_AREACODE")),
  @AttributeOverride(name="phone.telNo",column=@Column(name="HOLIDAY_TELEPHONE")),
  @AttributeOverride(name="address",column=@Column(name="HOLIDAY_ADDRESS"))}
)
public ContactCh4_5 getHolidayContact() {
  return holidayContact;
}

public void setHolidayContact(ContactCh4_5 holidayContact) {
  this.holidayContact = holidayContact;
}


}
```

Summary

In this chapter, you learned the four basic inheritance strategies: table per class hierarchy, table per subclass, table per concrete class with unions, and table per concrete class with implicit polymorphism.

You saw the implementation of these four inheritance mapping strategies and learned how to choose the appropriate strategy. Table 4-1 summarizes the relationship between the inheritance strategies and polymorphic associations.

Table 4-1. Polymorphic Associations Supported by Various Inheritance Strategies

Inheritance Strategy	Polymorphic Many-to-One	Polymorphic One-to-One	Polymorphic One-to-Many	Polymorphic Many-to-Many
Table per class hierarchy	`<many-to-one>`	`<one-to-one>`	`<one-to-many>`	`<many-to-many>`
Table per subclass	`<many-to-one>`	`<one-to-one>`	`<one-to-many>`	`<many-to-many>`
Table per concrete class with unions	`<many-to-one>`	`<one-to-one>`	`<one-to-many>` (for `Inverse="true"` only)	`<many-to-many>`
Table per concrete class with implicit polymorphism	`<any>`	Not supported	Not supported	`<many-to-any>`

You've seen how inheritance mapping enables polymorphic queries; Table 4-2 summarizes the polymorphic query capabilities supported by various inheritance strategies. You've also learned about the basic data types that Hibernate supports and the implementation of some custom data types.

Table 4-2. Polymorphic Queries Supported by Various Inheritance Strategies

Inheritance Strategy	Polymorphic load()/get()	Polymorphic Queries	Polymorphic Joins	Outer Join Fetching
Table per Class hierarchy	Supported	Supported	Supported	Supported
Table per subclass Sub class	Supported	Supported	Supported	Supported
Table per concrete class with unions	Supported	Supported	Supported	Supported
Table per concrete class with implicit polymorphism	Supported	Supported	Not supported	Not supported

CHAPTER 5

■■■

Many-to-One and One-to-One Mapping

In general, entities are related or associated to each other. For example, a `Customer` is associated with an `Address`. A `Customer` can have one or more than one `Address` (for example, `Billing` and `Shipping`). These relationships or associations are represented differently in a relational model and the domain/object model.

In a relational model, a foreign key column represents the dependency of one table on another. The `Customer` table has an `AddressId` as the foreign key column, which is the primary key of the `Address` table.

From the `Customer` perspective, because a `Customer` can have multiple addresses, so it's a many-to-one relationship. On the other hand, from the `Address` perspective, one address can belong to only one customer, so it's a one-to-one relationship.

The same relationship is represented in terms of classes and attributes in an object model. The `Customer` class has an attribute to hold multiple addresses belonging to that `Customer` (in Java, this is represented as a collection—`List`, `Set`, and so on). The `Address` class has an attribute of `Customer` type.

In the case of `Customer` and `Address` example, you consider the association from the view of both the `Customer` entity and the `Address` entity, so it's a *bidirectional association*. If you use the association from only one entity, it's a *unidirectional association*. In an object/relational mapping (ORM) framework, these relationships are represented using metadata in the configuration file as well using the entities/objects.

This chapter shows you how these associations are represented in Hibernate and also discusses the following features:

- Various ways to use the many-to-one and one-to-one mappings

- How to make unidirectional associations into bidirectional associations

- How to use features like lazy initialization and cascade

- How to map an association or a join table

5.1 Using Many-To-One Associations

Problem

Coming back to the online bookshop example, a publisher can publish many books. This relationship between the books and the publisher is a many-to-one relationship. How do you map objects in this case using the many-to-one association? How do you use the cascade option to persist the class hierarchy?

Solution

As already mentioned, the association from books to publisher is a many-to-one association. Because this association is navigable from book to publisher only, it's also a unidirectional association. You use the <many-to-one> element to establish this association.

How It Works

Your application has a **Publisher** class that hasn't been mapped to the database. Following the best practice of object identifiers discussed in Chapter 4, you can add an autogenerated **id** property on the class. Figure 5-1 shows the entity relationship drawing for a many-to-one unidirectional association.

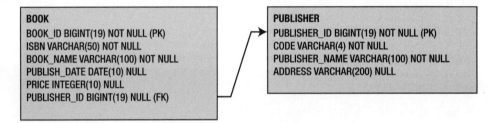

Figure 5-1. *Entity-relationship drawing showing a many-to-one unidirectional association*

```
public class Publisher implements Serializable{

        private Long publisher_id;
        private String code;
        private String name;
        private String address;
        // getters and setters
}

<hibernate-mapping package="com.hibernaterecipes.chapter5">
        <class name="Publisher" table="Publisher" schema="BOOK5">
                <id name="Publisher_id" type="long" column="PUBLISHER_ID" >
                        <generator class="native">
                        </generator>
                </id>
                <property name="code" type="string">
                        <column name="CODE" length="4" not-null="true" unique="true" />
                </property>
                <property name="name" type="string">
                        <column name="PUBLISHER_NAME" length="100" not-null="true" />
                </property>
                <property name="address" type="string">
```

```
                    <column name="ADDRESS" length="200" />
            </property>
        </class>
</hibernate-mapping>
```

Because you add a new persistent object to your application, you need to specify it in the Hibernate configuration file:

```
<mapping resource="com/hibernaterecipes/chapter5/Publisher.xml" />
```

For the Book class, you already have a Publisher property of type Publisher, which isn't used in the previous examples:

```
public class Book_5_1 implements Serializable{

        private Long book_id;
        private String isbn;
        private String name;
        private Publisher publisher;
        private Date publishDate;
        private Integer price;
        // getters and setters
}

<hibernate-mapping package="com.hibernaterecipes.chapter5">
        <class name="Book_5_1" table="Book" schema="BOOK5">
                <id name="book_id" type="long" column="BOOK_ID" >
                        <generator class="native">
                        </generator>
                </id>
                <property name="isbn" type="string">
                <column name="ISBN" length="50" not-null="true" unique="true" />
                </property>
                <property name="name" type="string">
                <column name="BOOK_NAME" length="100" not-null="true" />
                </property>
                <property name="publishDate" type="date" column="PUBLISH_DATE" />
                <property name="price" type="int" column="PRICE" />
                <many-to-one name="publisher" class="Publisher" column="PUBLISHER_ID"/>

        </class>
</hibernate-mapping>
```

After you created a new book object together with a new publisher object, you want to save them into the database. Will Hibernate save the publisher object when you save the book object? Unfortunately, an exception occurs if you save only the book object. That means you must save them one by one:

```
Session session = factory.openSession();
Transaction tx = null;
try {
```

```
        tx = session.beginTransaction();
        session.save(publisher);
        session.save(book);
        tx.commit();
} catch (HibernateException e) {
        if (tx != null) tx.rollback();
        throw e;
} finally {
        session.close();
}
```

It's a lot of trouble to save all the objects individually, especially for a large object graph. So, Hibernate provides a way to save them in one shot. Let's add a `cascade="save-update"` attribute to the `<many-to-one>` mapping, to make Hibernate cascade the save/update operations to the associated object:

```
<hibernate-mapping package="com.hibernaterecipes.chapter5">
        <class name="Book_5_1" table="Book" schema="BOOK5">
        .
.
.
.
.

                <many-to-one name="publisher" class="Publisher" column="PUBLISHER_ID"
cascade="save-update"/>

        </class>
</hibernate-mapping>
```

The save/update cascade is very useful when you persist a graph of objects, some of which are newly created and some of which have been updated. You can use the **saveOrUpdate()** method and let Hibernate decide which objects should be created and which should be updated:

```
session.saveOrUpdate(book);
```

In addition to the save/update cascade, you can also **cascade** the delete operation:

```
<many-to-one name="publisher" class="Publisher" column="PUBLISHER_ID" cascade="save-
update,delete" />
```

In JPA, the book and publisher classes are annotated as follows:

```
@Entity
@Table (name="PUBLISHER", schema="BOOK5")
public class Publisher implements Serializable{

        @Id
        @Column (name="PUBLISHER_ID")
        @GeneratedValue (strategy=GenerationType.AUTO)
        private Long publisher_id;
```

```
        @Column (name="CODE")
        private String code;
        @Column (name="PUBLISHER_NAME")
        private String name;
        @Column (name="ADDRESS")
        private String address;
        // getters and setters
}

@Entity
@Table (name="BOOK", schema="BOOK5")
public class Book_5_1 implements Serializable{
        @Id
        @Column (name="BOOK_ID")
        @GeneratedValue (strategy=GenerationType.AUTO)
        private Long book_id;
        @Column (name="isbn")
        private String isbn;
        @Column (name="BOOK_NAME")
        private String name;
        @ManyToOne
        @Cascade (value=CascadeType.SAVE_UPDATE)
        @JoinColumn (name="PUBLISHER_ID")
        private Publisher publisher;

        @Column (name="price")
        private Integer price;
        // getters and setters
    }
```

5.2 Using a Many-to-One Association with a Join Table

Problem

Let's say a set of books has been identified that will be published, but publishers haven't yet been allocated for those books. In the same way, you may have publishers that are ready to publish books, but the books haven't yet been written. In this case, if you use the same Book and Publisher entities, there will be rows in which the Book_Id is null in the PUBLISHER table and the Publisher_Id is null in the BOOK table. This isn't an efficient way to store data in a relational database and doesn't provide a normalized schema.

In this case, you use an additional table called a *join table* that contains the foreign key's Book_id and Publisher_Id as columns. This table includes all rows where a Book has a Publisher and a Publisher has published a Book.

How do you represent this data structure in Hibernate? And what are the additional features that it provides to manage this kind of association?

Solution

Hibernate provides the `<join>` mapping element to represent a join table.

How It Works

Use the following SQL queries to generate the tables:

```
CREATE TABLE "BOOK5"."BOOK_PUBLISHER"
(
    BOOK_ID bigint PRIMARY KEY NOT NULL,
    PUBLISHER_ID bigint NOT NULL
);
;
CREATE UNIQUE INDEX SQL091217230605770 ON BOOK_PUBLISHER(BOOK_ID)
;CREATE TABLE "BOOK5"."BOOK5_2"
(
    BOOK_ID bigint PRIMARY KEY NOT NULL,
    ISBN varchar(50) NOT NULL,
    BOOK_NAME varchar(100) NOT NULL,
    PUBLISH_DATE date,
    PRICE int
);

CREATE UNIQUE INDEX SQL091217225248451 ON BOOK5_2(BOOK_ID);

CREATE UNIQUE INDEX SQL091217225248450 ON BOOK5_2(ISBN);


CREATE TABLE "BOOK5"."PUBLISHER5_2"
(
    PUBLISHER_ID bigint PRIMARY KEY NOT NULL,
    CODE varchar(4) NOT NULL,
    PUBLISHER_NAME varchar(100) NOT NULL,
    ADDRESS varchar(200)
);

CREATE UNIQUE INDEX SQL091217225248980 ON PUBLISHER5_2(CODE);

CREATE UNIQUE INDEX SQL091217225248981 ON PUBLISHER5_2(PUBLISHER_ID);
```

The book mapping file is as follows:

```
<hibernate-mapping package="com.hibernaterecipes.chapter5">
        <class name="Book5_2" table="Book5_2" schema="BOOK5">
                <id name="book_id" type="long" column="BOOK_ID" >
                        <generator class="native">
                        </generator>
                </id>
                <property name="isbn" type="string">
```

```
            <column name="ISBN" length="50" not-null="true" unique="true" />
            </property>
            <property name="name" type="string">
            <column name="BOOK_NAME" length="100" not-null="true" />
            </property>
            <property name="publishDate" type="date" column="PUBLISH_DATE" />
            <property name="price" type="int" column="PRICE" />
            <join table="BOOK_PUBLISHER" optional="true" schema="BOOK5">
                    <key column="BOOK_ID" unique="true" />
                    <many-to-one name="publisher" class="Publisher5_2"
column="PUBLISHER_ID" not-null="true"
                    cascade="save-update" lazy="false"/>
            </join>

        </class>
</hibernate-mapping>
```

In the `<join>` mapping element, the `table` attribute holds the name of the join table—here it's `BOOK_PUBLISHER`. By setting `optional=true`, you tell Hibernate that it should insert a row into the join table only if the properties grouped by the mapping are non-null. `Book_Id` is the primary key in the join table and is implicitly unique. The `<many-to-one>` attribute specifies that this join table has a many-to-one relationship with the `Publisher` entity and the key column is `Publisher_id`. Figure 5-2 shows the entity relationship drawing for a many-to-one association with a join table.

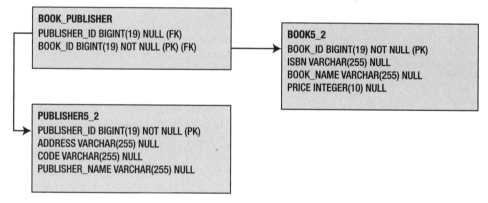

Figure 5-2. Entity-relationship drawing showing a many-to-one association with a join table

The JPA mapping for the book class is as follows. You use the `JoinTable` annotation to map the join table `BOOK_PUBLISHER`:

```
@Entity
@Table (name="BOOK5_2", schema="BOOK5")
public class Book_5_2 implements Serializable{
        @Id
        @Column (name="BOOK_ID")
        @GeneratedValue (strategy=GenerationType.AUTO)
        private Long book_id;
```

```
        @Column (name="isbn")
        private String isbn;
        @Column (name="BOOK_NAME")
        private String name;
        @ManyToOne
        @Cascade (value=CascadeType.SAVE_UPDATE)
        @JoinTable (schema="BOOK5",name="BOOK_PUBLISHER",
                        joinColumns=@JoinColumn(name="BOOK_ID"),
                        inverseJoinColumns=@JoinColumn(name="PUBLISHER_ID"))
        private Publisher5_2 publisher;

        @Column (name="price")
        private Integer price;
// getters and setters
}
```

The join table BOOK_PUBLISHER has a foreign key column named PUBLISHER_ID that points to the PUBLISHER table materialized by inverseJoinColumns, and a foreign key column named BOOK_ID pointing to the BOOK table materialized by the joinColumns attribute.

5.3 Using Lazy Initialization on Many-to-One Associations

Problem

In an association between two entities in an ORM framework, when the data of one entity is loaded from the database, the data of the dependent entity may be fetched along with it or loaded on demand.

For example, in the case of Book and Publisher, the BOOK table has the foreign key column Publisher_Id. If Book details are fetched from the database, should the Publisher details be loaded along with them, or should the Publisher details be retrieved only when you explicitly fetch them? When the dependent object's details are loaded only on demand, they're said to be *lazily loaded*. By lazily loading data, you can improve performance, because unnecessary queries aren't executed.

How is lazy initialization achieved in Hibernate? How effect does it have when you're retrieving an object graph? And what are the ways to deal with it?

Solution

Enabling lazy initialization defines what objects are available on the detached object. It's defined with the keyword lazy, which is different from the keyword fetch. The keyword fetch is used to define fetching strategies for tuning performance.

Hibernate provides lazy initialization of collections, associations, and even properties or value types. You learn about lazy initialization of collections in the next chapter. The value types of an entity can also be lazy initialized, but it's usually not required; it can be used with databases that have hundreds of columns.

How It Works

Suppose you have a method for retrieving a Book object given its ID. Because you added the <many-to-one> mapping, the Publisher object related to the Book should be retrieved at the same time:

```
Session session = factory.openSession();
try {
Book book = (Book) session.get(Book.class, id);
return book;
} finally {
session.close();
}
```

But when you access the Publisher object through book.getPublisher() outside this method, an exception occurs:

```
System.out.println(book.getName());
System.out.println(book.getPublisher().getName());
```

If you put the access code inside the try block of the method body, everything is OK. What's the reason for this exception? It happens because Hibernate doesn't load your Publisher object from the database until you first access the Publisher before the session is closed. This lazy initialization can avoid unnecessary database queries and thus enhance performance. Because the Publisher is first accessed outside the session (which has been closed), an exception is thrown.

If you want the Publisher object to be accessed from outside the session, there are two possible solutions. One is to initialize the Publisher explicitly by calling the method Hibernate.initialize(). Doing so forces the Publisher object to be loaded from the database:

```
Session session = factory.openSession();
try {
Book book = (Book) session.get(Book.class, id);
Hibernate.initialize(book.getPublisher());
return book;
} finally {
session.close();
}
```

Another solution is to turn off lazy initialization for this association. Doing so may decrease performance because the Publisher object is loaded together with the Book object every time:

```
<hibernate-mapping package="com.hibernaterecipes.chapter5">
        <class name="Book_5_1" table="Book" schema="BOOK5">
    .
.
.
.
.

                <many-to-one name="publisher" class="Publisher" column="PUBLISHER_ID"
cascade="save-update" lazy="false" />
```

```
        </class>
</hibernate-mapping>
```

5.4 Sharing Primary Key Associations

Problem

In what scenarios do you need to share the primary key, and how do you map it?

Solution

When rows in two tables are associated with the primary key value of one row, they're said to be *sharing* the primary key. You can use this kind of implementation when there is a requirement for tight coupling between two objects.

How It Works

Let's use the Customer and Address classes to create a one-to-one mapping with a shared primary key:

```
public class Customer5_1 implements Serializable {

        private static final long serialVersionUID = -3534434932962734600L;
        private Long id;
        private String countryCode;
        private String idCardNo;
        private String firstName;
        private String lastName;
        private Address5_1 address;
        private String email;
        //getters and setters
}

public class Address5_1 implements Serializable{

        private static final long serialVersionUID = -605474766287314591L;
        private Long id;
        private String city;
        private String street;
        private String doorplate;
        private Customer5_1 customer;
        //getters and setters
}
```

The Customer class is mapped like a regular class. It also contains the one-to-one mapping element that maps Customer to Address. You add the cascade option to save-update because you want to save the Address when you save the Customer object:

```
<hibernate-mapping package="com.hibernaterecipes.chapter5">
        <class name="Customer5_1" table="CUSTOMER" schema="BOOK5">
                <id name="id" type="long" column="ID">
                        <generator class="native"></generator>
                </id>
                <property name="firstName" type="string" column="FIRST_NAME" />
                <property name="lastName" type="string" column="LAST_NAME" />
                <property name="idCardNo" type="string" column="ID_CARD_NO" />
                <property name="countryCode" type="string" column="COUNTRY_CODE" />
                <property name="email" type="string" column="EMAIL" />
                <one-to-one name="address"
        class="com.hibernaterecipes.chapter5.Address5_1" cascade="save-update"></one-to-one>
        </class>
</hibernate-mapping>
```

By itself, this mapping establishes a unidirectional one-to-one mapping, provided the Address class is mapped as a separate entity. To achieve the sharing of the primary key, you need to map the Address class as shown here:

```
<hibernate-mapping package="com.hibernaterecipes.chapter5">
        <class name="Address5_1" table="ADDRESS" schema="BOOK5">
                <id name="id" type="long" column="ID" >
                        <generator class="foreign">
                                <param name="property">customer</param>
                        </generator>
                </id>
                <property name="city" type="string" column="CITY" />
                <property name="street" type="string" column="STREET" />
                <property name="doorplate" type="string" column="DOOR_PLATE" />
                <one-to-one name="customer" class="Customer5_1" constrained="true"></one-to-
one>

        </class>
</hibernate-mapping>
```

In the Address mapping file, you establish bidirectionality with the one-to-one element. Also note that you make constrained true, which adds a foreign key constraint. The constraint links the primary key of the ADDRESS table to the primary key of the CUSTOMER table. The generator of the primary key of the Address class is set to foreign with a property mapping to the Customer instance; this causes the primary key to be shared between the Customer and Address classes. In addition, you can't delete the Customer class without also deleting the Address class.

The JPA specification doesn't have a way to deal with a shared primary key. It has serious issues with establishing bidirectionality and a foreign key. In JPA annotations, the Customer class's Address property must be mapped with the annotations OneToOne and PrimaryKeyJoinColumn:

```
@Entity
@Table (name="CUSTOMER",schema="BOOK5")
public class Customer5_1 implements Serializable {

        private static final long serialVersionUID = -3534434932962734600L;
        @Column (name="ID")
```

```
        @Id
        @GeneratedValue (strategy=GenerationType.AUTO)
        private Long id;

        @Column (name="COUNTRY_CODE")
        private String countryCode;

        @Column (name="ID_CARD_NO")
        private String idCardNo;

        @Column (name="FIRST_NAME")
        private String firstName;

        @Column (name="LAST_NAME")
        private String lastName;

        @OneToOne
        @PrimaryKeyJoinColumn (name="ID")
        private Address5_1 address;
        // getters and setters
}
```

The **Address** class's **ID** property is annotated without any identity-generation strategy. Also note that the **Address** class doesn't have **customer** as a property:

```
@Entity
@Table (name="ADDRESS",schema="BOOK5")
public class Address5_1 implements Serializable
{

        private static final long serialVersionUID = -605474766287314591L;
        @Id
        @Column (name="ADDRESS_ID")
        private Long id;

        @Column(name="CITY")
        private String city;

        @Column(name="STREET")
        private String street;

        @Column(name="DOOR_PLATE")
        private String doorplate;
        // getters and setters
}
```

To persist the **Address** object, you have to manually set the associated **Customer** ID as the primary key of the **Address** object.

5.5 Creating a One-to-One Association Using a Foreign Key

Problem

Let's say that one Customer has only one Address and one Address belongs to only one Customer. This means there is a one-to-one relationship between Customer and an Address. How do you represent a one-to-one association in Hibernate?

Solution

The simplest way to map a one-to-one association is to treat it as a many-to-one association but add a unique constraint on it. You can declare the lazy, fetch, and cascade attributes in the same way.

How It Works

You can use the Customer and Address classes to create a one-to-one mapping with a foreign key association. (The classes Customer and Address remain the same—they're renamed for the sake of demonstration.) Customer's Hibernate mapping maps the Address property as many-to-one association. The unique constraint is set to true to change this association from many-to-one to one-to-one:

```
<hibernate-mapping package="com.hibernaterecipes.chapter5">
        <class name="Customer5_2" table="CUSTOMER" schema="BOOK5">
                <id name="id" type="long" column="ID">
                        <generator class="native"></generator>
                </id>
                <property name="firstName" type="string" column="FIRST_NAME" />
                <property name="lastName" type="string" column="LAST_NAME" />
                <property name="idCardNo" type="string" column="ID_CARD_NO" />
                <property name="countryCode" type="string" column="COUNTRY_CODE" />
                <property name="email" type="string" column="EMAIL" />
                <many-to-one name="address"
                                        class="com.hibernaterecipes.chapter5.Address5_2"
                                        column="ADDRESS_ID"
                                        cascade="save-update"
                                        unique="true">
                </many-to-one>
        </class>
</hibernate-mapping>
```

To obtain bidirectionality, you add a one-to-one mapping to the customer property in the Address class. You use the property_ref attribute to point Hibernate to the property to which the association is one-to-one; this is called an *inverse property reference*:

```
<hibernate-mapping package="com.hibernaterecipes.chapter5">
        <class name="Address5_2" table="ADDRESS" schema="BOOK5">
                <id name="id" type="long" column="ADDRESS_ID" >
                        <generator class="native">
```

```
                </generator>
            </id>
            <property name="city" type="string" column="CITY" />
            <property name="street" type="string" column="STREET" />
            <property name="doorplate" type="string" column="DOOR_PLATE" />
            <one-to-one name="customer" class="Customer5_2" property-
ref="address"></one-to-one>

        </class>
</hibernate-mapping>
```

In JPA annotations, the Address property of the Customer class is mapped with the annotations OneToOne and JoinColumn. Also note that you enable the cascade feature, which saves the address associated with the customer:

```
@Entity
@Table (name="CUSTOMER",schema="BOOK5")
public class Customer5_2 implements Serializable {

        private static final long serialVersionUID = -3534434932962734600L;
        @Column (name="ID")
        @Id
        @GeneratedValue (strategy=GenerationType.AUTO)
        private Long id;

        @Column (name="COUNTRY_CODE")
        private String countryCode;

        @Column (name="ID_CARD_NO")
        private String idCardNo;

        @Column (name="FIRST_NAME")
        private String firstName;

        @Column (name="LAST_NAME")
        private String lastName;

        @OneToOne (cascade=CascadeType.ALL)
        @JoinColumn (name="ADDRESS_ID")
        private Address5_2 address;

        @Column (name="EMAIL")
        private String email;
        // getters and setters
}
```

The Address class is as shown here. The customer is mapped with another one-to-one annotation, which makes it a bidirectional association. The inverse property reference is achieved with the mappedBy attribute:

```
@Entity
@Table (name="ADDRESS",schema="BOOK5")
public class Address5_2 implements Serializable
{

        private static final long serialVersionUID = -605474766287314591L;
        @Id
        @Column (name="ADDRESS_ID")
        @GeneratedValue (strategy=GenerationType.AUTO)
        private Long id;

        @Column(name="CITY")
        private String city;

        @Column(name="STREET")
        private String street;

        @Column(name="DOOR_PLATE")
        private String doorplate;

        @OneToOne (mappedBy="address")
        private Customer5_2 customer;
        // getters and setters
}
```

5.6 Creating a One-to-One Association Using a Join Table

Problem

Another strategy to represent a one-to-one association uses a join table. As explained in recipe 5.2, in some scenarios the foreign key in a table is null. To avoid storing the rows with null foreign keys, you can create a join table that holds the IDs of both the dependent entities. How do you use a join table to establish a one-to-one association in Hibernate?

Solution

The last method of mapping a one-to-one association uses a join-table element with a many-to-one association. Nothing is different unless both the <key> and <many-to-one> mappings need a unique constraint. This method is seldom used.

How It Works

You need to create the tables with scripts rather than use the hbm2ddl.auto option set to Create. You create the ADDRESS, CUSTOMER, and join (CUSTOMERADDRESS) tables as follows:

```
create table "BOOK5"."ADDRESS" ( address_Id bigint not null primary key,
```

```
                              CITY VARCHAR(50),
                              STREET VARCHAR(50),
                              DOOR_PLATE VARCHAR(50));


create table "BOOK5"."CUSTOMER" ( Id bigint not null primary key,
                          FIRST_NAME VARCHAR(50),
                          LAST_NAME VARCHAR(50),
                          ID_CARD_NO VARCHAR(50),
                          COUNTRY_CODE VARCHAR(50),
                          EMAIL VARCHAR(50));



create table "BOOK5"."CUSTOMERADDRESS" ( Id bigint not null primary key,
                              address_Id bigint not null unique );
```

The Address and Customer classes for the unidirectional association are as follows:

```
public class Address5_3 implements Serializable{

        private static final long serialVersionUID = -605474766287314591L;
        private Long addressId;
        private String city;
        private String street;
        private String doorplate;
        // getters and setters
}
```

```
public class Customer5_3 implements Serializable {

        private static final long serialVersionUID = -3534434932962734600L;
        private Long id;
        private String countryCode;
        private String idCardNo;
        private String firstName;
        private String lastName;
        private Address5_3 address;
        private String email;
        // getters and setters
}
```

The Hibernate mapping file for the Address class is like any simple entity mapping file, because this is a unidirectional mapping:

```
<hibernate-mapping package="com.hibernaterecipes.chapter5">
        <class name="Address5_3" table="Address" schema="BOOK5">
                <id name="addressId" type="long" column="ADDRESS_ID" >
                        <generator class="native">
                        </generator>
                </id>
```

```
                <property name="city" type="string" column="CITY" />
                <property name="street" type="string" column="STREET" />
                <property name="doorplate" type="string" column="DOOR_PLATE" />


        </class>
</hibernate-mapping>
```

The customer's Hibernate mapping file has the join element. The join element is mapped to the CUSTOMERADDRESS join table; it's mapped to have the customer ID as a primary key (see the create query). The join table contains the many-to-one element that maps to the ADDRESS table. The unique attribute is set to true in the many-to-one mapping element, which along with the key column establishes a one-to-one mapping. Also note that because you're dealing with multiple schemas, you use the schema attribute in the join element:

```
<hibernate-mapping package="com.hibernaterecipes.chapter5">
        <class name="Customer5_3" table="Customer" schema="BOOK5">
                <id name="id" type="long" column="ID">
                        <generator class="native"></generator>
                </id>
                <property name="firstName" type="string" column="FIRST_NAME" />
                <property name="lastName" type="string" column="LAST_NAME" />
                <property name="idCardNo" type="string" column="ID_CARD_NO" />
                <property name="countryCode" type="string" column="COUNTRY_CODE" />
                <property name="email" type="string" column="EMAIL" />
                <join table="CustomerAddress" optional="true" schema="BOOK5" >
                        <key column="ID" unique="true">
                        </key>
                        <many-to-one name="address"
                                        column="ADDRESS_ID"
                                        not-null="true"
                                        cascade="save-update"
                                        unique="true">
                        </many-to-one>
                </join>

        </class>
</hibernate-mapping>
```

Now, coming to bidirectionality, you have to add customer as a property in the address object:

```
public class Address5_3 implements Serializable{

        private static final long serialVersionUID = -605474766287314591L;
        private Long addressId;
        private String city;
        private String street;
        private String doorplate;
        private Customer5_3 customer;
        // getters and setters
}
```

111

And the address mapping file must having a `join` element similar to the one in the `CUSTOMER` table, to make it bidirectional one-to-one:

```
<hibernate-mapping package="com.hibernaterecipes.chapter5">
    <class name="Address5_3" table="Address" schema="BOOK5">
        <id name="addressId" type="long" column="ADDRESS_ID" >
            <generator class="native">
            </generator>
        </id>
        <property name="city" type="string" column="CITY" />
        <property name="street" type="string" column="STREET" />
        <property name="doorplate" type="string" column="DOOR_PLATE" />
        <join table="CustomerAddress" optional="true" inverse="true">
            <key column="ADDRESS_ID" unique="true" />
            <many-to-one name="customer"
                         class="com.hibernaterecipes.chapter5.Customer5_3"
                         column="ID"
                         unique="true"
                         not-null="true">
            </many-to-one>
        </join>


    </class>
</hibernate-mapping>
```

Using JPA annotations, the `Address` class is mapped to its `customer` property with the `OneToOne` annotation:

```
@Entity
@Table (name="ADDRESS",schema="BOOK5")
public class Address5_3 implements Serializable
{
        private static final long serialVersionUID = -605474766287314591L;
        @Id
        @Column (name="ADDRESS_ID")
        @GeneratedValue (strategy=GenerationType.AUTO)
        private Long id;

        @Column(name="CITY")
        private String city;
        @Column(name="STREET")
        private String street;
        @Column(name="DOOR_PLATE")
        private String doorplate;

        @OneToOne (mappedBy="address")
        private Customer5_2 customer;
        // getters and setters
}
```

The `Customer` table uses the `JoinTable` annotation to map the **address** object:

```
@Entity
@Table (name="CUSTOMER",schema="BOOK5")
public class Customer5_3 implements Serializable {

        private static final long serialVersionUID = -3534434932962734600L;
        @Column (name="ID")
        @Id
        @GeneratedValue (strategy=GenerationType.AUTO)
        private Long id;

        @Column (name="COUNTRY_CODE")
        private String countryCode;
        @Column (name="ID_CARD_NO")
        private String idCardNo;
        @Column (name="FIRST_NAME")
        private String firstName;

        @Column (name="LAST_NAME")
        private String lastName;

        @Column (name="EMAIL")
        private String email;

        @OneToOne (cascade=CascadeType.ALL)
        @JoinTable (name="CustomerAddress", schema="BOOK5",
                joinColumns=@JoinColumn(name="ID"),
                inverseJoinColumns=@JoinColumn(name="ADDRESS_ID"))
        private Address5_3 address;

        // getters and setters
}
```

Summary

In this chapter, you've seen how to represent and work with many-to-one and one-to-one associations using Hibernate. For a many-to-one association, you define the `<many-to-one>` mapping element in the class that has the many side of the relationship. In the case where there can be null foreign key values, you use a join table to map between the two dependent objects; the join table contains IDs of both the dependent objects.

You learned that you can use lazy initialization to increase performance: the data of the dependent object is retrieved from the database only on demand. You also learned that shared primary keys are used when rows in two tables are related by a primary key association.

You saw how to map a one-to-one association with a `<many-to-one>` element and then have a unique constraint on the one relationship. A one-to-one association can also be mapped using a join table.

CHAPTER 6

■ ■ ■

Collection Mapping

An object of **value** type has no database identity, and objects of **value** type are dependent on the owning entity object. The lifespan of the **value** type is bound by the lifespan of the owning entity. Entities that have a collection of **value** types need to be mapped to an appropriate collection interface from the Java API. For entities to have a collection of **value** types, you need to have a separate table with the entity's primary key as a foreign key.

Hibernate supports most of the collection interfaces provided by Java API. It's recommended that you use the collection interface to declare the type of the property and a matching implementation. Hibernate suggests using interfaces to declare collections because it supports Java collection, maps, and arrays; it has a **<set>** tag to support for all **java.util.Set** collections and **<bag>** or **<idbag>** to support **java.util.Collection**. You should initialize the implementation at the time of declaration to avoid uninitialized collections. The following code declares **chapters** to be type **java.util.Set** (which is an interface) and the matching implementation as **java.util.HashSet**:

```
Private Set<String> chapters = new HashSet<String>();
```

This chapter shows you how to map collections for **value** types. In Hibernate, collections can be lazily initialized, which means the state of the collection objects is loaded from the database only when the application needs it. This initialization is done transparently from the user. The chapter also deals with sorting collections in memory and at database level. You add a collection of chapters to your **Book** class as an example.

6.1 Mapping a Set

Problem

How do you map **value** types as collections of type **java.util.Set**?

Solution

The **<set>** mapping is the most common collection mapping that is used. You use the **<set>** element to map for **java.util.Set**. The property should be initialized to **HashSet**. The implementation doesn't allow duplicate elements, and the order of the elements isn't retained.

How It Works

The Book class has a property called chapters that is of type java.util.Set. The property is initialized as a HashSet:

```
public class Book6_1 implements Serializable{

  private Long book_id;
  private String isbn;
  private String name;
  private Date publishDate;
  private Integer price;
  private Set chapters = new HashSet();
  // getters and setters
}
```

Figure 6-1 shows the association between the BOOK table and the BOOK_CHAPTER table for this recipe.

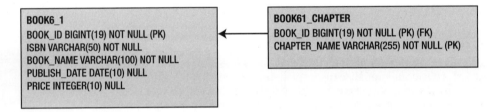

BOOK6_1
BOOK_ID BIGINT(19) NOT NULL (PK)
ISBN VARCHAR(50) NOT NULL
BOOK_NAME VARCHAR(100) NOT NULL
PUBLISH_DATE DATE(10) NULL
PRICE INTEGER(10) NULL

BOOK61_CHAPTER
BOOK_ID BIGINT(19) NOT NULL (PK) (FK)
CHAPTER_NAME VARCHAR(255) NOT NULL (PK)

Figure 6-1. Entity-relationship drawing between BOOK and BOOK_CHAPTER with a set association

In Book's Hibernate mapping file, the <set> element associates the chapters with the book. The <set> element contains the key column element that sets the book's ID (primary key as the foreign key). The association is mapped to a separate table, which has a composite key of the book's ID and the chapter name as the primary key.

```
<hibernate-mapping package="com.hibernaterecipes.chapter6">
  <class name="Book6_1" table="Book6_1" schema="BOOK6">
    <id name="book_id" type="long" column="BOOK_ID" >
      <generator class="native">
      </generator>
    </id>
    <property name="isbn" type="string">
    <column name="ISBN" length="50" not-null="true" unique="true" />
    </property>
    <property name="name" type="string">
    <column name="BOOK_NAME" length="100" not-null="true" />
    </property>
    <property name="publishDate" type="date" column="PUBLISH_DATE" />
    <property name="price" type="int" column="PRICE" />
    <set name="chapters" table="Book61_Chapter" schema="BOOK6">
      <key column="BOOK_ID"></key>
      <element type="string" column="CHAPTER_NAME" not-null="true"></element>
```

```
   </set>
  </class>
</hibernate-mapping>
```

If you print the CREATE TABLE script from the database GUI tool (Squirrel, in this case), it looks something like this:

```
CREATE TABLE "BOOK6"."BOOK61_CHAPTER"
(
    BOOK_ID bigint NOT NULL,
    CHAPTER_NAME varchar(255) NOT NULL,
    CONSTRAINT SQL091222210546110 PRIMARY KEY (BOOK_ID,CHAPTER_NAME)
);
ALTER TABLE BOOK61_CHAPTER
ADD CONSTRAINT FK3C070E729C936CD9
FOREIGN KEY (BOOK_ID)
REFERENCES BOOK6_1(BOOK_ID);
CREATE UNIQUE INDEX SQL091222210546110 ON BOOK61_CHAPTER
(
    BOOK_ID,
    CHAPTER_NAME
);
CREATE INDEX SQL091222210548040 ON BOOK61_CHAPTER(BOOK_ID);
```

In JPA, the Book class has the following annotations:

```
@Entity
@Table (name="BOOK6_1", schema="BOOK6")
public class Book_6_1 implements Serializable{

  @Id
  @Column (name="BOOK_ID")
  @GeneratedValue (strategy=GenerationType.AUTO)
  private Long book_id;

  @Column (name="isbn")
  private String isbn;

  @Column (name="BOOK_NAME")
  private String name;

  @Column (name="price")
  private Integer price;

  @CollectionOfElements (targetElement=java.lang.String.class)
  @JoinTable(
      name="Book61_Chapter",
      schema="BOOK6",
      joinColumns=@JoinColumn(name="BOOK_ID")
  )
  @Column(name="chapter_name")
```

```
    private Set chapters;
    // getters and setters
}
```

The `CollectionOfElements` annotation is used to declare what types of objects are being put in the collection that is being mapped. The `JoinTable` annotation provides details about the associated table and contains the join column that is used to map the two tables. The `Column` annotation provides the column name.

6.2 Mapping a Bag

Problem

A *bag* is a collection of objects that can have duplicates. It doesn't have any order. It's something like an `ArrayList`, but it doesn't retain its index. How do you map **value** types as collections of type **bag**? What is the difference between a **bag** and an **idbag**? How do you map using an **idbag**?

Solution

The Java Collections API doesn't have anything called a **bag**. Java developers who want to use bag-like semantics use the `java.util.List` implementation. Hibernate does the same by requiring the implementation to be an `ArrayList`. Hibernate recommends using `java.util.Collection` or `java.util.List` as the interface to map **bags**. The join table doesn't have a primary key when the mapping is done using the `<bag>` element. An **idbag** is similar to a **bag**, but it adds a primary key to the join table.

How It Works

The `Book` class has a property called `chapters` that is of type `java.util.Collection`. The property is initialized as an `ArrayList`:

```
public class Book6_2 implements Serializable{

    private Long book_id;
    private String isbn;
    private String name;
    private Date publishDate;
    private Integer price;
    private Collection chapters = new ArrayList();
    // getters and setters
}
```

In the book's Hibernate mapping file, the **bag** element is used to associate the chapters with the book. The association is mapped to a separate table that doesn't have a primary key. This is the impact of letting duplicate elements into the collection:

```
<hibernate-mapping package="com.hibernaterecipes.chapter6">
  <class name="Book6_2" table="Book6_2" schema="BOOK6">
    <id name="book_id" type="long" column="BOOK_ID" >
      <generator class="native">
      </generator>
    </id>
    <property name="isbn" type="string">
    <column name="ISBN" length="50" not-null="true" unique="true" />
    </property>
    <property name="name" type="string">
    <column name="BOOK_NAME" length="100" not-null="true" />
    </property>
    <property name="publishDate" type="date" column="PUBLISH_DATE" />
    <property name="price" type="int" column="PRICE" />
    <bag name="chapters" table="Book62_Chapter" schema="BOOK6">
      <key column="BOOK_ID"></key>
      <element type="string" column="CHAPTER_NAME" not-null="true"></element>
    </bag>

  </class>
</hibernate-mapping>
```

In JPA, the Book class has the following annotations:

```
@Entity
@Table (name="BOOK6_2", schema="BOOK6")
public class Book_6_2 implements Serializable{

  @Id
  @Column (name="BOOK_ID")
  @GeneratedValue (strategy=GenerationType.AUTO)
  private Long book_id;

  @Column (name="isbn")
  private String isbn;

  @Column (name="BOOK_NAME")
  private String name;

  @Column (name="price")
  private Integer price;

  @CollectionOfElements (targetElement=java.lang.String.class)
  @JoinTable(
      name="Book62_Chapter",
      schema="BOOK6",
      joinColumns=@JoinColumn(name="BOOK_ID")
  )
  @Column(name="chapter_name")
  private Collection chapters;
  // getters and setters
```

```
}
```

The CREATE TABLE query is shown here. Note that it doesn't have a primary key, and the book ID is a foreign key in the join table:

```
CREATE TABLE "BOOK6"."BOOK62_CHAPTER"
(
    BOOK_ID bigint NOT NULL,
    CHAPTER_NAME varchar(255) NOT NULL
);
ALTER TABLE BOOK62_CHAPTER
ADD CONSTRAINT FKD04B7D739C936CDA
FOREIGN KEY (BOOK_ID)
REFERENCES BOOK6_2(BOOK_ID);
CREATE INDEX SQL091227211955140 ON BOOK62_CHAPTER(BOOK_ID);
```

When you're mapping using the idbag, the Hibernate XML file has the collection-id element:

```xml
<hibernate-mapping package="com.hibernaterecipes.chapter6">
  <class name="Book6_21" table="Book6_21" schema="BOOK6">
    <id name="book_id" type="long" column="BOOK_ID" >
      <generator class="native">
      </generator>
    </id>
    <property name="isbn" type="string">
    <column name="ISBN" length="50" not-null="true" unique="true" />
    </property>
    <property name="name" type="string">
    <column name="BOOK_NAME" length="100" not-null="true" />
    </property>
    <property name="publishDate" type="date" column="PUBLISH_DATE" />
    <property name="price" type="int" column="PRICE" />
    <idbag name="chapters" table="Book621_Chapter" schema="BOOK6">
      <collection-id type="long" column="Book621_Chapter_id">
        <generator class="hilo"></generator>
      </collection-id>
      <key column="BOOK_ID"></key>
      <element type="string" column="CHAPTER_NAME" not-null="true"></element>
    </idbag>
  </class>
</hibernate-mapping>
```

Figure 6-2 shows the association between the BOOK table and the BOOK_CHAPTER table.

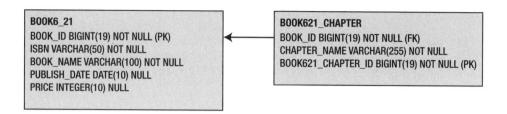

Figure 6-2. Entity-relationship drawing between BOOK *and* BOOK_CHAPTER *with an* idbag *association*

The JPA annotated Book class has the CollectionId and GenericGenerator annotations to define the primary key:

```
@Entity
@Table (name="BOOK6_21", schema="BOOK6")
public class Book_6_21 implements Serializable{

    @Id
    @Column (name="BOOK_ID")
    @GeneratedValue (strategy=GenerationType.AUTO)
    private Long book_id;

    @Column (name="isbn")
    private String isbn;

    @Column (name="BOOK_NAME")
    private String name;

    @Column (name="price")
    private Integer price;

    @CollectionOfElements (targetElement=java.lang.String.class)
    @JoinTable(
        name="Book621_Chapter",
        schema="BOOK6",
        joinColumns=@JoinColumn(name="BOOK_ID")
    )
    @GenericGenerator (name="hilo-gen",strategy="hilo")
    @CollectionId (columns=@Column(name = "Book621_Chapter_id"),
        type=@Type(type="long"),
        generator="hilo-gen")
    @Column(name="chapter_name")
    private Collection chapters = new ArrayList();
// getters and setters
}
```

The CREATE TABLE query looks something like this:

```
CREATE TABLE "BOOK6"."BOOK621_CHAPTER"
(
    BOOK_ID bigint NOT NULL,
    CHAPTER_NAME varchar(255) NOT NULL,
    BOOK621_CHAPTER_ID bigint PRIMARY KEY NOT NULL
);
ALTER TABLE BOOK621_CHAPTER
ADD CONSTRAINT FK574F883A8233ACD9
FOREIGN KEY (BOOK_ID)
REFERENCES BOOK6_21(BOOK_ID);
CREATE INDEX SQL091227214019670 ON BOOK621_CHAPTER(BOOK_ID);
CREATE UNIQUE INDEX SQL091227214017400 ON BOOK621_CHAPTER(BOOK621_CHAPTER_ID);
```

6.3 Mapping a List

Problem

A *list* is a list of objects. It's an ordered collection. The user of a list has precise control over where in the list each element is inserted. The user can access elements by their integer index (position in the list) and search for elements in the list. How do you map **value** types as collections of type **list**?

Solution

You use the list element **<list>** to map the **java.util.List** property. The property has to be initialized as an **ArrayList**. The index of the list is retained, and an additional column is added to define the index.

How It Works

The **Book** Java class has a property called **chapters** that is of type **java.util.List**. The property is initialized as an **ArrayList**:

```
public class Book6_3 implements Serializable{

    private Long book_id;
    private String isbn;
    private String name;
    private Date publishDate;
    private Integer price;
    private List chapters;
    // getters and setters
}
```

The **<list>** element maps the chapters, and the **index** element defines the index of the list. The **key** element defines the book ID as the foreign key:

```
<hibernate-mapping package="com.hibernaterecipes.chapter6">
  <class name="Book6_3" table="Book6_3" schema="BOOK6">
    <id name="book_id" type="long" column="BOOK_ID" >
      <generator class="native">
      </generator>
    </id>
    <property name="isbn" type="string">
    <column name="ISBN" length="50" not-null="true" unique="true" />
    </property>
    <property name="name" type="string">
    <column name="BOOK_NAME" length="100" not-null="true" />
    </property>
    <property name="publishDate" type="date" column="PUBLISH_DATE" />
    <property name="price" type="int" column="PRICE" />
    <list name="chapters" table="Book63_Chapter" schema="BOOK6">
      <key column="BOOK_ID"></key>
      <index column="CHAPTER_INDEX"></index>
      <element type="string" column="CHAPTER_NAME" not-null="true"></element>
    </list>
  </class>
</hibernate-mapping>
```

In the JPA annotation mapped Book class, IndexColumn defines the index of the list. Note the annotation's Base attribute: it makes the index start from 1 or any number you wish. The default for this attribute is zero. All the other annotations are very similar to those for the set mapping:

```
@Entity
@Table (name="BOOK6_3", schema="BOOK6")
public class Book_6_3 implements Serializable{

  @Id
  @Column (name="BOOK_ID")
  @GeneratedValue (strategy=GenerationType.AUTO)
  private Long book_id;

  @Column (name="isbn")
  private String isbn;

  @Column (name="BOOK_NAME")
  private String name;

  @Column (name="price")
  private Integer price;

  @CollectionOfElements (targetElement=java.lang.String.class)
  @JoinTable(
      name="Book63_Chapter",
      schema="BOOK6",
      joinColumns=@JoinColumn(name="BOOK_ID")
  )
```

```
@IndexColumn(
    name="CHAPTER_INDEX",
    base=0)
@Column(name="chapter_name")
private List chapters;
// getters and setters
}
```

The CREATE TABLE query is as follows:

```
CREATE TABLE "BOOK6"."BOOK63_CHAPTER"
(
    BOOK_ID bigint NOT NULL,
    CHAPTER_NAME varchar(255) NOT NULL,
    CHAPTER_INDEX int NOT NULL,
    CONSTRAINT SQL091227211951510 PRIMARY KEY (BOOK_ID,CHAPTER_INDEX)
);
ALTER TABLE BOOK63_CHAPTER
ADD CONSTRAINT FK648FEC749C936CDB
FOREIGN KEY (BOOK_ID)
REFERENCES BOOK6_3(BOOK_ID);
CREATE INDEX SQL091227214019790 ON BOOK63_CHAPTER(BOOK_ID);
CREATE UNIQUE INDEX SQL091227211951510 ON BOOK63_CHAPTER
(
    BOOK_ID,
    CHAPTER_INDEX
);
```

6.4 Mapping an Array

Problem

How do you map value types as Arrays?

Solution

An <array> has the same usage as a <list>. The only difference is that it corresponds to an array type in Java, not a java.util.List. It's seldom used unless you're mapping for legacy applications. In most cases, you should use <list> instead, because an array's size can't be increased or decreased dynamically, whereas a list's can.

How It Works

The Book Java class has a property called chapters that is of type String[]:

```
public class Book6_4 implements Serializable{

   private Long book_id;
   private String isbn;
   private String name;
   private Date publishDate;
   private Integer price;
   private String[] chapters;
         // getters and setters
}
```

You use the `<array>` element to map the property. All the other mapping elements are similar to those of a `List` mapping:

```xml
<hibernate-mapping package="com.hibernaterecipes.chapter6">
  <class name="Book6_4" table="Book6_4" schema="BOOK6">
    <id name="book_id" type="long" column="BOOK_ID" >
      <generator class="native">
      </generator>
    </id>
    <property name="isbn" type="string">
    <column name="ISBN" length="50" not-null="true" unique="true" />
    </property>
    <property name="name" type="string">
    <column name="BOOK_NAME" length="100" not-null="true" />
    </property>
    <property name="publishDate" type="date" column="PUBLISH_DATE" />
    <property name="price" type="int" column="PRICE" />
    <array name="chapters" table="Book64_Chapter" schema="BOOK6">
      <key column="BOOK_ID"></key>
      <index column="CHAPTER_INDEX"></index>
      <element type="string" column="CHAPTER_NAME" not-null="true"></element>
    </array>

  </class>
</hibernate-mapping>
```

The JPA annotations are exactly the same as the `List` mapping annotation. The type of **chapters** is changed from `List` to `String[]`, and the create queries on the DB level are the same as for `List`:

```java
@Entity
@Table (name="BOOK6_4", schema="BOOK6")
public class Book_6_4 implements Serializable{

   @Id
   @Column (name="BOOK_ID")
   @GeneratedValue (strategy=GenerationType.AUTO)
   private Long book_id;

   @Column (name="isbn")
```

```
    private String isbn;

    @Column (name="BOOK_NAME")
    private String name;

    @Column (name="price")
    private Integer price;

    @CollectionOfElements (targetElement=java.lang.String.class)
    @JoinTable(
        name="Book64_Chapter",
        schema="BOOK6",
        joinColumns=@JoinColumn(name="BOOK_ID")
    )
    @IndexColumn(
        name="CHAPTER_INDEX",
        base=0)
    @Column(name="chapter_name")
    private String[] chapters;
    // getters and setters
}
```

6.5 Mapping a Map

Problem

How do you map a value type as a map?

Solution

A <map> is very similar to a <list>. The difference is that a map uses arbitrary keys to index the collection, rather than the integer index used in a list. A map stores its entries in key/value pairs. You can look up the value by its key, which can be of any data types. The Java type corresponding to a <map> is java.util.Map.

How It Works

The chapters property is declared to be type Map in the Book class:

```
public class Book6_5 implements Serializable{

    private Long book_id;
    private String isbn;
    private String name;
    private Date publishDate;
    private Integer price;
```

```
  private Map chapters;
  // getters and settes
}
```

You use the `<map>` element to map the chapters. The `<map-key>` element defines the key for each chapter. All other elements are similar to those for the `List` implementation:

```
<hibernate-mapping package="com.hibernaterecipes.chapter6">
  <class name="Book6_5" table="Book6_5" schema="BOOK6">
    <id name="book_id" type="long" column="BOOK_ID" >
      <generator class="native">
      </generator>
    </id>
    <property name="isbn" type="string">
    <column name="ISBN" length="50" not-null="true" unique="true" />
    </property>
    <property name="name" type="string">
    <column name="BOOK_NAME" length="100" not-null="true" />
    </property>
    <property name="publishDate" type="date" column="PUBLISH_DATE" />
    <property name="price" type="int" column="PRICE" />
    <map name="chapters" table="Book65_Chapter" schema="BOOK6">
      <key column="BOOK_ID" />
      <map-key column="CHAPTER_KEY" type="string" />
      <element column="CHAPTER" type="string" length="100" />
    </map>

  </class>
</hibernate-mapping>
```

In the JPA, the `MapKey` annotation defines the key:

```
@Entity
@Table (name="BOOK6_5", schema="BOOK6")
public class Book_6_5 implements Serializable{
  @Id
  @Column (name="BOOK_ID")
  @GeneratedValue (strategy=GenerationType.AUTO)
  private Long book_id;

  @Column (name="isbn")
  private String isbn;

  @Column (name="BOOK_NAME")
  private String name;

  @Column (name="price")
  private Integer price;

  @CollectionOfElements (targetElement=java.lang.String.class)
  @JoinTable(name="Book65_Chapter",
```

```
        schema="BOOK6",
        joinColumns=@JoinColumn(name="BOOK_ID")
  )
  @MapKey (columns=@Column(name="CHAPTER_KEY"),
        targetElement=java.lang.String.class)
  @Column(name="chapter")
  private Map chapters;
        // getters and setters
}
```

The CREATE TABLE query looks something like this:

```
CREATE TABLE "BOOK6"."BOOK65_CHAPTER"
(
   BOOK_ID bigint NOT NULL,
   CHAPTER varchar(100),
   CHAPTER_KEY varchar(255) NOT NULL,
   CONSTRAINT SQL091227211951730 PRIMARY KEY (BOOK_ID,CHAPTER_KEY)
);
ALTER TABLE BOOK65_CHAPTER
ADD CONSTRAINT FK8D18CA769C936CDD
FOREIGN KEY (BOOK_ID)
REFERENCES BOOK6_5(BOOK_ID);
CREATE INDEX SQL091227214020070 ON BOOK65_CHAPTER(BOOK_ID);
CREATE UNIQUE INDEX SQL091227211951730 ON BOOK65_CHAPTER
(
  BOOK_ID,
  CHAPTER_KEY
);
```

6.6 Sorting Collections

Problem

What are the possible ways to sort collections?

Solution

One way to sort a collection is to use the sorting features provided by the Java Collections Framework. The sorting occurs in the memory of the Java virtual machine (JVM) when you run Hibernate, after the data is read from the database. Note that for large collections, this kind of sorting may not be efficient. Only <set> and <map> supports this kind of sorting.

You can also sort a collection at the query level using the **order-by** clause. If your collection is very large, it's more efficient to sort it in the database. You can specify the **order-by** condition to sort this collection upon retrieval. Notice that the **order-by** attribute should be a SQL column, not a property name in Hibernate.

How It Works

We'll see a number of ways to sort a collection, starting with the natural order.

Using the Natural Order

To sort a collection in natural order, you define the sort attribute to be natural in the collection. Hibernate uses the compareTo() method defined in the java.lang.Comparable interface to compare the elements. Many basic data types, such as String, Integer, and Double implement this interface.

The implementation for chapters is changed from HashSet to TreeSet. In the case of a Map, the implementation class needs to be changed to TreeMap:

```java
public class Book6_1 implements Serializable{

  private Long book_id;
  private String isbn;
  private String name;
  private Date publishDate;
  private Integer price;
  private Set chapters = new TreeSet();
  //getters and setters
}
```

In the Hibernate mapping file, the attribute sort is defined as natural:

```xml
<hibernate-mapping package="com.hibernaterecipes.chapter6">
  <class name="Book6_1" table="Book6_1" schema="BOOK6">
    <id name="book_id" type="long" column="BOOK_ID" >
      <generator class="native">
      </generator>
    </id>
    <property name="isbn" type="string">
    <column name="ISBN" length="50" not-null="true" unique="true" />
    </property>
    <property name="name" type="string">
    <column name="BOOK_NAME" length="100" not-null="true" />
    </property>
    <property name="publishDate" type="date" column="PUBLISH_DATE" />
    <property name="price" type="int" column="PRICE" />
    <set name="chapters" table="Book61_Chapter" schema="BOOK6" sort="natural" lazy="false">
      <key column="BOOK_ID"></key>
      <element type="string" column="CHAPTER_NAME" not-null="true"></element>
    </set>
  </class>
</hibernate-mapping>
```

In the JPA mapping file, you need to change the implementation to TreeSet and declare the annotation sort as natural. Also note that you disable lazy initialization. (Lazy initialization is discussed later in this chapter.)

```
@Entity
@Table (name="BOOK6_1", schema="BOOK6")
public class Book_6_1 implements Serializable{
  @Id
  @Column (name="BOOK_ID")
  @GeneratedValue (strategy=GenerationType.AUTO)
  private Long book_id;
  @Column (name="isbn")
  private String isbn;
  @Column (name="BOOK_NAME")
  private String name;
  @Column (name="price")
  private Integer price;
  @CollectionOfElements (targetElement=java.lang.String.class)
  @JoinTable(
      name="Book61_Chapter",
      schema="BOOK6",
      joinColumns=@JoinColumn(name="BOOK_ID")

  )
  @Column(name="chapter_name")
  @Sort (type=SortType.NATURAL)
  @LazyCollection (LazyCollectionOption.FALSE)
  private Set chapters = new TreeSet();
        //getters and setters
}
```

Writing Your Own Comparator

If you aren't satisfied with the natural ordering, you can write your own comparator instead by implementing the java.util.Comparator interface. The comparing logic should be put inside the overridden compare() method. To use this comparator, you pass it to the collection's **sort** attribute. The following is a sample implementation of the comparator:

```
public class ChapterComparator implements Comparator<String> {

  public int compare(String o1, String o2) {
    // if o1 and o2 don't instantiate the same class, throw an exception
    // if o1 is less than o2, return a negative number
    // if o1 is equal to o2, return a zero
    // if o1 is greater than o2, return a positive number
    if(o1.compareTo(o2)<1)
    {
      return 1;
    }else
    {
      return -1;
    }
  }
}
```

In the Hibernate XML mapping file, you declare the comparator implementation as the sorting mechanism:

```
<hibernate-mapping package="com.hibernaterecipes.chapter6">
  <class name="Book6_1" table="Book6_1" schema="BOOK6">
    <id name="book_id" type="long" column="BOOK_ID" >
      <generator class="native">
      </generator>
    </id>
    <property name="isbn" type="string">
    <column name="ISBN" length="50" not-null="true" unique="true" />
    </property>
    <property name="name" type="string">
    <column name="BOOK_NAME" length="100" not-null="true" />
    </property>
    <property name="publishDate" type="date" column="PUBLISH_DATE" />
    <property name="price" type="int" column="PRICE" />
    <set name="chapters" table="Book61_Chapter" schema="BOOK6"
      sort="com.hibernaterecipes.annotations.dao.ch6.ChapterComparator"
      lazy="false">
      <key column="BOOK_ID"></key>
      <element type="string" column="CHAPTER_NAME" not-null="true"></element>
    </set>
  </class>
</hibernate-mapping>
```

You also declare the comparator implementation to be the sorting mechanism in the JPA annotations:

```
@Entity
@Table (name="BOOK6_1", schema="BOOK6")
public class Book_6_1 implements Serializable{
  @Id
  @Column (name="BOOK_ID")
  @GeneratedValue (strategy=GenerationType.AUTO)
  private Long book_id;
  @Column (name="isbn")
  private String isbn;
  @Column (name="BOOK_NAME")
  private String name;
  @Column (name="price")
  private Integer price;
  @CollectionOfElements (targetElement=java.lang.String.class)
  @JoinTable(
      name="Book61_Chapter",
      schema="BOOK6",
      joinColumns=@JoinColumn(name="BOOK_ID")

  )
  @Column(name="chapter_name")
```

```
@Sort (type=SortType.COMPARATOR,
comparator=com.hibernaterecipes.annotations.dao.ch6.ChapterComparator.class)
@LazyCollection (LazyCollectionOption.FALSE)
private Set chapters = new TreeSet();
        // getters and setters
}
```

Sorting in the Database

If your collection is very large, it's more efficient to sort it in the database. You can specify the **order-by** condition to sort the collection when it's retrieved. Note that the **order-by** attribute should be a SQL column, not a property name:

```
<hibernate-mapping package="com.hibernaterecipes.chapter6">
  <class name="Book6_1" table="Book6_1" schema="BOOK6">
    :
            :
    <set name="chapters" table="Book61_Chapter" schema="BOOK6"
      lazy="false" order-by=" CHAPTER_NAME">
      <key column="BOOK_ID"></key>
      <element type="string" column="CHAPTER_NAME" not-null="true"></element>
    </set>
  </class>
</hibernate-mapping>
```

You can use any SQL expression that is valid in the **order by** clause for this **order-by** attribute—for example, using commas to separate multiple columns, or using **asc** or **desc** to specify sorting in ascending or descending order. Hibernate copies the **order-by** attribute to the **order by** clause during SQL generation:

```
<hibernate-mapping package="com.hibernaterecipes.chapter6">
  <class name="Book6_1" table="Book6_1" schema="BOOK6">
    <id name="book_id" type="long" column="BOOK_ID" >
      <generator class="native">
      </generator>
    </id>
    <property name="isbn" type="string">
    <column name="ISBN" length="50" not-null="true" unique="true" />
    </property>
    <property name="name" type="string">
    <column name="BOOK_NAME" length="100" not-null="true" />
    </property>
    <property name="publishDate" type="date" column="PUBLISH_DATE" />
    <property name="price" type="int" column="PRICE" />
    <set name="chapters" table="Book61_Chapter" schema="BOOK6"
      lazy="false" order-by="CHAPTER_NAME desc">
      <key column="BOOK_ID"></key>
      <element type="string" column="CHAPTER_NAME" not-null="true"></element>
    </set>
  </class>
```

```
</hibernate-mapping>
```

In the JPA annotations, you use the `OrderBy` annotation to declare the column name:

```java
@Entity
@Table (name="BOOK6_1", schema="BOOK6")
public class Book_6_1 implements Serializable{
  @Id
  @Column (name="BOOK_ID")
  @GeneratedValue (strategy=GenerationType.AUTO)
  private Long book_id;
  @Column (name="isbn")
  private String isbn;
  @Column (name="BOOK_NAME")
  private String name;
  @Column (name="price")
  private Integer price;
  @CollectionOfElements (targetElement=java.lang.String.class)
  @JoinTable(
      name="Book61_Chapter",
      schema="BOOK6",
      joinColumns=@JoinColumn(name="BOOK_ID")

  )
  @Column(name="chapter_name")
  @OrderBy (clause="chapter_name asc")
  @LazyCollection (LazyCollectionOption.FALSE)
  private Set chapters = new TreeSet();
//getters and setters
}
```

6.6 Using Lazy Initialization

Problem

How does lazy initialization work with collections? How do you avoid the `LazyInitializationException`?

Solution

An entity's mapped collection may not be needed every time the entity is loaded from the database into JVM memory. This mapped collection takes up unnecessary space in memory. To help with this, Hibernate provides the concept of *lazy initialization* in which associations and mapped collections aren't retrieved unless required by the user/application. The retrieval of the mapped collections is done transparently from the application. Hibernate by default has lazy initialization set to true, which saves a lot of memory usage.

Thus the collection of chapters isn't retrieved when a book is fetched. If the session is still open, you get the collection of chapters using `Hibernate.initialize(book.getChapters())`. And if the session isn't open, you have to load the collection when you load the owning entity; you configure this in the owning entity's mapping file by setting the property lazy to false.

How It Works

You can use the following code to retrieve a **book** object from the database. The collection of chapters is retrieved at the same time:

```
Session session = factory.openSession();
try {
  Book book = (Book) session.get(Book.class, id);
  return book;
} finally {
  session.close();
}
```

But when you access the chapter collection through **book.getChapters()** outside the session, an exception occurs:

```
for (Iterator iter = book.getChapters().iterator(); iter.hasNext();) {
  String chapter = (String) iter.next();
  System.out.println(chapter);
}
```

The reason for this exception is the lazy initialization of the collection. You can initialize it explicitly to access it outside the session:

```
Session session = factory.openSession();
try {
  Book book = (Book) session.get(Book.class, id);
  Hibernate.initialize(book.getChapters());
  return book;
} finally {
  session.close();
}
```

Or you can turn off lazy initialization for this collection. You must consider carefully before you do that, especially for a collection:

```
<hibernate-mapping package="com.hibernaterecipes.chapter6">
  <class name="Book6_1" table="Book6_1" schema="BOOK6">
    <id name="book_id" type="long" column="BOOK_ID" >
      <generator class="native">
      </generator>
    </id>
    <property name="isbn" type="string">
      <column name="ISBN" length="50" not-null="true" unique="true" />
    </property>
    <property name="name" type="string">
      <column name="BOOK_NAME" length="100" not-null="true" />
```

```
    </property>
    <property name="publishDate" type="date" column="PUBLISH_DATE" />
    <property name="price" type="int" column="PRICE" />
    <set name="chapters" table="Book61_Chapter" schema="BOOK6"
        lazy="false" order-by="CHAPTER_NAME desc">
      <key column="BOOK_ID"></key>
      <element type="string" column="CHAPTER_NAME" not-null="true"></element>
    </set>
  </class>
</hibernate-mapping>
```

In JPA, it's simply as follows:

```
@Entity
@Table (name="BOOK6_1", schema="BOOK6")
public class Book_6_1 implements Serializable{
  @Id
  @Column (name="BOOK_ID")
  @GeneratedValue (strategy=GenerationType.AUTO)
  private Long book_id;

  @CollectionOfElements (targetElement=java.lang.String.class)
  @JoinTable(
      name="Book61_Chapter",
      schema="BOOK6",
      joinColumns=@JoinColumn(name="BOOK_ID")

  )
  @Column(name="chapter_name")
  @OrderBy (clause="chapter_name asc")
  @LazyCollection (LazyCollectionOption.FALSE)
  private Set chapters = new TreeSet();
// getters and setters
}
```

Summary

This chapter has shown how to map a collection of **value** type objects to an entity. You've seen the implementation of <set>, <bag>, <idbag>, <list>, and <map> elements and their corresponding JPA annotations. You've learned the advantage of each collection mapping element and when it's a good idea to use each of these elements. You've also seen how to sort a collection using a comparator and using the order-by clause. Finally, you've learned how and when lazy initialization should be turned off.

■ ■ ■

CHAPTER 7

Many-Valued Associations

A many-valued association is by definition a collection of references to entities. The collection can be of type `List`, `Set`, `Map`, and so on in Java.

Why would you have a collection of references? When there is a parent/child relationship, and one parent can be associated to many children, the parent contains a collection of references to the child entities. In the case of a relational model, suppose two tables are dependent on each other, this can be represented as a foreign key column in the dependent table. For one row in the parent table, there exist many rows in the child table.

You've seen this in earlier chapters that specified how to use collections. This chapter discusses one-to-many and many-to-many relationships in detail, including how they're defined and how they're represented in Hibernate using the XML configuration and using JPA annotations. You also learn how data is loaded and updated from/in the database when such relationships are defined.

A one-to-many association is the most common and important type. A many-to-many association can be represented as two many-to-one associations. This model is more extensible, so it's used more widely in applications. These associations can be unidirectional as well as bidirectional.

7.1 Mapping a One-to-Many Association with a Foreign Key

Problem

How do you map objects using a one-to-many association with a foreign key? Can you establish this association from one direction only (unidirectional association)? When an operation such as update is executed on the parent object, users sometimes want the child object to be updated as well; this is called *cascading* in Hibernate. How do you use the cascading feature with a one-to-many association?

Solution

You can achieve a one-to-many relationship two ways in the database: by having a foreign key column in the dependent table or by creating a join table between the two tables. Each of these relationships can be unidirectional or bidirectional. The one-to-many unidirectional relationship is uncommon and isn't a recommended way to map using Hibernate.

How It Works

In the previous example, you treated each chapter of a book as a string and stored it in a collection. Now you extend this recipe by making each chapter a persistent object type. Because one **book** object can relate to many **chapter** objects, the association from **book** to **chapter** is a one-to-many association. You first define this association as unidirectional—navigable from **book** to **chapter** only—and then extend it to be bidirectional.

Remember that you have a **Chapter** class in your application that hasn't been mapped to the database. You first create a Hibernate mapping for it and then define an autogenerated identifier:

```
public class Chapter {

        private Long id;
        private String title;
        private int noOfPages;
        // getters and setters
}
```

```
<hibernate-mapping package="com.hibernaterecipes.chapter7">
        <class  name="Chapter"  table="CHAPTER"  dynamic-insert="true"  dynamic-update="true"
schema="BookShop">

                <id name="id"  column="id" type="long">
                        <generator class="native">
                        </generator>
                </id>
                <property name="title" type="string" column="title" />
                <property name="noOfPages" type="int" column="NUM_OF_PAGES" />

        </class>
</hibernate-mapping>
```

Because you added a new persistent object to the application, you also need to specify it in the Hibernate configuration file:

```
<mapping resource="com/hibernaterecipes/chapter7/chapter.xml" />
```

For the **Book** class, you already have a collection for storing chapters, although only the titles are stored. You can still use this collection, but you with **chapter** objects instead. Which collection type should you use? Because a book can't contain duplicated chapters, you choose the **<set>** collection type:

```
public class Book {

        private Long book_id;

        private String isbn;

        private String bookName;

        private Date publishDate;
```

```
    private Long price;

    private Set chapters;
    // getters and setters
}
```

To tell Hibernate that you're storing **chapter** objects and not strings in the collection, you can use the `<one-to-many>` mapping element instead of `<element>`:

```xml
<hibernate-mapping package="com.hibernaterecipes.chapter7">
    <class name="Book" table="BOOK" schema="BookShop7">
        <id name="book_id"  column="BOOK_ID" type="long">
            <generator class="native">
            </generator>
        </id>
        <property name="isbn" type="string" column="ISBN" />
        <property name="bookName" type="string" column="BOOK_NAME" />
        <property name="publishDate" type="date" column="PUBLISH_DATE" />
        <property name="price" type="long" column="PRICE" />
        <set name="chapters">
            <key column="BOOK_ID" />
            <one-to-many class="Chapter" />
        </set>
    </class>
</hibernate-mapping>
```

The following is the sample code to save the **book** and **chapter** objects:

```java
Transaction tx = session.beginTransaction();

Book book = new Book();
book.setIsbn("234234wef2323");
book.setBookName("Hibernate Recipes ");
book.setPrice(79l);
book.setPublishDate(new Date());
session.save(book);

Chapter chapter = new Chapter();
chapter.setBook_id(book.getBook_id());
chapter.setNoOfPages(10);
chapter.setTitle("One-To-Many Association");
session.save(chapter);

Set chapters = new HashSet<Chapter>();
chapters.add(chapter);
book.setChapters(chapters);
```

In this code, you save **book** and **chapter** separately: `session.save(book)` and `session.save(chapter)`. Also, you programmatically associate the chapters with the book: `book.setChapters(chapters)`. Hibernate resolves these statements into three queries and executes them as follows:

```
insert into BookShop7.BOOK (ISBN, BOOK_NAME, PUBLISH_DATE, PRICE, BOOK_ID) values (?, ?, ?,
?, ?)
```

```
insert into BookShop7.CHAPTER (BOOK_ID, title, NUM_OF_PAGES, id) values (?, ?, ?, ?)
```

```
update BookShop7.CHAPTER set BOOK_ID=? where id=?
```

The first SQL statement inserts the **book** record into the **BOOK** table. This is straightforward SQL and is associated with the statement **session.save(book)**.

The second SQL statement inserts the **chapter** object into the **CHAPTER** table. The code for this is **session.save(chapter)**.

The third SQL statement is the interesting one. It associates the **book** and **chapter** objects after they have been loaded individually. This is an **update** statement that updates the foreign key column in the **CHAPTER** table with the **book_id**, thus binding **Book** and **Chapter**.

Now, let's see how you save with the **cascade** option. This option specifies what operations should be cascaded from parent object to the associated object. For example, if you want to save **chapter** along with **book**, you can use **cascade=saveUpdate**. With this option, you don't have to invoke **session.save** but instead can just invoke **session.saveUpdate** once by passing the **book** object. The **chapters** collection is set to the **book** object, and finally the **book** object is inserted:

```xml
<hibernate-mapping package="com.hibernaterecipes.chapter7">
        <class name="Book" table="BOOK" schema="BookShop7">
                <id name="book_id"  column="BOOK_ID" type="long">
                        <generator class="native">
                        </generator>
                </id>
                <property name="isbn" type="string" column="ISBN" />
                <property name="bookName" type="string" column="BOOK_NAME" />
                <property name="publishDate" type="date" column="PUBLISH_DATE" />
                <property name="price" type="long" column="PRICE" />
                <set name="chapters" cascade="save-update">
                        <key column="BOOK_ID" />
                        <one-to-many class="Chapter" />
                </set>
        </class>
</hibernate-mapping>
```

Here's the code example:

```java
Book book = new Book();
book.setIsbn("234234wef2323");
book.setBookName("Hibernate Recipes ");
book.setPrice(79l);
book.setPublishDate(new Date());

Chapter chapter = new Chapter();
chapter.setBook_id(book.getBook_id());
chapter.setNoOfPages(10);
chapter.setTitle("One-To-Many Association");

Set chapters = new HashSet<Chapter>();
```

```
                chapters.add(chapter);

                book.setChapters(chapters);
                session.saveOrUpdate(book);
```

The statement `session.saveOrUpdate` generates two queries instead of the three you saw in the earlier example:

```
insert into BookShop7.BOOK7_1 (ISBN, BOOK_NAME, PUBLISH_DATE, PRICE, BOOK_ID) values (?, ?,
?, ?, ?)
insert into BookShop7.CHAPTER7_1 (title, NUM_OF_PAGES, book_id, id) values (?, ?, ?, ?)
```

Now, suppose you call a `delete` on the `book`, as follows:

```
Transaction tx = session.beginTransaction();
Book book = (Book) session.load(com.hibernaterecipes.chapter7.Book.class, new Long(294913));

session.delete(book);
tx.commit();
```

Hibernate issues two SQL statements on this `delete`:

- One to update the associated chapter record with a book's ID is null

- A delete on the book

After the `delete` is complete, you're left with an orphan chapter record. This isn't desirable. To avoid such orphan records, you need to use the `delete-orphan` option on `cascade`, as follows:

```
<hibernate-mapping package="com.hibernaterecipes.chapter7">
        <class name="Book7_1" table="BOOK7_1" schema="BookShop7">
                <id name="book_id"  column="BOOK_ID" type="long">
                        <generator class="native">
                        </generator>
                </id>
                <property name="isbn" type="string" column="ISBN" />
                <property name="bookName" type="string" column="BOOK_NAME" />
                <property name="publishDate" type="date" column="PUBLISH_DATE" />
                <property name="price" type="long" column="PRICE" />
                <set name="chapters" cascade="save-update,delete-orphan">
                        <key column="BOOK_ID" />
                        <one-to-many class="Chapter" />
                </set>
        </class>
</hibernate-mapping>
```

In JPA the mapping is as follows:

```
@Entity (name="bkch2")
@Table        (name="BOOK7_1", schema="BOOKSHOP")
public class Book7_1 {
```

```
@Id
@GeneratedValue (strategy=GenerationType.TABLE)
@Column (name="BOOK_ID")
private long book_id;

@Column (name="ISBN")
private String isbn;

@Column (name="book_Name")
private String bookName;

/*@Column (name="publisher_code")
String publisherCode;*/

@Column (name="publish_date")
private Date publishDate;

@Column (name="price")
private Long price;

@OneToMany(targetEntity=Chapter7_1.class)
@JoinColumn(name="book_id")
@Cascade (value={CascadeType.SAVE_UPDATE,CascadeType.DELETE_ORPHAN})
Set chapters;

// setters and gettes
}
```

7.2 Mapping a One-to-Many Bidirectional Association Using a Foreign Key

Problem

How do you map objects using a one-to-many bidirectional association with a foreign key?

Solution

In some cases, you want your associations to be bidirectional. Suppose you have a page that displays the detail of a Chapter inside a Book. You need to know which Book this Chapter belongs to, given a chapter object. You can do this by adding a reference to Book in the Chapter class. This association is a one-to-many association. The book-to-chapter and chapter-to-book associations combine to form a bidirectional association.

How It Works

In the previous example, you treated each chapter of a Book as a string and stored it in a collection. Now, you extend this recipe by making each Chapter of a persistent object type. One book object can relate to many chapter objects, so this is a one-to-many association. You first define this association as unidirectional—navigable from book to chapter only—and then extend it to be bidirectional.

The Chapter class is updated to include the book as follows:

```
public class Chapter7_1 {

        private Long id;
        private Book7_1 book;
        private String title;
        private int noOfPages;
        // Getters and Setters

}
```

The Hibernate mapping for Chapter is as follows:

```
<hibernate-mapping package="com.hibernaterecipes.chapter7">
        <class    name="Chapter7_1"    table="CHAPTER7_1"    dynamic-insert="true"    dynamic-
update="true" schema="BookShop7">

                <id name="id"  column="id" type="long">
                        <generator class="native">
                        </generator>
                </id>
                <property name="title" type="string" column="title" />
                <property name="noOfPages" type="int" column="NUM_OF_PAGES" />
                <many-to-one name="book"
                 column="book_id" class="Book7_1"
                ></many-to-one>
        </class>
</hibernate-mapping>
```

You get three SQL statements to save one book with one chapter from the unidirectional association. Ideally, you want to avoid the update query. This can be achieved by setting the inverse attribute to true in the book mapping class:

```
<hibernate-mapping package="com.hibernaterecipes.chapter7">
        <class name="Book7_1" table="BOOK7_1" schema="BookShop7">
                <id name="book_id"  column="BOOK_ID" type="long">
                        <generator class="native">
                        </generator>
                </id>
                <property name="isbn" type="string" column="ISBN" />
                <property name="bookName" type="string" column="BOOK_NAME" />
                <property name="publishDate" type="date" column="PUBLISH_DATE" />
                <property name="price" type="long" column="PRICE" />
                <set name="chapters" inverse="true">
```

```
                        <key column="BOOK_ID" />
                        <one-to-many class="Chapter7_1" />
              </set>
        </class>
</hibernate-mapping>
```

The foreign key BOOK_ID has two representations in memory: the **Book** property of **Chapter** and the element of the **chapters** collection held by **Book**. Suppose you add a **chapter** to a **book** object. Also say you haven't initially set inverse="true", and you established bidirectionality as follows:

```
chapter.setBook(book);
book.getChapters().add(chapter);
```

If you save the **chapter** object, two SQL statements are executed, because Hibernate doesn't know that the mapping of BOOK_ID in the **book** and **chapter** mapping files refers to the same database column. The SQL statements executed are shown here:

```
insert into BookShop7.CHAPTER7_1 (title, NUM_OF_PAGES, book_id, id) values (?, ?, ?, ?)
update BookShop7.CHAPTER7_1 set BOOK_ID=? where id=?
```

Now, add inverse="true". When you save the **chapter**, you see that only one insert on the **chapter** is executed. This is because you tell Hibernate that BOOK_ID is the same in both mapping files.

In JPA, the **Chapter** class is as follows:

```
@Entity (name="chapter")
@Table        (name="Chapter7_1", schema="BOOKSHOP")
public class Chapter7_1 {

        @Id
        @GeneratedValue (strategy=GenerationType.TABLE)
        @Column (name="id")
        private long id;

        @ManyToOne
        @JoinColumn (name="book_id")
        private Book7_1 book;

        @Column (name="title")
        private String title;

        @Column (name="NUM_OF_PAGES")
        private int numOfPages;

        // getters and setters
}
```

In annotations, the inverse attribute is replaced by the mappedBy attribute:

```
@Entity (name="bkch2")
@Table        (name="BOOK7_1", schema="BOOKSHOP")
public class Book7_1 {
```

```
    @Id
    @GeneratedValue (strategy=GenerationType.TABLE)
    @Column (name="BOOK_ID")
    private long book_id;

    @Column (name="ISBN")
    private String isbn;

    @Column (name="book_Name")
    private String bookName;

    /*@Column (name="publisher_code")
    String publisherCode;*/

    @Column (name="publish_date")
    private Date publishDate;

    @Column (name="price")
    private Long price;

    @OneToMany(targetEntity=Chapter7_1.class,mappedBy="book")
    @JoinColumn(name="BOOK_ID")
    @Cascade (value={CascadeType.SAVE_UPDATE,CascadeType.DELETE_ORPHAN})
    Set chapters;
    // getters and setters
}
```

7.3 Mapping a One-to-Many Bidirectional Association Using a Join Table

Problem

How do you map objects using a one-to-many association with a join table?

Solution

Remember that you can use a join table for a many-to-one association and also for a one-to-many association. You can do so by using a <many-to-many> association type and marking unique="true".

How It Works

One book object can relate to many chapter objects, so the association from Book to Chapter is one-to-many. You first define this association as unidirectional—navigable from book to chapter only—and then extend it to be bidirectional.

The Book mapping is as follows:

```
<hibernate-mapping package="com.hibernaterecipes.chapter7">
        <class name="Book7_3" table="BOOK7_3" schema="BookShop7">
                <id name="book_id"  column="BOOK_ID" type="long">
                        <generator class="native">
                        </generator>
                </id>
                <property name="isbn" type="string" column="ISBN" />
                <property name="bookName" type="string" column="BOOK_NAME" />
                <property name="publishDate" type="date" column="PUBLISH_DATE" />
                <property name="price" type="long" column="PRICE" />
                <set name="chapters" table="BOOK_CHAPTER" schema="BookShop7" cascade="save-
update,delete-orphan">
                        <key column="BOOK_ID" />
                        <many-to-many column="CHAPTER_ID" class="Chapter7_3" unique="true"/>
                </set>
        </class>
</hibernate-mapping>
```

The join table BOOK_CHAPTER is defined as the collection table. BOOK_ID and CHAPTER_ID form the composite primary key of the join table. Instead of one-to-many, you need to use the <many-to-many> element, because one-to-many doesn't know about join tables. By setting the unique attribute to true, you say that one Book can have a Chapter only once (determined by the hashCode() and equals() methods), and you indirectly implement a one-to-many association.

Using JPA annotations, the Book class is mapped as follows. Note that the mappedby attribute isn't set because this is a unidirectional example. Also, Chapter doesn't have an instance of Book:

```
@Entity (name="bkch73")
@Table        (name="BOOK7_3", schema="BOOKSHOP7")
public class Book7_3 {

        @Id
        @GeneratedValue (strategy=GenerationType.TABLE)
        @Column (name="BOOK_ID")
        private long book_id;

        @Column (name="ISBN")
        private String isbn;

        @Column (name="book_Name")
        private String bookName;

        /*@Column (name="publisher_code")
        String publisherCode;*/

        @Column (name="publish_date")
        private Date publishDate;

        @Column (name="price")
```

```
        private Long price;

        @OneToMany(targetEntity=Chapter7_3.class)
        @JoinTable(name = "Book_Chapter",schema="BOOKSHOP7",
                        joinColumns = {
                                @JoinColumn(name="book_id")
                        }
        )
        @Cascade (value={CascadeType.SAVE_UPDATE,CascadeType.DELETE_ORPHAN})
        private Set chapters;

        // getters and setters
}
```

If you want to make a bidirectional one-to-many/many-to-one association using a join table, you can define the many-to-one end the same way as before. It's important to note that you should mark one end of the bidirectional association as inverse. This time, you make the Chapter end inverse, but it's OK to choose the other end:

```
<hibernate-mapping package="com.hibernaterecipes.chapter7">
        <class    name="Chapter7_3"    table="CHAPTER7_3"    dynamic-insert="true"    dynamic-
update="true" schema="BookShop7">
                <id name="id"  column="id" type="long">
                        <generator class="native">
                        </generator>
                </id>
                <property name="title" type="string" column="title" />
                <property name="noOfPages" type="int" column="NUM_OF_PAGES" />

                <join          table="BOOK_CHAPTER"          optional="true"          inverse="true"
schema="BookShop7">
                        <key column="CHAPTER_ID" unique="true" />
                        <many-to-one  name="book"  class="Book7_3"  column="BOOK_ID"  not-
null="true" />
                </join>
        </class>
</hibernate-mapping>
```

In JPA, you update the Book class with the mappedBy attribute:

```
@Entity (name="bkch73")
@Table        (name="BOOK7_3", schema="BOOKSHOP7")
public class Book7_3 {

    .
.
.
.
.
}
```

```
            @OneToMany(targetEntity=Chapter7_3.class,mappedBy="book")
            @JoinTable(name = "Book_Chapter",schema="BOOKSHOP7",
                        joinColumns = {
                                @JoinColumn(name="book_id")
                    }
            )
            @Cascade (value={CascadeType.SAVE_UPDATE,CascadeType.DELETE_ORPHAN})
            private Set chapters;

// getters and setters
}
```

And the Chapter class is as follows:

```
@Entity (name="chapter73")
@Table        (name="Chapter7_3", schema="BOOKSHOP7")
public class Chapter7_3 {

        @Id
        @GeneratedValue (strategy=GenerationType.TABLE)
        @Column (name="id")
        private long id;

        @ManyToOne
        @JoinTable(
                        name="Book_Chapter",
                        schema="BOOKSHOP7",
                        joinColumns=@JoinColumn(name="id")
        )
        @JoinColumn (name="book_id")
        private Book7_3 book;

        @Column (name="title")
        private String title;

        @Column (name="NUM_OF_PAGES")
        private int numOfPages;
        // getters and setters
}
```

7.4 Mapping a Many-to-Many Unidirectional Association with a Join Table

Problem

How do you map objects using a many-to-many unidirectional association with a join table?

Solution

The last type of association this chapter discusses is the many-to-many association. Suppose Books and Chapters can have a many-to-many relationship. That means a chapter can be a part of more than one book. It isn't common, but it's definitely possible. Let's see how it works.

How It Works

The Book XML mapping file uses the set element (`<set>`) with a many-to-many association to map a set of chapters. Neither the Chapter class nor the XML file references book, because this association is unidirectional:

```
<hibernate-mapping package="com.hibernaterecipes.chapter7">
        <class name="Book7_4" table="BOOK7_4" schema="BookShop7">
                <id name="book_id"  column="BOOK_ID" type="long">
                        <generator class="native">
                        </generator>
                </id>
                <property name="isbn" type="string" column="ISBN" />
                <property name="bookName" type="string" column="BOOK_NAME" />
                <property name="publishDate" type="date" column="PUBLISH_DATE" />
                <property name="price" type="long" column="PRICE" />
                <set name="chapters" table="BOOK_CHAPTER" schema="BookShop7" cascade="save-
update,delete-orphan">
                        <key column="BOOK_ID" />
                        <many-to-many column="ID" class="Chapter7_4" unique="true"/>
                </set>
        </class>
</hibernate-mapping>
```

The Chapter XML file is unchanged:

```
<hibernate-mapping package="com.hibernaterecipes.chapter7">
        <class    name="Chapter7_4"    table="CHAPTER7_4"    dynamic-insert="true"    dynamic-
update="true" schema="BookShop7">
                <id name="id"   column="id" type="long">
                        <generator class="native">
                        </generator>
                </id>
                <property name="title" type="string" column="title" />
                <property name="noOfPages" type="int" column="NUM_OF_PAGES" />

        </class>
</hibernate-mapping>
```

In JPA, the Book class is as follows:

```
@Entity (name="bkch74")
@Table          (name="BOOK7_4", schema="BOOKSHOP7")
public class Book7_4 {
```

```
@Id
@GeneratedValue (strategy=GenerationType.TABLE)
@Column (name="BOOK_ID")
private long book_id;

@Column (name="ISBN")
private String isbn;

@Column (name="book_Name")
private String bookName;

/*@Column (name="publisher_code")
String publisherCode;*/

@Column (name="publish_date")
private Date publishDate;

@Column (name="price")
private Long price;

@ManyToMany(targetEntity=Chapter7_4.class)
@JoinTable(name = "Book_Chapter",schema="BOOKSHOP7",
            joinColumns = {@JoinColumn(name="book_id")},
        inverseJoinColumns={@JoinColumn(name="chapter_id")}
)
@Cascade (value={CascadeType.SAVE_UPDATE,CascadeType.DELETE_ORPHAN})
private Set chapters;
}
```

The join table BOOK_CHAPTER has two columns that form the composite key for the table.

7.5 Creating a Many-to-Many Bidirectional Association with a Join Table

Problem

How do you map objects using a many-to-many bidirectional association with a join table?

Solution

To achieve bidirectionality, you need to update the Chapter class to have a collection of book object. You use the set element to map both sides.

How It Works

Update the Chapter class to include a set:

```java
public class Chapter7_41 {

        private Long id;
        private Set book;
        private String title;
        private int noOfPages;
        // getters and setters
}
```

The XML mapping for the Chapter class is as follows:

```xml
<hibernate-mapping package="com.hibernaterecipes.chapter7">
        <class name="Chapter7_41" table="CHAPTER7_41" dynamic-insert="true" dynamic-
update="true" schema="BookShop7">
                <id name="id"   column="id" type="long">
                        <generator class="native">
                        </generator>
                </id>
                <property name="title" type="string" column="title" />
                <property name="noOfPages" type="int" column="NUM_OF_PAGES" />
                <set name="book" table="BOOK_CHAPTER" inverse="true" cascade="save-update">
                        <key column="id"></key>
                        <many-to-many class="Book7_41" column="BOOK_ID" />

                </set>
        </class>
</hibernate-mapping>
```

The XML for the Book class is as follows:

```xml
<hibernate-mapping package="com.hibernaterecipes.chapter7">
        <class name="Book7_41" table="BOOK7_41" schema="BookShop7">
                <id name="book_id"   column="BOOK_ID" type="long">
                        <generator class="native">
                        </generator>
                </id>
                <property name="isbn" type="string" column="ISBN" />
                <property name="bookName" type="string" column="BOOK_NAME" />
                <property name="publishDate" type="date" column="PUBLISH_DATE" />
                <property name="price" type="long" column="PRICE" />
                <set name="chapters" table="BOOK_CHAPTER" schema="BookShop7" cascade="save-
update,delete-orphan">
                        <key column="BOOK_ID" />
                        <many-to-many column="ID" class="Chapter7_41" unique="true"/>
                </set>
        </class>
</hibernate-mapping>
```

In JPA, the Book and Chapter classes are as shown here:

```java
@Entity (name="bkch741")
@Table        (name="BOOK7_41", schema="BOOKSHOP7")
public class Book7_41 {

        @Id
        @GeneratedValue (strategy=GenerationType.TABLE)
        @Column (name="BOOK_ID")
        private long book_id;

        @Column (name="ISBN")
        private String isbn;

        @Column (name="book_Name")
        private String bookName;

        /*@Column (name="publisher_code")
        String publisherCode;*/

        @Column (name="publish_date")
        private Date publishDate;

        @Column (name="price")
        private Long price;

        @ManyToMany
        @JoinTable(name = "Book_Chapter",schema="BOOKSHOP7",
                        joinColumns = {@JoinColumn(name="book_id")},
                    inverseJoinColumns={@JoinColumn(name="id")}
        )
        @Cascade (value={CascadeType.SAVE_UPDATE})
        private Set<Chapter7_41> chapters = new HashSet<Chapter7_41>();
        // getters and setters
}


@Entity (name="chapter741")
@Table        (name="Chapter7_41", schema="BOOKSHOP7")
public class Chapter7_41 {

        @Id
        @GeneratedValue (strategy=GenerationType.TABLE)
        @Column (name="id")
        private long id;

        @ManyToMany (mappedBy="chapters")
        private Set<Book7_41> book = new HashSet<Book7_41>();

        @Column (name="title")
```

```
        private String title;

        @Column (name="NUM_OF_PAGES")
        private int numOfPages;
        // getters and setters
}
```

Summary

In this chapter, you've learned how to create and use many-valued associations. The many-valued associations are of type one-to-many and many-to-many. The more widely used of these is the one-to-many association. Both one-to-many and many-to-many can be mapped in two ways: using a foreign key or using a join table.

When you use a foreign key, you map the key in the parent table using the `<set>` mapping element with the key attribute as the foreign key column. The class to which it's associated is specified by the `<one-to-many>` mapping element. With the `cascade` option, operations are cascaded from the parent entity to the associated entity.

A many-to-many association is mapped using a join table. You create a join table to hold the IDs from the parent entity and the associated entity.

A bidirectional association in both one-to-many and many-to-many mappings is represented using `inverse="true"`, which specifies that the inverse directional mapping from the associated entity to the parent entity can be traversed.

CHAPTER 8

HQL and JPA Query Language

When you use JDBC to access databases, you write SQL statements for the query and update tasks. In such cases, you're dealing with tables, columns, and joins. When you use Hibernate, most update tasks can be accomplished through the APIs provided by Hibernate. However, you still need to use a query language for the query tasks. Hibernate provides a powerful query language called Hibernate Query Language (HQL).

HQL is database independent and translated into SQL by Hibernate at runtime. When you write HQL, you can concentrate on the objects and properties without knowing much detail about the underlying database. You can treat HQL as an object-oriented variant of SQL.

In this chapter, you see how to query the database using HQL and JPA Query Language (JPA QL). Hibernate basically provides three ways to query a database:

- HQL and JPA QL, which is a subset of HQL

- Criteria API (Criteria and Example)

- Direct SQL

This chapter looks at HQL, JPA QL, and Direct SQL. You see how to form a query, bind parameters (named and position), and execute the query. You learn how to manipulate the result, which can help you deal with large result sets. You also query associated objects.

8.1 Using the Query Object

Problem

How do you create a `Query` object in hibernate? How do you enable pagination? What are the various ways to bind parameters to a query?

Solution

A `Query` is an object-oriented representation of an actual query. The Hibernate interface `org.hibernate.Query` and the JPA interface `javax.persistence.Query` provide methods to control the execution of a query and bind values to query parameters. In Hibernate, you can obtain an instance of the `Query` object by calling `Session.createQuery()`. And in JPA, the EntityManager provide an instance of the `Query` object with a call like `EntityManager.createQuery()`.

How It Works

Let's see how to use the Query object, starting with how to create it.

Creating a Query Object

In the previous chapters, you've seen some basic HQL statements for querying objects. For example, returning to the bookshop example, you can use the following HQL to query for all books, and then call the list() method to retrieve the result list that contains book objects:

```
Query query = session.createQuery("from Book");
List books = query.list();
```

The from Clause

Now, let's look at the from clause, which is the only required part of a HQL statement. The following HQL statement queries for books whose name is "Hibernate". Notice that name is a property of the Book object:

```
from Book
where name = 'Hibernate'
```

Or, you can assign an alias for the object. This is useful when you're querying multiple objects in one query. You should use the naming conventions for classes and instances in Java. Note that the as keyword is optional:

```
from Book as book
where book.name = 'Hibernate'
```

You can then integrate the alias with the query:

```
Query query = session.createQuery("from Book where book.name='Hibernate'");
List books = query.list();
```

You need to use the EntityManager to create a javax.persistence.Query instance in JPA QL. The select clause is required in Java persistence, as shown here:

```
public List<Book> readFromManager() {

    EntityManager manager = SessionManager.getEntityManager();
    EntityTransaction tran = manager.getTransaction();
    tran.begin();
    Query query = manager.createQuery("select b from Book b");
    List<Book> list = query.getResultList();
    return list;
}
```

Note that you need to place the persistence.xml file in the META-INF folder. Also remember to place all the required jars in the classpath.

The where Clause

In HQL, you can use where clauses to filter results, just as you do in SQL. For multiple conditions, you can use *and*, *or*, and *not* to combine them. This is called *applying restrictions*:

```
from Book book
where book.name like '%Hibernate%' and book.price between 100 and 200
```

You can check whether an associated object is null or not by using is null or is not null:

```
from Book book
where book.publisher is not null
```

Notice that the null check can't be performed on a collection. So, if you have a query like the following, you get an exception from Hibernate:

```
from Book8_1 book
where book.chapters is not null
```

Hibernate provides the empty key word, which you can use to check if a collection is empty:

```
from Book8_1 book
where book.chapters is not empty
```

Let's say you want to retrieve all books published by the publishers "Apress" and "friendsOfED". In technical terms, you want to retrieve based on a property (publisher's name) of the association (publisher). For this kind of requirement, you can use *implicit joins* in the where clause. You create an implicit join by using the . *dot* operator:

```
from Book book
where book.publisher.name in ('Apress', 'friendsOfED')
```

Remember that for a collection association, if you reference it more than one time, you should use an *explicit join* to avoid duplicated joins. Explicit joins require the use of the join keyword. Querying using joins is described in detail later in this chapter.

Hibernate provides a function that lets you check the size of a collection. You can use the special property size or the special size() function. Hibernate uses a select count(...) subquery to get the size of the collection:

```
from Book book
where book.chapters.size > 10
from Book book
where size(book.chapters) > 10
```

Pagination

When the number of records returned by a query is large, it's desirable to retrieve only a subset of the actual number of records. The subset is usually equal to the page size (number of records); this feature is called *pagination*. The Hibernate and JPA Query interfaces provide two methods to enable pagination:

- setFirstResult(int beginPoint): Sets the first row with the given **beginPoint**

- setMaxResult(int size): Sets the returned result-set size

The implementation looks like this:

```
public List<Book> readFromManager() {

    EntityManager manager = SessionManager.getEntityManager();
    EntityTransaction tran = manager.getTransaction();
    tran.begin();
    Query query = manager.createQuery("select b from Book b");
    query.setFirstResult(5);
    query.setMaxResults(15);
    List<Book> list = query.getResultList();
    return list;
  }
```

In this example, the records starting with the fifth row and the next 15 records after that are retrieved.

Parameter Binding

You use *parameter binding* to bind values to the query parameters. Parameter binding makes the code look cleaner; the code is also safer. It isn't recommended that you inject user input into a query using string concatenation; this can lead to a security issue called *SQL injection*.

SQL Injection

A SQL injection attack is an "injection" of a SQL query into the application via user input. A successful SQL injection exploit can, among other things, read sensitive data from the database, modify database data (insert/update/delete), and execute administrative operations on the database.

Let's look at a simple example. The following main() method invokes a method called exampleSQLInjection(), which takes a user input string:

```
public static void main(String[] args) {

    List books = exampleSQLInjection("Hibernate");
    if(books!=null)
    {
      System.out.println("Size- "+books.size());
      Iterator it = books.iterator();
      while(it.hasNext())
      {
        System.out.println("book- "+it.next());
      }
    }
```

```
}
```

The implementation of the exampleSQLInjection() method is as follows:

```
public static List exampleSQLInjection(String userInput)
{
  Session session = getSession();
  String q="from Book8_1 book where book.bookName='"+userInput+"'";
  Query query = session.createQuery(q);
  List books = query.list();
  return books;
}
```

exampleSQLInjection() is only supposed to return a list of books with the name "Hibernate". If the user input changes from "Hibernate" to something like

```
Hibernate' or 'x'='x
```

and the method is invoked like this

```
List books = exampleSQLInjection("Hibernate' or 'x'='x");
```

then it returns all the books in the table, which violates the query's purpose. Imagine a similar attack on a user table that contains passwords or other secure information.

This is a very basic example of SQL injection. Of course, user input should be validated before it reaches this point, but you should never entirely depend on it being validated properly. Hence, it's a very good habit to use parameter binding.

Hibernate and JPA support two types of parameter binding:

- Named parameter binding
- Positional parameter binding

You can specify query parameters the same way you do for SQL queries. If you're sure only one unique object will be returned as a result, you can call the uniqueResult() method to retrieve it. Null is returned if nothing matches:

```
query = session.createQuery("from Book where isbn = ?");
query.setLong(0, 520);
Book bookCh8 = (Book) query.uniqueResult();
```

This example uses ? to represent a query parameter and set it by index (which is zero-based, not one-based as in JDBC). This kind of parameter binding is called *positional* parameter binding. You can also use *named* parameter binding for queries. The advantages of using named parameters is that they're easy to understand and can occur multiple times:

```
Query query = session.createQuery("from Book where isbn =:isbn");
query.setLong("isbn", 520);
Book bookCh8 = (Book) query.uniqueResult();
System.out.println(bookCh8);
```

Named Queries

You can put query statements in any mapping definitions and refer them by name in the code. These are called *named queries.* But for easier maintenance, you should centralize all your named queries in one mapping definition, say `NamedQuery.hbm.xml`. In addition, setting up a mechanism for naming queries is also beneficial—you need to assign each query a unique name. You should also put the query string in a `<![CDATA[...]]>` block to avoid conflicts with special XML characters. Named queries don't have to be HQL or JPA QL strings—they can be native SQL queries:

```
<hibernate-mapping>
  <query name="Book.by.isbn">
    <![CDATA[from Book where isbn = ?]]>
  </query>
</hibernate-mapping>
```

To reference a named query, you use the `session.getNamedQuery()` method:

```
Query query = session.getNamedQuery("Book.by.isbn");
query.setString(0, "1932394419");
Book book = (Book) query.uniqueResult();
```

The JPA specifies the `@NamedQuery` and `@NamedNativeQuery` annotations. The `name` and `query` attributes are required. You can place these annotations in the metadata of a particular entity or into a JPA XML file:

```
@NamedQueries({
  @NamedQuery(
  name="Book.by.isbn",
  query="from Book where isbn = ?"
  )
})
@Entity (name="book")
@Table  (name="BOOK", schema="BOOKSHOP")
public class Book{…}
```

8.2 Using the Select Clause

Problem

How and where do you use the `select` clause?

Solution

The previous examples query for entire persistent objects. You can instead query for particular fields by using the `select` clause. The `select` clause picks which objects and properties to return in the query result set.

How It Works

The following query returns all the book names in a list:

```
select book.name
from Book book
```

You can use the SQL aggregate functions, such as `count()`, `sum()`, `avg()`, `max()`, and `min()`, in HQL. They're translated in the resulting SQL:

```
select avg(book.price)
from Book book
```

Implicit joins can also be used in the `select` clause. In addition, you can use the keyword `distinct` to return distinct results:

```
select distinct book.publisher.name
from Book book
```

To query multiple fields, use a comma to separate them. The result list contains elements of `Object[]`:

```
select book.isbn, book.name, book.publisher.name
from Book book
```

You can create custom types and specify them in the `select` clause to encapsulate the results. For example, let's create a `BookSummary` class for the `bookIsbn`, `bookName`, and `publisherName` fields. The custom type must have a constructor of all the fields:

```
public class BookSummary {
  private String bookIsbn;
  private String bookName;
  private String publisherName;
  public BookSummary(String bookIsbn, String bookName, String publisherName) {
    this.bookIsbn = bookIsbn;
```

```
      this.bookName = bookName;
      this.publisherName = publisherName;
   }
   // Getters and Setters
}
```

```
select new BookSummary(book.isbn, book.name, book.publisher.name)
from Book book
```

The results can be encapsulated in collections such as lists and maps. Then, the query result is a list of collections. For example, if you use a list, the result is a List of List objects, as shown here:

```
String queryString = "select new list(book.isbn, book.name, book.publisher.name)
from Book book";
Query query = session.createQuery(queryString);
List books = query.list();

if(books!=null)
{
  System.out.println("Size- "+books.size());
  Iterator it = books.iterator();
  while(it.hasNext())
  {
    List book = (List)it.next();
    Iterator listIt = book.iterator();
    while(listIt.hasNext())
    {
      System.out.println("Inside book- "+listIt.next());
    }//end of second(inner) while loop
    System.out.println(" ");
  }//end of first while loop
}//end of if
```

For the map collection, you need to use the keyword **as** to specify the map key for each field. In the case of a map, the result is a List of Map objects:

```
String queryString =
  "select new map(
      book.isbn as bookIsbn, book.name as bookName, book.publisher.name as publisherName
  ) from Book book";
Query query = session.createQuery(queryString);
List books = query.list();

if(books!=null)
{
  System.out.println("Size- "+books.size());
  Iterator it = books.iterator();
  while(it.hasNext())
  {
    Map book = (Map)it.next();
    Set bookSet = book.keySet();
```

```
    Iterator listIt = bookSet.iterator();
    while(listIt.hasNext())
    {
      String key = (String)listIt.next();
      System.out.println("Inside chapter{ Key- "+key+" },{ Value- "+book.get(key)+"}");
    }
      System.out.println(" ");
  }
}
```

8.3 Joining

Problem

How do you create various types of joins in HQL and JPA QL?

Solution

Hibernate and JPA support both inner and outer joins. You use the dot operator (.) to express implicit association joins.

How It Works

Let's look at all the different types of joins you can take advantage of.

Explicit Joins

In HQL, you can use the `join` keyword to join associated objects. The following query finds all the books published by the publisher "Apress". The result contains a list of object pairs in the form of an array of `Objects(Object[])`. Each pair consists of a **book** object and a **publisher** object:

```
from Book book join book.publisher publisher
where publisher.name = 'Apress'
```

In addition to many-to-one associations, all other kinds of associations can be joined. For example, you can join the one-to-many association from **book** to **chapters**. The following query finds all the books containing a chapter titled "Hibernate Basics". The result contains a list of object pairs; each pair consists of a **book** object and a collection of **chapters**:

```
from Book book join book.chapters chapter
where chapter.title = 'Hibernate Basics'
```

Implicit Joins

In the previous joins, you specify the `join` keyword to join associated objects. This kind of join is called an *explicit join*. You can also reference an association directly by name: this causes an *implicit join*. For example, the previous two queries can be expressed as follows. The result contains only a list of **book** objects, because no join is specified in the `from` clause:

```
from Book book
where book.publisher.name = 'Manning'
```

Note that implicit joins are directed along many-to-one or one-to-one associations. They're never directed along many-to-many associations. This means you can never use something like

```
String QueryString3 =
    "from Book8_1 book where book.chapters.title = 'Many-To-Many Association'";
Query query1 = session.createQuery(QueryString3);
List<Chapter8_1> chptrs = query1.list();
```

The correct usage is as follows:

```
String queryString =
    "from Book8_1 book join book.chapters chapter where chapter.title=:title";
Query query = session.createQuery(queryString);
query.setString("title", "Many-To-Many Association");
List books = query.list();
```

Outer Joins

If you use the following HQL to query for books joined with publishers, books with null publisher aren't included. This type of join is called an *inner join*, and it's the default if you don't specify a join type or if you specify `inner join`. It has the same meaning as an inner join in SQL:

```
from Book book join book.publisher
```

If you want to get all books regardless of whether the publisher is null, you can use a left join by specifying `left join` or `left outer join`:

```
from Book book left join book.publisher
```

HQL supports two other types of joins: right joins and full joins. They have the same meaning as in SQL but are seldom used.

Matching Text

The following HQL retrieves books and their associated chapters where at least one of the chapter titles includes the word *Hibernate*. The result contains pairs consisting of a **book** and a **chapter**:

```
from Book book join book.chapters chapter
where chapter.title like '%Hibernate%'
```

Fetching Associations

You can use `join fetch` to force a lazy association to be initialized. It differs from a pure `join` in that only the parent objects are included in the result:

```
from Book book join fetch book.publisher publisher
```

An `inner join fetch` query doesn't return `book` objects with a null `publisher`. If you want to include them, you must use `left join fetch`:

```
from Book book left join fetch book.publisher publisher
```

8.4 Creating Report Queries

Problem

How do you create queries that group and aggregate data?

Solution

You use the `select` clause to generate report queries. The `groupby` and `having` clauses are used for aggregation. You saw how to use the `select` clause earlier in this chapter.

How It Works

Let's see how to aggregate and group data.

Projection with Aggregation Functions

HQL and JPA QL support the aggregate functions `count()`, `min()`, `max()`, `sum()`, and `avg()`. If you want to know how many books are in your bookshop, you have to do something like this:

```
String q2 = "select count(i) from Book i";
Query query = session.createQuery(q2);
Long count = (Long) query.uniqueResult();
```

To find the minimum and maximum prices of the books in the bookshop, you can use a query like the following:

```
String q3 = "select min(i.price),max(i.price) from Book i";
Query query = session.createQuery(q3);
Object[] count = (Object[]) query.uniqueResult();
System.out.println("Minimum price-  "+count[0]);
System.out.println("Maximum price- "+count[1]);
```

Note that this query's return type is an `Object[]` array.

Grouping Aggregated Results

You can sort the result list with an **order** by clause. Multiple fields and ascending/descending order can be specified:

```
from Book book
order by book.name asc, book.publishDate desc
```

HQL also supports the **group by** and **having** clauses. They're translated into SQL by Hibernate:

```
select book.publishDate, avg(book.price)
from Book book
group by book.publishDate
```

```
select book.publishDate, avg(book.price)
from Book book group by book.publishDate
having avg(book.price) > 10
```

Summary

In this chapter, you've learned how to query a database using Hibernate Query Language. You've seen how to use the `from`, `select`, and `where` clauses that form the backbone of most queries. And you've learned how to bind parameters to the query parameters. You should be able to externalize queries by using named queries. If the result set size is large, you can use pagination to retrieve a subset of the original result set. You've learned to use the dot (`.`) operator to create implicit joins and the `join` keyword to create explicit joins. You've also seen how to use aggregate functions like `min()`, `max()`, `avg()`, `count()`, and `sum()`.

CHAPTER 9

■ ■ ■

Querying with Criteria and Example

In the previous chapter, you saw how to use Hibernate Query Language (HQL) and Java Persistence Query Language (JPA QL). HQL forces you to interact with the database using SQL-like syntax. You must have some knowledge of SQL to create complex queries, which makes it difficult to develop applications that use multicriteria queries.

With HQL and JPA QL, it's easy to make mistakes with string concatenation and SQL syntax. Sometimes, errors occur due to the simple fact that there is no space between two clauses in SQL. Because these errors are uncovered only at runtime, if you have no unit test, you must go through the long process of build and deployment on an application server to catch them.

Unlike HQL, Hibernate Criteria is completely object oriented. It uses objects and their interfaces to load data from Hibernate-supported databases. It presents an elegant and cleaner way to build dynamic queries. For example, the following code invokes the Criteria API to fetch the **Book** details from the database given a book's name and publisher:

```
        Criteria criteria = session.createCriteria(Book.class);
if (startDate != null) {
                criteria.add(Expression.ge("bookName",bookName));
}
if (endDate != null) {
        criteria.add(Expression.le("publisher",publisher));
}
List results = criteria.list();
```

The same code when used with HQL must deal with string concatenation and setting parameters:

```
        String queryString = "from Book where bookName=? and publisher=?";

        Session session = SessionManager.getSessionFactory().getCurrentSession();
        Query query = session.createQuery(arg0);

        query.setParameter(0, "Recipes");
        query.setParameter(1, "APress");
        List<Book7_1> list = query.getResultList();
```

As you can see, accessing the data using Criteria is simpler and easy.

In this chapter, you learn how to use Criteria and the Example API. The Java Persistence API version 2.0 (JSR-317 JPA 2.0) has introduced a similar Criteria API to support dynamic queries. This is still

evolving; you can find the documentation at
`http://openjpa.apache.org/builds/latest/docs/manual/jpa_overview_criteria.html`.

The chapter shows how to apply restrictions to criterion objects to fetch data. These restrictions act like the `where` clause in HQL or SQL. You learn how to use a `criteria` object that isn't in a session: this is called a `DetachedCriteria`.

9.1 Using Criteria

Problem

How do you create a basic `criteria` object and use it to load data from a database?

Solution

As with HQL, you get the `criteria` object from the session. If you don't have a session to create a `criteria` object, then you can use `DetachedCriteria`. This `DetachedCriteria` object is later used with the session to get the results. This recipe demonstrates the basic implementation of the Criteria API.

How It Works

A basic Criteria query looks like this:

```
Criteria criteria = session.createCriteria(Book.class)
List books = criteria.list();
```

This query corresponds to the following HQL query:

```
from Book book
```

Most methods in the `Criteria` class return an instance of themselves, so you can build up your criteria as follows. Here you add a restriction to your criteria, which says that the name of the book should be equal to "Hibernate Quickly":

```
Criteria criteria = session.createCriteria(Book.class)
.add(Restrictions.eq("name", "Hibernate Quickly"));
List books = criteria.list();
```

If you don't have an open session, you can instantiate a detached criteria by using the `forClass()` method and later attach it to a session for execution. When you have a session to run the query, you call `getExecutableCriteria()` and pass the session as a method argument. The `getExecutableCriteria()` method returns an executable instance of `criteria`:

```
DetachedCriteria criteria = DetachedCriteria.forClass(Book.class);
List books = criteria.getExecutableCriteria(session).list();
```

9.2 Using Restrictions

Problem

How do you filter data when using criteria? How do you apply restriction to criteria?

Solution

You can add a series of restrictions to your Criteria query to filter the results, just as you build up the where clause in HQL. The Restrictions class provides a variety of methods to build restrictions.

How It Works

Each restriction you add is treated as a logical conjunction. The Criterion interface is an object-oriented representation of a query criterion that may be used as a restriction in a Criteria query. The Restrictions class provides static factory methods that return built-in criterion types. The org.hibernate.criterion package provides an API for creating complex queries:

```
Criteria criteria = session.createCriteria(Book.class);
Criterion nameRest = Restrictions.eq("name", "Hibernate Recipes");
criteria.add(nameRest);
List books = criteria.list();
```

This is equivalent to the following HQL:

```
from Book book where name='Hibernate Recipes'
```

eq is an equals implementation that takes two input method arguments: the name of the property of the Book class and the value to be compared with. To get a unique result, you can use the uniqueResult() method:

```
Criteria criteria = session.createCriteria(Book.class);
Criterion nameRest = Restrictions.eq("name", "Hibernate Recipes");
criteria.add(nameRest);
Book book = (Book)criteria.uniqueResult();
```

You can use the ignoreCase() method to add case insensitivity to the query:

```
Criterion nameRest = Restrictions.eq("name", "Hibernate Recipes").ignoreCase();
```

The Restrictions class has many other methods, including the following:

- gt (greater than)
- lt (less than)
- ge (greater than or equal to)

- idEq (ID is equal to)

- ilike (a case-insensitive like, similar to PostgreSQL's ilike operator)

- isNull

- isNotNull

- isEmpty

- isNotEmpty

- between

- in (applies an "in" constraint to the named property)

- le (less than or equal to)

Here's an example:

```
Criteria criteria = session.createCriteria(Book.class)
        .add(Restrictions.like("name", "%Hibernate%"))
        .add(Restrictions.between("price", new Integer(100), new Integer(200)));
List books = criteria.list();
```

This Criteria query corresponds to the following HQL query:

```
from Book book
where (book.name like '%Hibernate%') and (book.price between 100 and 200)
```

The % character is a wildcard. Because it's added before and after the word *Hibernate*, it enables you to search for all books that have the word *Hibernate* in a book name. If you want to look for all books whose name starts with *Hibernate*, the query is as follows:

```
Criteria criteria = session.createCriteria(Book.class)
        .add(Restrictions.like("name", "Hibernate%"))
.add(Restrictions.between("price", new Integer(100), new Integer(200)));
List books = criteria.list();
```

Notice that there is no % character before the word *Hibernate* in the search string. You can also group some of the restrictions with logical disjunction. How do you achieve the following query using the Criteria API?

```
from Book book
where (book.name like '%Hibernate%' or book.name like '%Java%') and (book.price between 100
and 200)
```

You can directly translate it into something like this:

```
Criteria criteria = session.createCriteria(Book.class)
        .add(Restrictions.or(
                        Restrictions.like("name", "%Hibernate%"),
                        Restrictions.like("name", "%Java%")
                )
```

```
        )
    .add(Restrictions.between("price", new Integer(100), new Integer(200)));
List books = criteria.list();
```

This query can also be written using Restrictions' disjunction() method:

```
Criteria criteria = session.createCriteria(Book.class)
            .add(Restrictions.disjunction()
                        .add(Restrictions.like("name", "%Hibernate%"))
                        .add(Restrictions.like("name", "%Java%"))
            )
            .add(Restrictions.between("price", new Integer(100), new Integer(200)));
List books = criteria.list();
```

If you want to search using wildcards, you can use the MatchMode class. It provides a convenient way to express a substring match without using string manipulation:

```
Criteria criteria = session.createCriteria(Book.class);
Criterion nameRest = Restrictions.like("name", "Hibernate",MatchMode.START);
criteria.add(nameRest);
Book books = (Book)criteria.uniqueResult();
```

This Criteria statement is the same as

```
Criterion nameRest = Restrictions.like("name", "Hibernate%");
```

The following MatchMode values are available:

- START: Matches the start of the string with the pattern

- END: Matches the end of the string with the pattern

- ANYWHERE: Matches the pattern anywhere in the string

- EXACT: Matches the complete pattern in the string

Writing Subqueries

Using Criteria, you can also execute subqueries. A *subquery* is a query that is nested inside another query. It's also called as *inner query* or *inner select*.

For example, here's a subquery in SQL:

```
select publisher_name, address from Publisher pub where pub.code=(select publisher_code from Book book where book.publish_date=current_timestamp)
```

This query fetches the name and address of any publisher whose book was published today. The second **select** query is nested in the main SQL query.

You can write this using Criteria as follows:

```
DetachedCriteria todaysBook = DetachedCriteria.forClass(Book.class)
.setProjection( (Projection) Property.forName("publishDate").eq("current_timestamp") );
List =manager.createCriteria(Publisher.class)
            .add( Property.forName("publisherCode").eq(todaysBook) )
            .list();
```

9.3 Using Criteria in Associations

Problem

How do you express a join restriction using the Criteria API when there are associated objects? How do you use dynamic fetching?

Solution

When you have associated objects, you need to join them in order to retrieve data from them. In HQL, you use an alias and an equijoin on the foreign key in the **where** clause:

```
from Book b, Publisher p where b.publisherId = p.publisherId
```

This query joins the **Publisher** object and **Book** object with **publisherId**, which is the foreign key in **Book**.

Let's see how this is achieved using the Criteria API. Hibernate provides two methods to enable joining of associated entities: **createCriteria()** and **createAlias()**. The difference between the two is that **createCriteria()** returns a new instance of **Criteria**. It means you can nest calls to **createCriteria()**. The **createAlias()** method doesn't create a new instance of **Criteria** and is very similar to the alias you declare in the HQL **from** clause.

How It Works

You can reference an association property by its name to trigger an implicit join. For example, suppose you have an **Order** class that contains a **Price** object, which holds details as **unitPrice** and **currency**:

```
public class Order {

        Price price;
}

public class Price {

                String currency;
                float unitPrice;
}
```

If you need to fetch the **unitPrice** of an **Order**, you can use **Order.price.unitPrice** in HQL:

```
from Order order where order.price.unitPrice > 50
```

Can the same implicit join work using `Criteria`?

```
Criteria criteria = session.createCriteria(Book.class,"book")
.add(Restrictions.like("name", "%Hibernate%"))
.add(Restrictions.eq("book.publisher.name", "Manning"));
List books = criteria.list();
```

If you execute this code, the following exception is thrown:

Exception in thread "main" org.hibernate.QueryException: could not resolve property:
publisher.name of: com.hibernaterecipes.chapter5.Book
       at
org.hibernate.persister.entity.AbstractPropertyMapping.propertyException(AbstractPropertyMap
ping.java:67)

Hibernate can't resolve the property `publisher.name`. That means an implicit join isn't supported for Criteria queries. To join an association explicitly, you need to create a new **criteria** object for it:

```
Criteria criteria = session.createCriteria(Book.class)
        .add(Restrictions.like("name", "%Hibernate%"))
        .createCriteria("publisher")
        .add(Restrictions.eq("name", "Manning"));
List books = criteria.list();
```

In this example, the createCriteria() method has a **string** attribute, where you pass the name of the associated property. Because you're creating a **criteria** on the **publisher** property of the Book object, you need to pass "publisher" in this case. You can also use createAlias() to generate the same query:

```
Criteria criteria = session.createCriteria(Book.class)
            .createAlias("publisher", "publisherAlias")
            .add(Restrictions.like("name", "%Hibernate%"))
            .add(Restrictions.eq("publisherAlias.name", "Manning"));
            List books = criteria.list();
```

In HQL, the query is as follows:

```
from Book book
where book.name like '%Hibernate%' and book.publisher.name = 'Manning'
```

As in HQL, you can specify the fetching strategy that Hibernate should follow when it loads data in case of associations. This strategy can also be set in the metadata configuration file. If the configuration needs to be overridden, then you can use the FetchMode **API** when you retrieve data using **Criteria**.

Following are the FetchMode options are available:

- **DEFAULT**: The default setting that is used from the configuration file.

- **EAGER**: Deprecated. Use `FetchMode.JOIN` instead.

- **JOIN**: Retrieves the associated object's data by using an outer join.

- LAZY: Deprecated. Use `FetchMode.SELECT` instead.

- SELECT: Fetches eagerly using an additional `SELECT` query. Unless the `lazy` option is disabled explicitly in the configuration file, the second `SELECT` query is executed when the association is accessed.

The following code uses the `FetchMode.JOIN` and `FetchMode.SELECT` options:

```
Criteria criteria = session.createCriteria(Book.class)
.add(Restrictions.like("name", "%Hibernate%"))
.setFetchMode("publisher", FetchMode.JOIN)
.setFetchMode("chapters", FetchMode.SELECT);
List books = criteria.list();
```

In this case, the associated `Publisher` object is fetched using an outer join, where `Chapters` is retrieved with a second `SELECT` query.

9.4 Using Projections

Problem

What are projections, and how do you use them in the Criteria API?

Solution

Until now, when you retrieved objects using Criteria, you fetched the complete object in the result set. What if you want to fetch only certain fields or columns in a table, and you don't want the complete object?

Projections help you filter data and return only those fields you need. You can use projections when you don't want the entire fetched entity and its associations. You can also use them when there is a requirement to get the results in a flat manner (not in an object graph). This approach improves performance, especially when you're dealing with lot of columns and the object graph is very deep.

How It Works

To customize the fields of the result, you can use projections to specify the fields to be returned:

```
Criteria criteria = session.createCriteria(Book.class)
.setProjection(Projections.property("name"));
List books = criteria.list();
```

This is similar to the following SQL statement:

```
select book.name from Book book
```

This is better than

```
from Book book
```

which fetches the complete book object although you need only the book name.

Aggregate Functions and Groupings with Projections

Aggregate functions in SQL summarize data and return a single value by calculating it from values in a column. Here are some examples:

- SUM: Returns the summation of the column values on which it's applied

- AVG: Returns the average of the column values

- MIN: Returns the minimum of the specified column values

- MAX: Returns the maximum of the specified column values

In HQL, you can use these directly just as in SQL:

```
select min(book.price) from Book book
```

This query returns the minimum price of all the books in the BOOK table.

When you're querying with the Criteria API, you can use projections to apply the aggregated functions. These functions are encapsulated in the Projections class as static methods:

```
Criteria criteria = session.createCriteria(Book.class)
.setProjection(Projections.avg("price"));
List books = criteria.list();
```

This is similar to the following:

```
select avg(book.price) from Book book
```

The results can be sorted in ascending or descending order:

```
Criteria criteria = session.createCriteria(Book.class)
.addOrder(Order.asc("name"))
.addOrder(Order.desc("publishDate"));
List books = criteria.list();
```

This is something like

```
from Book book
order by book.name asc, book.publishDate desc
```

Grouping is also supported for Criteria queries. You can assign any properties as group properties, and they appear in the group by clause:

```
Criteria criteria = session.createCriteria(Book.class)
.setProjection(Projections.projectionList()
```

```
.add(Projections.groupProperty("publishDate"))
.add(Projections.avg("price")));
List books = criteria.list();
```

Thisresults in

```
select book.publishDate, avg(book.price)
from Book book
group by book.publishDate
```

9.5 Querying by Example

Problem

What is Query by Example (QBE), and how do you use it to retrieve data?

Solution

Suppose you need to retrieve data based on different input. The search criteria can be complex filtering data on various columns. Using `Criteria`, it might look like this:

```
Criteria criteria = getSession().createCriteria(Book.class);
criteria.add(Restrictions.eq("name", "Hibernate")).
        add(Restrictions.eq("price",100))
```

If you have more columns to be filtered, the list increases. QBE makes this easy for you.

QBE returns a result set depending on the properties that were set on an instance of the queried class. You can also specify the properties that need to be excluded. This approach greatly reduces the amount of code you have to write.

How It Works

Criteria queries can be constructed through an `Example` object. The object should be an instance of the persistent class you want to query. All null properties are ignored by default:

```
Book book = new Book();
book.setName("Hibernate");
book.setPrice(new Integer(100));
Example exampleBook = Example.create(book);
Criteria criteria = session.createCriteria(Book.class)
.add(exampleBook);
List books = criteria.list();
```

The HQL is similar to the following:

```
from Book book
```

```
where book.name = 'Hibernate' and book.price = 100
```

In this example, the instance of Book is created, and the search criteria are set: they include name and price. This Book instance is then passed while creating an Example object. Finally, the Criteria interface accepts the Example instance to retrieve the data based on the values set on the Book instance.

You can specify creation rules for the construction of the Example object. For example, you can exclude some of the properties or enable like for a string comparison:

```
Book book = new Book();
book.setName("%Hibernate%");
book.setPrice(new Integer(100));
Example exampleBook = Example.create(book)
.excludeProperty("price")
.enableLike();
Criteria criteria = session.createCriteria(Book.class)
.add(exampleBook);
List books = criteria.list();
```

The corresponding HQL is as follows:

```
from Book book
where book.name like '%Hibernate%'
```

Summary

This chapter has introduced the Criteria API and how to use it to retrieve data. You can use restrictions to filter data. The Restrictions interface has several methods that let you filter data: equal, like, greater than, and less than. It also provides disjunctions. The MatchMode interface provides variables that you can use for string comparisons. Subqueries also can be implemented using the DetachedCriteria object. You can use the createCriteria() and createAlias() methods can be used to fetch data when there are associated objects. And you can use projections for aggregated functions and groupings. Finally, Query by Example makes it easy to fetch data when the data has to be filtered on various search criteria.

CHAPTER 10

Working with Objects

This chapter discusses the states an object goes through during its lifecycle. The session is responsible for managing object state in Hibernate, and the EntityManager does the same in Java Persistence. Hibernate provides a persistence mechanism that is transparent to the entities and the application; the application has to know the state of an object.

The chapter also discusses the persistence context provided by Hibernate. The persistence context manages objects and caches object states within a transaction (unit of work). You will learn how to use data filtering and interceptors.

10.1 Identifying Persistent Object States

Problem

What are the states that an object can have in Hibernate? How does the object lifecycle work?

Solution

Hibernate defines four object states: transient, persistent, detached, and removed. You look into each state and what methods in Hibernate or JPA take an object to that state.

How It Works

Let's begin with the transient object before moving on to look at the other states.

Transient Objects

Objects instantiated using the new operator are called *transient objects*. The Hibernate persistence context isn't aware of operations performed on transient objects. Their state is lost when they aren't referenced by any other object and become available for garbage collection. They don't have any association with any database table row. JPA doesn't have this state. Figure 10-1 provides a graphical representation.

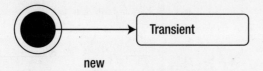

Figure 10-1. Objects instantiated using the new operator are called transient

Persistent Objects

An object that has a database identity associated with it is called a *persistent object*. The key for an object to be in a persistent state is to be associated with a *persistent context*. The persistent context caches the object state and can identify changes made, if any.

You can create persistent objects two ways: you can retrieve a database table row as an entity by calling API methods like get(), load(), and list(); or you can persist a transient object using API methods like save() and saveOrUpdate(). Figure 10-2 illustrates the possible ways for an object to become persistent.

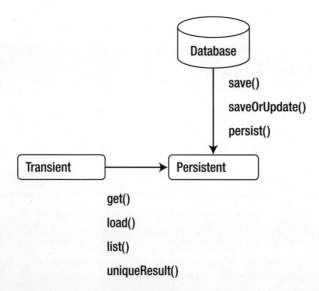

Figure 10-2. Possible ways for an object to become persistent

Detached Objects

In the previous section, you learned that a persistent object is associated with a persistent context. The persistent context no longer exists after the transaction is closed. If the application retains a reference to the persistent object, then the object is said to be in the *detached state*. The state of a detached object can be modified and can be persisted back to the database. This is very common when you're working with applications that have a multilayered architecture.

Hibernate provides a reattached mode and a merging mode to make a detached object persistent. JPA has merging mode only. Figure 10-3 illustrates the relationship between detached and persistent objects.

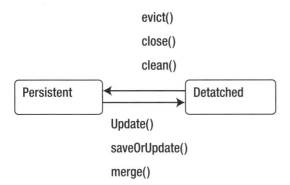

Figure 10-3. Relationship between detached and persistent objects

Removed Objects

A persistent object is considered to be in the *removed* state when a `delete()` or `remove()` operation is called on it. The `delete()` method is provided by a Hibernate session, whereas the `remove()` method is provided by the JPA EntityManager.

Note that when an object is removed, the persistence context then deletes the object from the database. This means you shouldn't use any references to the removed object in the application. For example, in the following code, after the `book` object has been deleted, the code tries to call `update()` to use the reference to the deleted book, but this isn't correct:

```
public static void deletePersistentObject()
{
  Session session = getSession();
  Transaction tx = session.beginTransaction();
  Book book = (Book) session.get(Book.class, new Long(294912));
  session.delete(book);
  tx.commit();
  // cannot use the reference to book as it has been deleted from database.
  session.update(book);
  session.close();
}
```

Figure 10-4 shows how to reach the removed state.

181

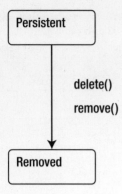

Figure 10-4. Creating an object in the removed state

10.2 Working with Persistent Objects

Problem

How do you make a persistent object? How do you perform CRUD operations on it?

Solution

The `Session` interface provides methods to perform CRUD operations on an entity to make it a persistent object.

How It Works

Let's start by seeing how to create a persistent object, and then carry out other operations on it.

Creating a Persistent Object

In Hibernate, you need an instance of the session from the application's session factory. The session is a factory for transactions and keeps track of all the changes to object within its scope. The session factory is an immutable cache of compiled mappings for a single database; it's a factory for providing session instances. So, if your application interacts with two databases, you need to configure two separate session factories.

Here's how to do it in Hibernate:

```
sessionFactory = new Configuration().configure().buildSessionFactory();
Session hibernateSession = sessionFactory.openSession();
```

The first line in this code looks for a `hibernate.cfg.xml` file in its path. It compiles and loads the mapping listed in the file. Creating a session factory is an expensive task, so you should create it only once—preferably at application startup. Creating a session is relatively inexpensive; it doesn't even open a database connection.

Let's create the persistent object:

```
Transaction tx = session.beginTransaction();
Book book = new Book();
book.setName("Book Name - hibernate ");
book.setPrice(79);
book.setPublishDate(new Date());
Serializable bookId = session.save(book);
tx.commit();
session.close();
```

On the first line, an instance of Transaction is retrieved from the session. By default, the session provides a Java Database Connectivity (JDBC) transaction. The other two possible types of transaction that a session can provide are Java Transaction API (JTA) and container-managed transaction. For the session to provide either of these two types, you need to declare the hibernate.transaction_factory property in the hibernate.cfg.xml file.

The next couple of lines create a transient book object using the new keyword. You make the transient object into a persistent object by calling the save() method. Then, the book object is associated with the session and its persistent context. Note that until this point, a database record hasn't been created.

The save() method returns the primary key of the newly inserted record. Only by calling commit() on the transaction is a database connection created and a record inserted into the database. The last line closes the session, which means its persistent context is no longer active. The book object is now in a detached state.

Next, here's how you do it in JPA:

```
EntityManagerFactory managerFactory = Persistence.createEntityManagerFactory("book");
EntityManager manager = managerFactory.createEntityManager();
```

In JPA, you use the createEntityManagerFactory() method of the class javax.persistence.Persistence to get an instance of the EntityManagerFactory class. This method call looks for a persistence.xml file in the META-INF folder. EntityManagerFactory is similar to Hibernate's sessionFactory class; it provides you with an EntityManager. The EntityManager has a new persistent context, which is used to save and load objects:

```
Book newBook = new Book();
newBook.setBookName("HIbernate Recipes Phase1");
newBook.setPublishDate(new Date());
newBook.setPrice(50l);
EntityTransaction tran = manager.getTransaction();
tran.begin();
manager.persist(book);
tran.commit();
manager.close();
```

In JPA, the EntityManager replaces the session: it's a factory that provides transactions (EntityTransactions in this case). The save() method is replaced by the persist() method, which moves the book object from the transient state to the persistent state. After the persist() method is called, the state of the **book** object is managed by the persistence context. Note that **persist()** doesn't return the serializable ID of the newly created record.

Retrieving a Persistent Object

In Hibernate, you need an instance of the session to retrieve an entity by its ID. Hibernate provides two methods for this: get() and load(). Both methods take the entity class and the ID as input parameters:

```
Session session = getSession();
Transaction tx = session.beginTransaction();
//Book book = (Book) session.load(Book.class, new Long(294912));
Book book1 = (Book) session.get(Book.class, new Long(294912));
tx.commit();
session.close();
System.out.println(book1);
```

The get() method makes a call to the database and does a lookup for the primary key. If it finds the primary key, it retrieves and returns the object. If it can't, it returns null.

The load() method, on the other hand, looks in the current persistence context. If it can find the entity, it returns the entity object. If the object isn't being managed in the current persistence context, then a proxy placeholder is returned without hitting the database. This means if you request an entity object that isn't in the database (or, of course, the current persistence context), then the load() method returns a proxy. You get an org.hibernate.ObjectNotFoundException when you try to read/retrieve properties other than the primary key within the same persistence context, and you get an org.hibernate.LazyInitializationException when you try to read/retrieve properties after the session is closed (the persistence context has ended). The load() method is useful when you only need a proxy and don't need to make a database call. You need just a proxy when, in a given persistence context, you need to associate an entity before persisting.

In JPA, you use the EntityManager to read/retrieve persistent entities. JPA provides two methods: find() and getReference(). Both methods take the entity class and the ID as input parameters:

```
EntityManager manager = SessionManager.getEntityManager();
EntityTransaction tran = manager.getTransaction();
tran.begin();
Book book = manager.find(Book.class, new Long(294912));
//Book book1 = manager.getReference(Book.class, new Long(294912));
tran.commit();
manager.close();
```

The find() method is similar to the get() method in Hibernate. A call to the database is made when this method is invoked. If it doesn't find the persistent entity, the find() method returns null. Note that you haven't cast the return value from the find() method. It isn't required, because find() is a generic method, and the first parameter is set as the return type.

The getReference() method is similar to the load() method in Hibernate. You should use it when you only need a proxy.

Modifying a Persistent Object

You can modify any persistent object that is associated with a session and a persistence context. Its state is then synchronized with the database:

```
Session session = getSession();
Transaction tx = session.beginTransaction();
Book book = (Book) session.get(Book.class, new Long(294912));
book.setName("Book Name - hibernate 2");
tx.commit();
session.close();
```

The entity is retrieved from the database and modified in the same transaction. The modifications are propagated to the database when the commit() method is called. The persistence context identifies the changes that have been made to the entity's state and synchronizes with the database. This is called *automatic dirty checking*.

The implementation in JPA is as follows:

```
EntityManager manager = SessionManager.getEntityManager();
EntityTransaction tran = manager.getTransaction();
tran.begin();
Book book = manager.find(Book.class, new Long(294912));
book.setBookName("Book Name - hibernate 22");
tran.commit();
manager.close();
```

Deleting a Persistent Object

You can delete from the database any persistent object that is associated with a session and a persistence context. To do so, you call the delete() method:

```
Session session = getSession();
Transaction tx = session.beginTransaction();
Book book = (Book) session.get(Book.class, new Long(294912));
session.delete(book);
tx.commit();
session.close();
```

The entity is in the removed state after the call to delete(). The database record is deleted after the transaction is committed, and the object is in the transient state after the session is closed.

In JPA, the remove() method performs the same function as the delete() method:

```
EntityManager manager = SessionManager.getEntityManager();
EntityTransaction tran = manager.getTransaction();
tran.begin();
Book book = manager.find(Book.class, new Long(294912));
manager.remove(book);
tran.commit();
manager.close();
```

10.3 Persisting Detached Objects

Problem

How do you persist a detached object?

Solution

You can persist a detached object two ways: by reattaching it or by merging it.

How It Works

You first reattach a detached object and then merge one.

Reattaching a Detached Object

In Hibernate, you use the session's `update()` method to reattach a detached object to the session and persistence context:

```
Session session = getSession();
Transaction tx = session.beginTransaction();
Book book = (Book) session.get(Book.class, new Long(294912));
tx.commit();
session.close();
book.setName("Detached Hibernate");
Session session2 = getSession();
Transaction tx2 = session2.beginTransaction();
session2.update(book);
tx2.commit();
session2.close();
```

Hibernate keeps track of modifications made to the detached object. Hence, when the `update()` method is called, it always schedules an `update` SQL command. If you don't want to make an `update` call, you can configure the class mapping to have `select-before-update='true'`. Then, a `get()` call is made to check whether the object has been updated , before the call to the `update()` method.

JPA doesn't have an `update()` method. It only supports merging detached objects.

Merging a Detached Object

In Hibernate, you use the session's `merge()` method to persist a detached object. The `merge()` method call results in a complex set of actions. Hibernate first looks to see if the instance of the entity is in the current persistence context. If it finds an instance of the entity equal to the detached object, then it copies the state from the detached object to the instance in the persistence context:

```
Session session = getSession();
```

```
Transaction tx = session.beginTransaction();
Book book = (Book) session.get(Book.class, new Long(294912));
tx.commit();
session.close();
book.setName("Detached Hibernate");
Session session2 = getSession();
Transaction tx2 = session2.beginTransaction();
Book book2 = (Book) session2.merge(book);
tx2.commit();
session2.close();
```

If the persistence context doesn't contain an equal instance of the entity, Hibernate makes a `get()` call internally to load the persistent entity object into the persistence context. Then, the detached object state is copied onto the newly created persistent entity object.

Note that if a transient object is passed to the `merge()` method, a new persistent instance is created and the state is copied to the new instance. The same applies to JPA. Here's the implementation:

```
EntityManager manager = SessionManager.getEntityManager();
EntityTransaction tran = manager.getTransaction();
tran.begin();
Book book = manager.find(Book.class, new Long(262144));
tran.commit();
manager.close();
book.setBookName("Detached Hibernate merged");
EntityManager manager2 = SessionManager.getEntityManager();
EntityTransaction tran2 = manager2.getTransaction();
tran2.begin();
Book book2 = (Book) manager2.merge(book);
tran2.commit();
manager2.close();
```

10.4 Using Data Filters

Problem

Suppose your bookshop has a lot of children and teenagers as users. You want to make the bookshop kid friendly by classifying users according to their age range. (You don't want a child to be able to buy a book meant for an adult reader.) How can you achieve this by using the data-filtering mechanism provided by Hibernate?

Solution

Every `Book` class has a `UserRank` class that specifies the lowest rank that can access a book. Books for adults have a user rank of 3, and books for children have a user rank of 1.

You define a filter definition (`<filter-def>`) in the metadata, which can be declared in any XML mapping file as long as it's inside a `<hibernate-mapping>` element. You need to provide a globally unique name to the filter definition. You apply and implement the filter in **Book**'s mapping XML file. And finally, you enable the filter on the session that is used to query.

How It Works

First, you create the **UserRank** class and the **Book** class. The **UserRank** class includes the user rank and the user type. The **Book** class is associated with the **UserRank** class:

```
public class UserRank {

  private long rank;
  private String userType;

  // getters and setters
}

public class Book {

  private Long book_id;
  private String isbn;
  private String name;
  private String publisher;
  private Date publishDate;
  private Integer price;
  private UserRank userRank;
  // getters and setters
}
```

The mapping files for **UserRank** and **Book** are shown next. You define the filter in the **UserRank** mapping file by providing a globally unique name and the filter parameters it requires. You use the `<filter-def>` element and `<filter-param>` elements to define a filter:

```
<hibernate-mapping package="com.hibernaterecipes.chapter10" auto-import="false" >
  <import class="UserRank" rename="userRank"/>
  <class name="UserRank" table="UserRank" dynamic-insert="true" dynamic-update="true"
schema="BOOK">
    <id name="rank"  column="RANK" type="long">
      <generator class="assigned">
      </generator>
    </id>
    <property name="userType" type="string" column="USERTYPE" />

  </class>
  <filter-def name="filterByRank">
    <filter-param name="currentRank" type="long"/>
    <filter-param name="requestedRank" type="long"/>
  </filter-def>
</hibernate-mapping>
```

In the Book mapping class, you apply the defined filter to instances of the Book class. You use `<filter>` to implement the filter. The condition attribute is a SQL expression that must evaluate to true if the results must pass the filter. In this case, you compare the user's rank with the rank of the book the user is requesting. If the user's current rank is greater than or equal to the requested book's rank, then the results are returned to the user:

```
<hibernate-mapping package="com.hibernaterecipes.chapter10" auto-import="false" >
  <import class="Book" rename="book"/>
  <class name="Book" table="Book" dynamic-insert="true" dynamic-update="true" schema="BOOK">
    <id name="isbn" type="string" column="ISBN" />
    <property name="name" type="string" column="BOOK_NAME" />
    <property name="publishDate" type="date" column="PUBLISH_DATE" />
    <property name="price" type="int" column="PRICE" />
    <many-to-one name="userRank" class="UserRank" column="RANK" cascade="save-update"/>

    <filter name="filterByRank"
      condition=":currentRank>=(select distinct(b.RANK)
                        from Book b
                        where b.rank=:requestedRank)">
    </filter>
  </class>
</hibernate-mapping>
```

So far, all you've done is define and apply the filter. The results of a query are filtered only after the filter is enabled and parameterized in the application for a particular session. The EntityManager doesn't support this API, so you have to use interfaces provided by Hibernate. You enable the filter by calling the enableFilter() method on the session, which takes the globally unique filter name as an input parameter. This method returns a Filter instance. The returned Filter instance accepts runtime arguments; you set the parameters you've defined. The session also has other methods, getEnabledFilter(String filterName) and disableFilter(String filterName). The implementation method is as follows:

```
static void fetchKidsbooks(Long userRank,Long requestedRank)
{
  Session session = getSession();
  Filter filter = session.enableFilter("filterByRank");
  filter.setParameter("currentRank", userRank);
  filter.setParameter("requestedRank", requestedRank);
  List<Book> books =
    session.createQuery("from book where userRank<="+requestedRank.toString()).list();
  if(books != null)
  {
    for(Book book:books)
    {
      System.out.println("Name "+book.getName());
    }
  }
}
```

The other methods that the `Filter` provides are as follows:

- `getFilterDefinition()` gets the filter definition containing additional information about the filter (such as its default condition and expected parameter names/types).

- `validate()` performs validation of the filter state. This is used to verify the state of the filter after it's enabled and before it's used. It throws a Hibernate exception if the filter isn't valid.

You can also apply filters to collections:

```
<set ...>
  <filter name="myFilter" condition=":myFilterParam = MY_FILTERED_COLUMN"/>
</set>
```

Data filtering can also be used to filter regional or temporal data.

10.5 Using Interceptors

Problem

You want to save the date on any insert made into the `BookShop` database. For example, if a new publisher is inserted, you want to save the created date. The same is true for books: if a new book is entered into the database, you want to know when it was created by referring to the created date. How can you do this by using interceptors provided by Hibernate?

Solution

Because the created date is a property that is used in many classes, you can create an `Auditable` class and have all classes that need to have a created date extend that class. You create an interceptor that extends Hibernate's `EmptyInterceptor` and override the `onSave()` method. In the `onSave()` method, you assign the date if the object is an instance of `Auditable`. Because interceptors are session scoped, every time you request a session from `sessionFactory`, you need to assign the interceptor to the session when you open the session.

How It Works

You first create a simple `Auditable` class with one property: `createDate`. The entity classes that need a created date to be persisted in the database extend this class:

```
public class Auditable {
  private Date createDate;
  // getter and setter
}
```

In this case, let's use the `Book` class. Update the `Book` class to extend `Auditable`:

```
public class Book extends Auditable implements Serializable{
    ...
}
```

Then, update the XML mapping file to include the created date:

```
<hibernate-mapping package="com.hibernaterecipes.chapter10" auto-import="false" >
  <import class="Book" rename="book"/>
  <class name="Book" table="Book" dynamic-insert="true" dynamic-update="true" schema="BOOK">
    <id name="isbn" type="string" column="ISBN" />
    <property name="name" type="string" column="BOOK_NAME" />
    <property name="publishDate" type="date" column="PUBLISH_DATE" />
    <property name="price" type="int" column="PRICE" />
    <property name="createDate" type="date" column="CREATE_DATE" />
  </class>
</hibernate-mapping>
```

Now, you create the interceptor class. For the bookshop application, it's called
BookShopInterceptor, and it extends Hibernate's EmptyInterceptor class. EmptyInterceptor doesn't do
anything—it's provided by Hibernate for use as a base class for application-defined custom interceptors.
In the BookShopInterceptor implementation, you need to override the onSave() method. In this method,
you set createDate if the object is of type Auditable:

```
public class BookShopInterceptor extends EmptyInterceptor {

  @Override
  public boolean onSave(Object entity, Serializable id, Object[] state,
                        String[] propertyNames, Type[] types) {
    if ( entity instanceof Auditable ) {
      for ( int i=0; i<propertyNames.length; i++ ) {
        if ( "createDate".equals( propertyNames[i] ) ) {
          state[i] = new Date();
          return true;
        }
      }
    }
    return false;
  }
}
```

You need to assign the interceptor to a Hibernate session when you open the session:

```
Session hibernateSession = sessionFactory.openSession(new BookShopInterceptor());
Transaction tx = session.beginTransaction();
System.out.println(" Started ");
Book2 book = new Book2();
book.setIsbn("PBN123");
book.setName("Spring Recipes ");
book.setPrice(30);
book.setPublishDate(new Date());
```

```
book.setPublisher("Apress");
session.saveOrUpdate(book);
tx.commit();
session.close();
```

If you have to use `sessionFactory.getCurrentSession()`, then you don't control the opening of the session. You must write an implementation that extends Hibernate's `CurrentSessionContext` implementation.

You can also assign the interceptor at the global level. If you choose to do that, then all sessions are assigned the interceptor:

```
Configuration config = new Configuration();
config.setInterceptor(new BookShopInterceptor());
sessionFactory = config.configure().buildSessionFactory();
Session hibernateSession = sessionFactory.openSession();
```

Interceptors are also used in audit logging.

Summary

Now you have a good understanding of the persistence lifecycle and the states an object can have during its lifecycle. When you're working with a detached object, you can either reattach or merge the object. You should be able to use dynamic data filtering to provide security or to access temporal/regional data. You've also learned to use interceptors to persist common properties like created date and created by.

CHAPTER 11

■■■

Batch Processing and Native SQL

Batch processing is the execution of a series of programs. From an application standpoint, batch processing means reading data from a persistent store, doing something with the data, and then possibly storing the processed data in the persistent store. Batch processing allows for the automation and sharing of computer resources. It's usually run when computer resources are less busy.

Let's say that for the bookshop application, you want to increase sales by putting all books in the shop on sale on the 27th and 28th of the month. This is a classic case for implementing batch processing. The night before 27th, you list all the books that are in stock and implement the required discount. And on the night of 28th, the discount is removed.

During batch processing, you generally need to insert, update, and delete a lot of database records. This chapter discusses Hibernate's batch-update and batch-delete features. For example, the following code snippet tries to insert a million books. This isn't a good approach—it may lead to `OutOfMemory` issues, because Hibernate caches the instances in its cache:

```
Session session = getSession();
Transaction tx = session.beginTransaction();
for(int i =0;i<100000;i++)
{
        BookCh2 book = new BookCh2();
        book.setName("Book Name "+(i+1));
        book.setPrice(79);
        book.setPublishDate(new Date());
        session.save(book);
}

tx.commit();
session.close();
```

If you're processing one million books in one session, you should call the `flush()` and `clear()` methods of the `session` after every 100 or 200 books; `flush()` and `clear()` clear the first-level cache. If the second-level cache is enabled at the entity level, and if you want it to be disabled for the batch-insert method, you need to call `session.setCacheMode (CacheMode.IGNORE)`. By setting the `session`'s `cacheMode` to `IGNORE`, you tell Hibernate not to interact with the second-level cache for that particular session.

On a global level, you can enable the JDBC batch size by setting the `jdbc.batch_size` attribute (recommended values are 5 to 30). You can also disable the second-level caching on the global level in the mapping file by setting the `cache.use_second_level_cache` attribute to `false`:

```
<property name="hibernate.jdbc.batch_size">25</property>
<property name="hibernate.cache.use_second_level_cache">false</property>
```

This chapter also looks into using native SQL to query databases. Native SQL is useful when you want to use database-specific features. You work with named SQL queries that are defined in the mapping document and are used just like Hibernate Query.

11.1 Performing Batch Inserts

Problem

How do you perform batch inserts?

Solution

To do a batch insert, you use the `flush()` and `clear()` methods of the Session API. These methods are called regularly to control the size of the first-level cache. To have Hibernate not interact with second-level cache, you need to call `session.setCacheMode.(CacheMode.IGNORE)`.

How It Works

The code for a batch insert is as follows. An additional `if` condition is added to call the `flush()` and `clear()` methods when the iteration reaches the size of the JDBC batch:

```
Session session = getSession();
Transaction tx = session.beginTransaction();
session.setCacheMode(CacheMode.IGNORE);
for(int i =0;i<100;i++)
{

        BookCh2 book = new BookCh2();
        book.setName("Book Name "+(i+1));
        book.setPrice(79);
        book.setPublishDate(new Date());
        session.save(book);
        if(i % 25 == 0)
        {
                System.out.println("Flushing in batches");
                session.flush();
                session.clear();
                System.out.println("get isbn "+book.getIsbn());
        }

}
tx.commit();
session.close();
```

By setting CacheMode to Ignore, you tell Hibernate not to interact with the second-level cache. You need to do this only if the second-level cache is enabled at the global or entity level.

11.2 Performing Batch Updates and Deletes

Problem

How do you perform batch updates and deletes?

Solution

You can accomplish batch updates in two ways. One way is to use the flush() and clear() methods to free the first-level cache and save in batches. The second way is to use the update statement with a where clause.

How It Works

Suppose you're planning a promotion for the Hibernate books in your online bookshop. All books with the word *Hibernate* in the name will have a $10 discount. You can do this by querying the matched books first and then updating them one by one:

```
Session session = getSession();
Transaction tx = null;
try {
        tx = session.beginTransaction();
        Query query = session.createQuery("from bkch2 where name like ?");
        query.setString(0, "%Hibernate%");
        List books = query.list();
        for (Iterator iter = books.iterator(); iter.hasNext();)
        {
                BookCh2 book = (BookCh2) iter.next();
                book.setPrice(new Integer(book.getPrice()- 10));
                session.saveOrUpdate(book);
        }
                tx.commit();
} catch (HibernateException e) {
        if (tx != null)
                tx.rollback();

        throw e;
} finally {
        session.close();
}
```

The disadvantage of this technique is that you load the complete result set returned by `query.list()` into memory and then save the records one at a time. Instead, you can use the `session.flush()` and `session.clear()` methods to update in batches. You can also use `scroll` to get a JDBC `ResultSet`, which is a table of data representing a database result set that is usually generated by executing a statement that queries the database. A default `ResultSet` maintains a cursor that is navigated from the first row to the last row. Setting `CacheMode.IGNORE` makes Hibernate not interact with the second-level cache for that particular session:

```
Session session = getSession();
Transaction tx = null;
tx = session.beginTransaction();
ScrollableResults books = session.createQuery("from bkch2 where name like 'Book%'")
.setCacheMode(CacheMode.IGNORE)
.scroll(ScrollMode.FORWARD_ONLY);

int count=0;
while ( books.next() ) {
        BookCh2 book = (BookCh2) books.get(0);
        book.setPrice(new Integer(book.getPrice()- 10));
if ( ++count % 25 == 0 ) {
        //flush a batch of updates and release memory:
                System.out.println("Flushing in batches");
                session.flush();
                session.clear();
}
}
tx.commit();
session.close();
```

You can also accomplish batch updates by using the `UPDATE` query. The execution of the query is at the SQL level and doesn't involve changing the object state in memory. HQL supports parameter binding. The syntax for an `UPDATE` or `DELETE` is as follows:

```
( UPDATE | DELETE ) FROM? EntityName (WHERE where_conditions)?.
```

The following rules apply to this query:

- The `FROM` clause is optional.

- The `WHERE` clause is optional.

- No joins, either implicit or explicit, can be specified in a bulk HQL query.

- Only a single entity can be named in the `FROM` clause.

So here is `UPDATE`:

```
Session session = getSession();
Transaction tx = null;
try {
tx = session.beginTransaction();
Query query = session.createQuery("update bkch2 set price = price - ? where name like ?");
```

```
query.setInteger(0, 10);
query.setString(1, "%Hibernate%");
int count = query.executeUpdate();

tx.commit();
} catch (HibernateException e) {
        if (tx != null)
                tx.rollback();

                        throw e;
} finally {
        session.close();
}
```

The DELETE query looks very similar to the UPDATE query:

```
Session session = getSession();
Transaction tx = null;
try {
        tx = session.beginTransaction();
        Query query = session.createQuery("delete from Book where name like ?");
        query.setString(0, "%Hibernate%");
        int count = query.executeUpdate();
        tx.commit();
} catch (HibernateException e) {
if (tx != null) tx.rollback();
throw e;
} finally {
        session.close();
}
```

11.3 Using Native SQL

Problem

Hibernate provides HQL, and it supports JPA QL and criteria queries to execute most queries. But what if you need to use database-specific features like query hints or keywords? In such scenarios, you need to use Hibernate's support for native SQL. How do you query using native SQL?

Solution

The Session API provides the createSQLQuery() method, which returns the SQLQuery interface. This interface provides methods you can use to query databases using native SQL.

How It Works

Let's say you need to compile some statistics for your top-selling books. This process is very complicated and requires some native features provided by the database. HQL isn't much help in this case. but Hibernate supports using native SQL to query for objects. For demonstration purposes, this recipe doesn't implement complicated statistics—you just create a view to emulate the result of the query. You create the view TOP_SELLING_BOOK by joining the BOOK and PUBLISHER tables:

```
CREATE VIEW TOP_SELLING_BOOK (
ID, ISBN, BOOK_NAME, PUBLISH_DATE, PRICE,
PUBLISHER_ID, PUBLISHER_CODE, PUBLISHER_NAME, PUBLISHER_ADDRESS
) AS
SELECT book.ID, book.ISBN, book.BOOK_NAME, book.PUBLISH_DATE, book.PRICE,
book.PUBLISHER_ID, pub.CODE, pub.PUBLISHER_NAME, pub.ADDRESS
FROM BOOK book LEFT OUTER JOIN PUBLISHER pub ON book.PUBLISHER_ID = pub.ID
```

First, you retrieve the book objects from that view only and ignore the associated publishers. You use native SQL to select all the columns related to a book. The addEntity() method specifies the type of resulting persistent objects:

```
String sql = "SELECT ID, ISBN, BOOK_NAME, PUBLISH_DATE, PRICE, PUBLISHER_ID
FROM TOP_SELLING_BOOK
WHERE BOOK_NAME LIKE ?";
Query query = session.createSQLQuery(sql)
.addEntity(Book.class)
.setString(0, "%Hibernate%");
List books = query.list();
```

Because all the columns in the result have the same names as in the mapping definition of Book, you can specify {book.*} in the SELECT clause. Hibernate replaces {book.*} with all the column names in your mapping definition:

```
String sql = "SELECT {book.*}
FROM TOP_SELLING_BOOK book
WHERE BOOK_NAME LIKE ?";
Query query = session.createSQLQuery(sql)
.addEntity("book", Book.class)
.setString(0, "%Hibernate%");
List books = query.list();
```

Next, let's consider the associated publishers. Because not all the column names are identical to those in the mapping definition of Publisher, you need to map them manually in the SQL SELECT clause. The addjoin() method specifies the joined associations:

```
String sql = "SELECT {book.*},
book.PUBLISHER_ID as {publisher.id},
book.PUBLISHER_CODE as {publisher.code},
book.PUBLISHER_NAME as {publisher.name},
book.PUBLISHER_ADDRESS as {publisher.address}
FROM TOP_SELLING_BOOK book
WHERE BOOK_NAME LIKE ?";
```

```
Query query = session.createSQLQuery(sql)
.addEntity("book", Book.class)
.addJoin("publisher", "book.publisher")
.setString(0, "%Hibernate%");
List books = query.list();
```

If you want to query for some simple values only, you can use the addScalar() method:

```
String sql = "SELECT max(book.PRICE) as maxPrice
FROM TOP_SELLING_BOOK book
WHERE BOOK_NAME LIKE ?";
Query query = session.createSQLQuery(sql)
.addScalar("maxPrice", Hibernate.INTEGER)
.setString(0, "%Hibernate%");
Integer maxPrice = (Integer) query.uniqueResult();
```

11.4 Using Named SQL Queries

Problem

How do you use named queries?

Solution

You can define named SQL queries in the mapping document and call them exactly like named HQL queries.

How It Works

Native SQL statements can also be put in a mapping definition and referred to by name in the Java code. You can use <return> and <return-join> to describe the resulting objects. The return-join element is used to join associations. Note that Hibernate doesn't support return-join on stored procedures. In the following query, the publisher of a book is retrieved with the book:

```
<hibernate-mapping package="com.hibernaterecipes.bookstore">
<sql-query name="TopSellingBook.by.name">
<return alias="book" class="Book" />
<return-join alias="publisher" property="book.publisher"/>
<![CDATA[
SELECT {book.*},
book.PUBLISHER_ID as {publisher.id},
book.PUBLISHER_CODE as {publisher.code},
book.PUBLISHER_NAME as {publisher.name},
book.PUBLISHER_ADDRESS as {publisher.address}
FROM TOP_SELLING_BOOK book
WHERE BOOK_NAME LIKE ?
]]>
```

```
</sql-query>
</hibernate-mapping>
Query query = session.getNamedQuery("TopSellingBook.by.name")
.setString(0, "%Hibernate%");
List books = query.list();
```

You can also wrap a query for simple values as a named query. In this case, you use `<return-scalar>` instead:

```
<hibernate-mapping package="com.hibernaterecipes.bookstore">
...
<sql-query name="TopSellingBook.maxPrice.by.name">
<return-scalar column="maxPrice" type="int" />
<![CDATA[
SELECT max(book.PRICE) as maxPrice
FROM TOP_SELLING_BOOK book
WHERE BOOK_NAME LIKE ?
]]>
</sql-query>
</hibernate-mapping>
Query query = session.getNamedQuery("TopSellingBook.maxPrice.by.name")
.setString(0, "%Hibernate%");
Integer maxPrice = (Integer) query.uniqueResult();
```

For a named SQL query, you can group `<return>` and `<return-join>` in a *result set mapping* and reference them in `<sql-query>`. The advantage of a result set mapping is that it can be reused for multiple queries:

```
<hibernate-mapping package=" com.hibernaterecipes.bookstore ">
<resultset name="bookPublisher">
<return alias="book" class="Book" />
<return-join alias="publisher" property="book.publisher" />
</resultset>
<sql-query name="TopSellingBook.by.name" resultset-ref="bookPublisher">
<![CDATA[
SELECT {book.*},
book.PUBLISHER_ID as {publisher.id},
book.PUBLISHER_CODE as {publisher.code},
book.PUBLISHER_NAME as {publisher.name},
book.PUBLISHER_ADDRESS as {publisher.address}
FROM TOP_SELLING_BOOK book
WHERE BOOK_NAME LIKE ?
]]>
</sql-query>
</hibernate-mapping>
```

In the result set mapping, you can further map each database column to an object property. Doing so can simplify your SQL statements by removing the mapping from the SELECT clause:

```
<hibernate-mapping package=" com.hibernaterecipes.bookstore ">
<resultset name="bookPublisher">
```

```
<return alias="book" class="Book" />
<return-join alias="publisher" property="book.publisher">
<return-property name="id" column="PUBLISHER_ID" />
<return-property name="code" column="PUBLISHER_CODE" />
<return-property name="name" column="PUBLISHER_NAME" />
<return-property name="address" column="PUBLISHER_ADDRESS" />
</return-join>
</resultset>
<sql-query name="TopSellingBook.by.name" resultset-ref="bookPublisher">
<![CDATA[
SELECT {book.*},
book.PUBLISHER_ID as {publisher.id},
book.PUBLISHER_CODE as {publisher.code},
book.PUBLISHER_NAME as {publisher.name},
book.PUBLISHER_ADDRESS as {publisher.address}
FROM TOP_SELLING_BOOK book
WHERE BOOK_NAME LIKE ?
]]>
</sql-query>
</hibernate-mapping>
```

After you move the column mappings to the result set mapping, you can simplify the SELECT clause to a "select all":

```
<hibernate-mapping package=" com.hibernaterecipes.bookstore ">
...
<sql-query name="TopSellingBook.by.name" resultset-ref="bookPublisher">
<![CDATA[
SELECT *
FROM TOP_SELLING_BOOK book
WHERE BOOK_NAME LIKE ?
]]>
</sql-query>
</hibernate-mapping>
```

Summary

In this chapter, you've seen when to use batch processing. You've learned how to perform batch inserts, updates, and deletes. You've also learned how to manage the first-level and second-level cache during batch processing. And you can now use native SQL and named queries with other Hibernate HQL and criteria queries.

CHAPTER 12

■■■

Cashing in Hibernate

Caching is one of the important features implemented by an application for better performance. In an ORM perspective, data retrieved from a database is cached in memory or to disk so that there is no need to make a call to the database for every request. A *cache* is a local copy of the information from the database that may be used to avoid a database call whenever:

- The application performs a lookup by identifier.
- The persistence layer resolves an association or collection lazily.

In Figure 12-1, when an application queries for data, the first time Hibernate fetches it from the database; from then on, it fetches data from the cache if the same data is requested.

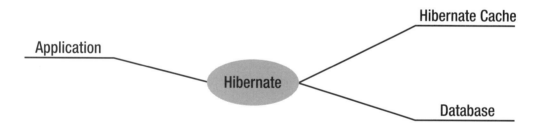

Figure 12-1. How Hibernate caches

Hibernate provides a way to configure caching at the class level, at the collection level, and also at the query result-set level. Cached data is available at three different scopes in an application:

- *Transaction scope:* As you've seen in earlier chapters, a transaction is defined as a unit of work. How does caching affect data in a transaction? If data is fetched in one session, and the same query is executed again in that same session before that unit of work is completed, is that data stored in memory/disk? Does this avoid a call to the database? Yes. This data is stored in memory/disk by default, so the call to the database for the second query is avoided. Because a unit of work is for one request, this data isn't shared or accessed concurrently.

- *Process scope:* Data is cached across sessions or across units of work. If a query is executed in one session and the same query is executed in a second session after closing the first, this data is cached so that the second call to the database is avoided. Because two requests can access the same data in these two sessions, this data is accessed concurrently. You should use this scope with caution.

- *Cluster scope:* Data is shared between multiple processes on the same machine or different machines in a cluster.

A process-scoped cache makes data retrieved from the database in one unit of work visible to another unit of work. This may have some unwanted consequences that you need to avoid. If an application has non-exclusive access to the database, you shouldn't use process scope. That means the application has concurrent access to the database, and one request can share data with another request. In this case, process scope should be used when data doesn't change often and also if it can be refreshed safely when the local cache expires.

Any application that is designed to be scalable should support caching at the cluster level. Process scope doesn't maintain consistency of data between machines, so you should use cluster-level caching.

Hibernate has a two-level cache architecture:

- The first-level cache is the *persistence context cache*. This is at the unit-of-work level. It corresponds to one session in Hibernate for a single request and is by default enabled for the Hibernate session.

- The second-level cache is either at the *process scope or the cluster scope*. This is the cache of the state of the persistence entities. A cache-concurrency strategy defines the transaction isolation details for a particular item of data, and the cache provider represents the physical cache implementation.

Hibernate also implements caching for query result sets. This requires two additional physical cache regions that hold the cached query result sets and the timestamp when a table was last updated.

This chapter first shows how to use and configure the second-level cache and then looks at the query-level cache in Hibernate.

Using the Second-Level Cache in Hibernate

At the second-level cache, all persistence contexts that have been started from the same `SessionFactory` share the same cached data. Different kinds of data require different cache policies: for example, how long the cache should be maintained before evicting data, at what scope the data should be cached, whether the data should be cached in memory, and so on. The cache policy involves setting the following:

- Whether the second-level cache is enabled

- The Hibernate concurrency strategy

- Cache expiration policies (such as timeout, least recently used, and memory sensitive)

- The physical format of the cache (memory, indexed files, or cluster-replicated)

To reiterate, the second-level cache is more useful when there is less data that is often updated. In other words, it's useful when there is more read-only data.

You set up the second-level cache in two steps. First, you have to decide on the concurrency strategy; then, you configure the cache expiration and physical cache attributes using the cache provider.

Concurrency Strategies

There are four built-in concurrency strategies:

- *Transactional:* This strategy should be used when there is more data to read. It prevents stale data in concurrency strategies. It's equivalent to isolation level: repeatable read.

- *Read-write:* This maintains a read-committed isolation level.

- *Non-strict read-write:* This doesn't guarantee that you won't read stale data. It doesn't guarantee consistency between cache and database.

- *Read-only:* This is appropriate for data that never changes.

Cache Providers

The following built-in providers are available in Hibernate:

- *EHCache:* This is an open source standards-based cache that supports process-scope cache. It can cache in memory or to disk, and it supports query cache. EHCache Distributed supports the cluster-scope cache. It has its own configuration file (ehcache.xml) where all the required parameters are set for caching. You can check out the tutorial at http://ehcache.org/.

- *OSCache:* This is also open source caching provider that writes to memory and disk. It also has cluster cache support. The URL www.opensymphony.com/oscache/ has documentation.

- *SwarmCache:* This is a simple but effective distributed cache. It uses IP multicast to communicate with any number of hosts in a distributed system. The documentation is at http://swarmcache.sourceforge.net.

- *JBoss cache:* This is a distributed cache system. It replicates data across different nodes in a distributed system. State is always kept in synch with other servers in the system. The documentation is at www.jboss.org/jbosscache/.

Table 12-1 summarizes these cache providers.

Table 12-1. Cache Providers

Cache	Provider Class	Type	Cluster Safe	Query Cache Supported
Hashtable	org.hibernate.cache.HashtableCacheProvider	Memory	Yes	
EHCache	org.hibernate.cache.EHCacheProvider	Memory, disk	Yes	
OSCache	org.hibernate.cache.OSCacheProvider	Memory, disk	Yes	
JBoss Cache	org.hibernate.cache.JBossCacheProvider	Clustered, ip-multicast	Yes	
SwarmCache	org.hibernate.cache.SwarmCacheProvider	Clustered, ip-multicast	Yes	

You can develop an adapter for your application by implementing org.hibernate.cache.CacheProvider. All of the listed cache providers implement this interface.

Not every cache provider is compatible with every concurrency strategies. The compatibility matrix is given in Table 12-2.

Table 12-2. Cache Providers' Concurrency Strategies

Cache Provider	Read-Only	Non-Strict Read-Write	Read-Write	Transactional
EHCache	Yes	Yes	Yes	
OSCache	Yes	Yes	Yes	
SwarmCache	Yes	Yes	Yes	
JBoss Cache	Yes			Yes

You can configure the cache for a specific class or a collection. The <cache> element is used to configure cache in the hibernate.cfg.xml file. The <cache> element is defined as follows:

```
<cache  usage="transactional|read-write|nonstrict-read-write|read-only"
        region="RegionName" include="all|lazy"/>
```

Table 12-3 defines its attributes.

Table 12-3. <cache> Element Attributes

Attribute	Description
usage	The caching strategy.
region	The region name. Region names are references to actual cached data.
include	Specifies that properties of the entity mapped with lazy=true can't be cached when the attribute level lazy fetching is enabled.

What Are Cache Regions?

Cache regions are handles by which you can reference classes and collections in the cache provider configuration and set the expiration policies applicable to that region. Regions are buckets of data of two types: one type contains disassembled data of entity instances, and the other contains only identifiers of entities that are linked through a collection.

The name of the region is the class name in the case of a class cache or the class name together with the property name in the case of a collection cache.

Caching Query Results

A query's result set can be configured to be cached. By default, caching is disabled, and every HQL, JPA QL, and Criteria query hits the database. You enable the query cache as follows:

```
hibernate.cache.use_query_cache = true
```

In addition to setting this configuration property, you should use the org.hibernate.Query interface:

```
Query bookQuery = session.createQuery("from Book book where book.name < ?");
bookQuery.setString("name","HibernateRecipes");
bookQuery.setCacheable(true);
```

The setCacheable() method enables the result to be cached.

12.1 Using the First-Level Cache

Problem

What is the first-level cache, and how is it used in Hibernate?

Solution

The first-level cache is at the transaction level or the unit of work. It's enabled by default in Hibernate. Caching at the first level is associated with a session. If the same query is executed multiple times in the same session, the data associated with the query is cached.

How It Works

The general concept of caching persistent objects is that when an object is first read from external storage, a copy of it is stored in the cache. Subsequent readings of the same object can be retrieved from the cache directly. Because caches are typically stored in memory or on local disk, it's faster to read an object from cache than external storage. If you use it properly, caching can greatly improve the performance of your application.

As a high-performance ORM framework, Hibernate supports the caching of persistent objects at different levels. Suppose you retrieve an object more than once within a session: does Hibernate query the database as many times as the query is invoked?

```
Session session = factory.openSession();
try {
        Book book1 = (Book) session.get(Book.class, id);
        Book book2 = (Book) session.get(Book.class, id);
} finally {
        session.close();
}
```

If you inspect the SQL statements executed by Hibernate, you find that only one database query is made. That means Hibernate is caching your objects in the same session. This kind of caching is called *first-level caching*, and its caching scope is a session.

But how about getting an object with same identifier more than once in two different sessions?

```
Session session1 = factory.openSession();
try {
        Book book1 = (Book) session1.get(Book.class, id);
} finally {
        session1.close();
}
Session session2 = factory.openSession();
try {
        Book book2 = (Book) session2.get(Book.class, id);
} finally {
        session2.close();
}
```

Two database queries are made. That means Hibernate isn't caching the persistent objects across different sessions by default. You need to turn on this *second-level caching*, whose caching scope is a session factory.

12.2 Configuring the Second-Level Cache

Problem

What is the second-level cache, and how is it configured and used in Hibernate?

Solution

Second-level cache is configured at the process level or the cluster level. In Hibernate, you can configure it for a particular class or for a collection to improve performance. You can use the second-level cache with large and complex object graphs that may be loaded often. It's associated with one `SessionFactory` and can be reused in multiple `Sessions` created from the same `SessionFactory`.

How It Works

To turn on the second-level cache, the first step is to choose a cache provider in the Hibernate configuration file `hibernate.cfg.xml`. Hibernate supports several cache implementations, such as EHCache, OSCache, SwarmCache and JBoss Cache, as discussed earlier. In a nondistributed environment, you can choose EHCache, which is Hibernate's default cache provider:

```
<hibernate-configuration>
<session-factory>
...
<property name="cache.provider_class">
org.hibernate.cache.EhCacheProvider
</property>
...
</session-factory>
</hibernate-configuration>
```

You can configure EHCache through the configuration file `ehcache.xml`, located in the source root folder. You can specify different settings for different cache regions, which store different kinds of objects. If the parameter `eternal` is set to false, the elements will be expired in a time period. The parameter `timeToIdleSeconds` is the time to idle for an element before it expires; it's the maximum amount of time between accesses before an element expires and is used only if the element isn't eternal. The parameter `timeToLiveSeconds` is time to live for an element before it expires; it's the maximum time between creation and when the element expires and is used only if the element isn't eternal:

```
<ehcache>
<diskStore path="java.io.tmpdir" />
<defaultCache maxElementsInMemory="10000" eternal="false" timeToIdleSeconds="120"
timeToLiveSeconds="120" overflowToDisk="true"
/>
<cache name="com.metaarchit.bookshop.Book" maxElementsInMemory="10000"
eternal="false" timeToIdleSeconds="300" timeToLiveSeconds="600"
overflowToDisk="true"
/>
```

```
</ehcache>
```

To monitor Hibernate's caching activities at runtime, add the following line to the log4j configuration file `log4j.properties`:

```
log4j.logger.org.hibernate.cache=debug
```

Now, you need to enable caching for a particular persistent class. Let's look at what goes on behind the scenes when caching is enabled in Hibernate.

When you enable a class with the second-level cache, Hibernate doesn't store the actual instances in cache. Instead it caches the individual properties of that object. In the example, the instance of `Book` isn't cached—rather, the properties in the `book` object like `name` and `price` are cached. The cached objects are stored in a region that has the same name as the persistent class, such as `com.metaarchit.bookshop.Book`.

You can choose several cache usages for a persistent class. If the persistent objects are read-only and never modified, the most efficient usage is `read-only`:

```
<hibernate-mapping package="com.metaarchit.bookshop">
<class name="Book" table="BOOK">
<cache usage="read-only" />
...
</class>
</hibernate-mapping>
```

When the `Book` class is cached, only one SQL query is made, even though the `book` object is loaded more than once in two different sessions. Because the second call to the database is avoided, the query's performance improves:

```
Session session1 = factory.openSession();
try {
        Book book1 = (Book) session1.get(Book.class, id);
} finally {
        session1.close();
}
Session session2 = factory.openSession();
try {
        Book book2 = (Book) session2.get(Book.class, id);
} finally {
        session2.close();
}
```

However, if you modify the `book` object in one session and flush the changes, an exception will be thrown for updating a read-only object.

```
Session session1 = factory.openSession();
try {
        Book book1 = (Book) session1.get(Book.class, id);
        book1.setName("New Book");
        session1.save(book1);
        session1.flush();
} finally {
```

```
        session1.close();
}
```

So, for an updatable object, you should choose another cache usage: **read-write**. Hibernate invalidates the object from cache before it's updated:

```
<hibernate-mapping package="com.metaarchit.bookshop">
<class name="Book" table="BOOK">
<cache usage="read-write" />
...
</class>
</hibernate-mapping>
```

In some cases, such as when the database updated by other applications, you may want to invalidate the cached objects manually. You can do it through the methods provided by the session factory. You can invalidate either one instance or all instances of a persistent class:

```
factory.evict(Book.class);
factory.evict(Book.class, id);
factory.evictEntity("com.metaarchit.bookshop.Book");
factory.evictEntity("com.metaarchit.bookshop.Book", id);
```

After the cached object is evicted from cache, when you need to fetch data from the database, the query is executed and the updated data is retrieved. This avoids having stale data in cache. Note that the eviction from the second-level cache is nontransactional, meaning that the cache region isn't locked during the eviction process.

CacheMode options are provided to control the interaction of Hibernate with the second level cache:

```
Session session1 = factory.openSession();
Session.setCacheMode(CacheMode.IGNORE);
try {
Book book1 = new Book();
book1.setName("New Book");
session1.save(book1);
session1.flush();
} finally {
session1.close();
}
```

CacheMode.IGNORE tells Hibernate not to interact with second level cache for that session. Options available in CacheMode are as follows:

- CacheMode.NORMAL: The default behavior.

- CacheMode.IGNORE: Hibernate doesn't interact with the second-level cache. When entities cached in the second-level cache are updated, Hibernate invalidates them.

- CacheMode.GET: Hibernate only reads and doesn't add items to the second-level cache. When entities cached in the second-level cache are updated, Hibernate invalidates them.

- CacheMode.PUT: Hibernate only adds and doesn't add read from the second-level cache. When entities cached in the second-level cache are updated, Hibernate invalidates them.

- CacheMode.REFRESH: Hibernate only adds and doesn't read from the second-level cache. In this mode, the setting of hibernate.cache.use_minimal_puts is bypassed, as the refresh is forced.

12.3 Caching Associations

Problem

Can associated objects be cached? How do you configure them?

Solution

Associated objects have a parent-child relationship in the database. How does caching work in this case? If the parent object is cached, is the child object also cached? By default, associated objects aren't cached. If you need to cache these objects, you can configure it explicitly. The primary reason to cache associations is to avoid additional calls to the database.

How It Works

Is a book's associated publisher object cached when its parent book object is cached?

```
<hibernate-mapping package="com.metaarchit.bookshop">
<class name="Book" table="BOOK">
<cache usage="read-write" />
...
<many-to-one name="publisher" class="Publisher" column="PUBLISHER_ID" />
</class>
</hibernate-mapping>
```

If you initialize the association in two different sessions, it's loaded as many times as the initialization is made. This is because Hibernate caches only the identifier of publisher in Book's region:

```
Session session1 = factory.openSession();
try {
        Book book1 = (Book) session1.get(Book.class, id);
        Hibernate.initialize(book1.getPublisher());
} finally {
session1.close();
}
Session session2 = factory.openSession();
try {
        Book book2 = (Book) session2.get(Book.class, id);
        Hibernate.initialize(book2.getPublisher());
```

```
} finally {
        session2.close();
}
```

To cache the `publisher` objects in their own region, you need to enable caching for the `Publisher` class. You can do it the same way as for the `Book` class. The cached `publisher` objects are stored in a region with the name `com.metaarchit.bookshop.Publisher`:

```
<hibernate-mapping package="com.metaarchit.bookshop">
        <class name="Publisher" table="PUBLISHER">
                <cache usage="read-write" />
...
        </class>
</hibernate-mapping>
```

When the `Publisher` class is configured to be cached along with `Book`, for all the join queries between `Publisher` and `Book`, if the `Publisher` data is cached, it doesn't fetch the data from the database but fetches from the cache.

12.4 Caching Collections

Problem

How do you cache collections?

Solution

Collections also can be cached explicitly in Hibernate. If a persistent object contains associated objects in a collection, the collection can also be cached explicitly. If the collection contains `value` types, they're stored by their values. If the collection contains objects, the object's identifiers are cached.

How It Works

For the associated chapters of a book to be cached, you enable caching for the `Chapter` class. The cached `chapter` objects are stored in a region names `com.metaarchit.bookshop.Chapter`:

```
<hibernate-mapping package="com.metaarchit.bookshop">
        <class name="Book" table="BOOK">
                <cache usage="read-write" />
                ...
                <set name="chapters" table="BOOK_CHAPTER">
                <key column="BOOK_ID" />
                <one-to-many class="Chapter" />
                </set>
        </class>
</hibernate-mapping>
```

```
<hibernate-mapping package="com.metaarchit.bookshop">
        <class name="Chapter" table="CHAPTER">
                <cache usage="read-write" />
                ...
                <many-to-one name="book" class="Book" column="BOOK_ID" />
        </class>
</hibernate-mapping>
```

Then, you can try initializing the collection in two different sessions. No query should be made for the second session:

```
Session session1 = factory.openSession();
try {
        Book book1 = (Book) session1.get(Book.class, id);
        Hibernate.initialize(book1.getChapters());
} finally {
        session1.close();
}
Session session2 = factory.openSession();
try {
        Book book2 = (Book) session2.get(Book.class, id);
        Hibernate.initialize(book2.getChapters());
} finally {
        session2.close();
}
```

Inspecting the SQL statements, you see that one query is still made. The reason is that, unlike a many-to-one association, a collection isn't cached by default. You need to turn on caching manually by specifying cache usage to the collection. For a book's chapter collection, it's stored in a region named com.metaarchit.bookshop.Book.chapters.

How can Hibernate cache a collection? If the collection is storing simple values, the values themselves are cached. If the collection is storing persistent objects, the identifiers of the objects are cached in the collection region, and the persistent objects are cached in their own region:

```
<hibernate-mapping package="com.metaarchit.bookshop">
        <class name="Book" table="BOOK">
                <cache usage="read-write" />
                ...
                <set name="chapters" table="BOOK_CHAPTER">
                <cache usage="read-write" />
                <key column="BOOK_ID" />
                <one-to-many class="Chapter" />
                </set>
        </class>
</hibernate-mapping>
```

To invalidate a particular collection or all the collections in a region, you can use the following methods provided by the session factory:

```
factory.evictCollection("com.metaarchit.bookshop.Book.chapters");
factory.evictCollection("com.metaarchit.bookshop.Book.chapters", id);
```

For a bidirectional one-to-many/many-to-one association, you should call the `evictCollection()` method on the collection end after the single end is updated. That means you need to remove the **Book** reference from the **Chapter** and update the **Chapter** first. Then, call the `evictCollection()` method:

```
Session session1 = factory.openSession();
try {
        Book book1 = (Book) session1.get(Book.class, id);
        Chapter chapter = (Chapter) book1.getChapters().iterator().next();
        chapter.setBook(null);
        session1.saveOrUpdate(chapter);
        session1.flush();
        factory.evictCollection("com.metaarchit.bookshop.Book.chapters", id);
} finally {
        session1.close();
}
Session session2 = factory.openSession();
try {
        Book book2 = (Book) session2.get(Book.class, id);
        Hibernate.initialize(book2.getChapters());
} finally {
        session2.close();
}
```

12.5 Caching Queries

Problem

Can queries be cached? How is this achieved in Hibernate?

Solution

Query result sets can be cached. This is useful when you run a particular query often with the same parameters.

How It Works

In addition to caching objects loaded by a session, a query with HQL can be cached. Suppose you're running the same query in two different sessions:

```
Session session1 = factory.openSession();
try {
        Query query = session1.createQuery("from Book where name like ?");
        query.setString(0, "%Hibernate%");
        List books = query.list();
} finally {
```

```
        session1.close();
}
Session session2 = factory.openSession();
try {
        Query query = session2.createQuery("from Book where name like ?");
        query.setString(0, "%Hibernate%");
        List books = query.list();
} finally {
        session2.close();
}
```

By default, the HQL queries aren't cached. You must first enable the query cache in the Hibernate configuration file:

```
<hibernate-configuration>
        <session-factory>

        ...

        <property name="cache.use_query_cache">true</property>

        ...

        </session-factory>
</hibernate-configuration>
```

The setting cache.use_query_cache creates two cache regions: one holding the cached query result sets and the other holding timestamps of the more recent updates to queryable tables.

By default, the queries aren't cached. In addition to using the previous setting, to enable caching, you need to call Query.setCacheable(true). This allows the query to look for existing cache results or add the results of the query to the cache.

Then, you need to set the query to be cacheable before execution. The query result is cached in a region named org.hibernate.cache.QueryCache by default.

How can a query be cached by Hibernate? If the query returns simple values, the values themselves are cached. If the query returns persistent objects, the identifiers of the objects are cached in the query region, and the persistent objects are cached in their own region:

```
Session session1 = factory.openSession();
try {
        Query query = session1.createQuery("from Book where name like ?");
        query.setString(0, "%Hibernate%");
        query.setCacheable(true);
        List books = query.list();
} finally {
        session1.close();
}
Session session2 = factory.openSession();
try {
        Query query = session2.createQuery("from Book where name like ?");
        query.setString(0, "%Hibernate%");
        query.setCacheable(true);
        List books = query.list();
} finally {
        session2.close();
}
```

You can also specify the cache region for a query. Doing so lets you separate query caches in different regions and reduce the number of caches in one particular region:

```
...
query.setCacheable(true);
query.setCacheRegion("com.metaarchit.bookshop.BookQuery");
```

Summary

In this chapter, you've seen what caching is and the different levels of caching in Hibernate. Caching can be enabled at the transaction level, where data is cached for one unit of work; this is the default behavior in Hibernate. Multiple queries in a particular session share the cached data.

You've learned that at the second level, caching is enabled for a process, and the cache is associated with a `SessionFactory`. Multiple sessions within a `SessionFactory` share the same data. Configuring the second-level cache is a two step process: first, you decide on the concurrent strategy, and then you choose the provider that implements the caching strategy.

You've also learned that you can use four concurrent strategies: read-only, read-write, transactional, and not-strict read-write. There are many open source cache providers, including OSCache, EHCache, SwarmCache, and JBoss Cache. Each of these provides different concurrent strategies.

Query result sets also can be cached. You do so through configuration and by invoking `setCacheable(true)`. Associated objects and collections can also be cached explicitly.

CHAPTER 13

∎∎∎

Transactions and Concurrency

Let's say a buyer logs in to the bookshop application and purchases a book. The following actions should take place in the event of purchase:

- Charge the buyer the cost of the book

- Reduce the stock of the book

If the charge on the credit card fails, the stock shouldn't be reduced. Also, when the book is out of stock, the buyer shouldn't be charged. That means either both actions should be successfully completed, or they should have no effect. These actions collectively are called a *transaction* or *unit of work*. In essence, transactions provide an all-or-nothing proposition.

The concept of transactions is inherited from database management systems. By definition, a transaction must be **a**tomic, **c**onsistent, **i**solated, and **d**urable (ACID):

- *Atomicity* means that if one step fails, then the whole unit of work fails.

- *Consistency* means that the transaction works on a set of data that is consistent before and after the transaction. The data must be clean after the transaction. From a database perspective, the clean and consistent state is maintained by integrity constraints. From an applications perspective, the consistent state is maintained by the business rules.

- *Isolation* means one transaction isn't visible to other transactions. Isolation makes sure the execution of a transaction doesn't affect other transactions.

- *Durability* means that when data has been persisted, it isn't lost.

In an application, you need to identify when a transaction begins and when it ends. The starting point and ending point of a transaction are called *transaction boundaries*, and the technique of identifying them in an application is called *transaction demarcation*. You can set the transaction boundaries either programmatically or declaratively. This chapter shows you how.

Multiuser systems like databases need to implement concurrency control to maintain data integrity. There are two main approaches to concurrency control:

- *Optimistic:* Involves some kind of versioning to achieve control

- *Pessimistic:* Uses a locking mechanism to obtain control

Some of the methods that are used in concurrency control are as follows:

- *Two-phase locking:* This is a locking mechanism that uses two distinct phases to achieve concurrency. In the first phase of transaction execution, called the *expanding* phase, locks are acquired, and no locks are released. In the second phase, called the *shrinking phase*, locks are released, and no new locks acquired. This guarantees serializability. The transactions are serialized in the order in which the locks are acquired. *Strict two-phase locking* is a subset of two-phase locking. All the write locks are released only at the end (after committing or aborting), and read locks are released regularly during phase 2. With both these locking mechanisms, a deadlock is possible but can be avoided if you maintain a canonical order for obtaining locks. So, if two processes need locks on A and B, then they both request first A and then B.

- *Serialization:* A *transaction schedule* is a sequential representation of two or more concurrent transactions. The transaction schedules have a property called *serializability*. Two transactions that are updating the same record are executed one after the other and don't overlap in time.

- *Time-stamp-based control:* This is a nonlocking mechanism for concurrency control. Every transaction is given a timestamp when it starts. Every object or record in the database also has a read timestamp and a write timestamp. These three timestamps are used to define the isolation rules that are used in this type of concurrency control.

- *Multiversion concurrency control:* When a transaction does a read on a database, a snapshot is created, and the data is read from that snapshot. This isolates the data from other concurrent transactions. When the transaction modifies a record, the database creates a new record version instead of overwriting the old record. This mechanism gives good performance because lock contention between concurrent transactions is minimized—in fact, lock contention is eliminated between read locks and write locks, which means read locks never block a write lock. Most current databases, such as Oracle, MySQL, SQL Server, and PostgreSQL, implement the multiversion concurrent control for concurrency.

This chapter shows how Hibernate implements the optimistic and pessimistic concurrency approaches.

13.1 Using Programmatic Transactions in a Standalone Java Application

Problem

If you're working on a standalone Java application, how do you achieve transaction demarcation?

Solution

In a multiuser application, you need more than one connection to support multiple concurrent users. It's also expensive to create new connections when you need to interact with the database. For this, you need to have a connection pool that creates and manages database connections. Every thread that needs to interact with the database requests a connection from the pool and executes its queries. After it's done, the connection is returned to the pool. Then, if another thread requests a connection, the connection pool may provide it with same connection.

Usually, an application server provides a connection pool. When you're working in a standalone Java application, you need to use a third-party solution that provides connection pools. Hibernate comes with an open source third-party connection pooling framework called C3P0. Apache also provides a connection-pooling framework called Commons DBCP. You need to configure Hibernate to use one of these frameworks. After the connection pool is configured, you can use the Hibernate's Transaction API for transaction demarcation and use connections from the connection pool.

How It Works

You need to add the Java `c3p0-0.9.1.jar` file that comes with Hibernate to the build path. In your Eclipse IDE, select your Java project, and right-click to edit build path. (See the explanation in Chapter 1 if you have trouble adding the jar to the build path.) In the `Hibernate.cfg.xml` file, add the following configuration:

```
<property name="connection.provider_class">org.hibernate.connection.C3P0ConnectionProvider
</property>
<property name="hibernate.c3p0.min_size">5</property>
<property name="hibernate.c3p0.max_size">10</property>
<property name="hibernate.c3p0.timeout">300</property>
<property name="hibernate.c3p0.max_statements">50</property>
<property name="hibernate.c3p0.acquire_increment">1</property>
<property name="hibernate.c3p0.idle_test_period">3000</property>
```

Here's an explanation for each of the parameters you set:

- `connection.provider_class` specifies that `C3P0ConnectionProvider` is the class providing the connections.

- `min_size` is the minimum number of connections that are ready at all times.

- `max_size` is the maximum number of connections in the pool. This is the only property that is required for C3P0 to be enabled.

- `timeout` is the maximum idle time for a connection, after which the connection is removed from the pool.

- `max_statements` is the maximum number of prepared statements that can be cached.

- `idle_test_period` is the time in seconds before which a connection is automatically validated.

- `acquire_increment` is the number of connections acquired when the pool is exhausted.

These are all the settings required in the configuration file. Hibernate also provides a property called `hibernate.transaction.factory_class` that you can set in the configuration file. It provides the factory to use to instantiate transactions, and it defaults to `JDBCTransactionFactory`:

```
SessionFactory sessionFactory = new Configuration().configure().buildSessionFactory();
Session session = sessionFactory.openSession();
Transaction tx = null;
try {
        tx = session.beginTransaction();
        BookCh2 book = new BookCh2();
        book.setName("Hibernate Recipes Book  ");
        book.setPrice(200);
        book.setPublishDate(new Date());
        session.saveOrUpdate(book);
        tx.commit();

        } catch (RuntimeException e) {
                try{
                        if(tx != null)
                        {
                                tx.rollback();
                        }
                }catch(RuntimeException ex)
                {
                        log.error("Cannot rollback transaction");
                }
                throw e;
        } finally {
                session.close();
        }
```

The session is provided by the sessionFactory.openSession() call. A database connection isn't opened when the session is created; this keeps the session creation a non-expensive task. The database connection is retrieved from the connection pool when the call session.beginTransaction() is made, and all queries are executed using this connection. The entities to be persisted are cached in the persistent context of the session. The commit() on the Transaction flushes the persistent context and completes the save of the entities. Another Transaction can be opened after the current Transaction is committed. Then, a new connection is provided by the connection pool. All resources and connections are release when close() is called on the Session.

The exceptions thrown by Hibernate are RuntimeExceptions and subtypes of RuntimeExceptions. These exceptions are fatal, and hence you have to roll back your transactions. Because rolling back a transaction can also throw an exception, you have to call the rollback method within a try/catch block.

In JPA, you have to define the same configurations as for Hibernate, and the EntityTransaction API is used to manage transactions:

```
EntityManager manager = null;
EntityTransaction tx = null;
try {
        EntityManagerFactory managerFactory =
Persistence.createEntityManagerFactory("book");
        manager = managerFactory.createEntityManager();
         tx = manager.getTransaction();
        tx.begin();
        BookCh2 newBook = new BookCh2();
```

```
        newBook.setBookName("Hibernate Recipes Phase1");
        newBook.setPublishDate(new Date());
        newBook.setPrice(new Long(50));
        manager.persist(newBook);
        tx.commit();
        log.debug("Transaction committed");
}catch (RuntimeException e)
{
        try
        {
                if(tx != null)
                {
                        tx.rollback();
                }
        }catch(RuntimeException ex)
        {
                log.error("Cannot rollback transaction");
        }

        throw e;
} finally
{
        manager.close();
}
```

getTransaction() is called on the EntityManager to get a transaction. The actual connection is requested from the pool with the transaction's begin() method. The commit() on the transaction flushes the persistent context and completes the save of the entities. The EntityManager's close() method is called in the finally block to make sure the session is closed even in the case of an exception.

13.2 Using Programmatic Transactions with JTA

Problem

Suppose you're using an application server that provides support to manage resources. Application servers like WebLogic, WebSphere, and JBoss can provide connections from a connection pool and manage transactions. How do you achieve programmatic transaction demarcation using the Java Transaction API (JTA)?

Solution

You have to configure a Java enterprise application with Hibernate as the persistent framework. You also need to configure Hibernate to use JTATransactionFactory to provide JTATransaction objects. You then need to use the UserTransaction interface to manage transactions programmatically.

How It Works

You use WebLogic (version 9.2) as the application server to demonstrate using JTA for programmatic transaction demarcation. The assumption is that you're well versed with building and deploying your application.

To begin, you need to configure the data source on the application server. To do so, you need to start the WebLogic server, log in to the console, and configure the data source. You must also add the database driver to the server library. For Derby, you add **derbyClient.jar** to the server library. Make sure you test connectivity from the console!

You need to the provide the following information (with your values):

- *JNDI Name:* local_derby. The application uses this to obtain database connections.

- *Database Name:* BookShopDB

- *Host Name:* localhost. If you're pointing to a remote database, then this value is something like the IP of that machine.

- *Port:* 1527.

- *User:* book.

- *Password:* book.

After you successfully configure the data source on the application server, you need to configure Hibernate. The key properties you're required to provide are as follows:

- **Hibernate.connection.datasource**: The value of this property must be the same as the JNDI name of the data source you configured on the application server.

- **Hibernate.transaction.factory_class**: The default value for this is **JDBCTransactionFactory**. But because you want to use a JTA transaction for transaction demarcation, you need to define this as **JTATransactionFactory**.

- **Hibernate.transaction.manager_lookup_class**: The value of this transaction manager is dependent on the application server. Each application server has a different JTA implementation, so you have to tell Hibernate which JTA implementation to use. Hibernate supports most major application server implementation; you use **org.hibernate.transaction.WeblogicTransactionManagerLookup** for WebLogic.

The following is the Hibernate configuration:

```
<?xml version="1.0" encoding="UTF-8"?>
<!DOCTYPE hibernate-configuration PUBLIC
            "-//Hibernate/Hibernate Configuration DTD 3.0//EN"
            "http://hibernate.sourceforge.net/hibernate-configuration-3.0.dtd">
<hibernate-configuration>
    <session-factory name="book">
        <property name="hibernate.connection.datasource">local_derby</property>
        <property
name="hibernate.transaction.factory_class">org.hibernate.transaction.JTATransactionFactory</
property>
```

```
    <property
name="hibernate.transaction.manager_lookup_class">org.hibernate.transaction.WeblogicTransact
ionManagerLookup</property>
        <property name="hibernate.dialect">org.hibernate.dialect.DerbyDialect</property>
        <property name="hibernate.show_sql">true</property>
        <property name="hibernate.cache.use_second_level_cache">false</property>
    <mapping resource="book.xml" />

  </session-factory>
 </hibernate-configuration>
```

You now need to write a class that provides SessionFactory for the complete application. To do so, you defined a utility class that has a static method to return the SessionFactory. Here's the code implementation:

```
import org.hibernate.SessionFactory;
import org.hibernate.cfg.Configuration;

public class HibernateUtil {

        private HibernateUtil(){}

        public static SessionFactory getSessionFactory()
        {
                SessionFactory factory = null;;
                try {

                        factory = new Configuration().configure().buildSessionFactory();

                } catch (Exception e) {

                        e.printStackTrace();
                }
                return factory;
        }
}
```

Now you're ready to use JTA for transaction demarcation. You get the UserTransaction by looking up the JNDI registry:

```
public void saveBook(Book book) throws NotSupportedException, SystemException,
NamingException, Exception {
                System.out.println("Enter DAO Impl");
                Session session = null;
                UserTransaction tx = (UserTransaction)new InitialContext()
                .lookup("java:comp/UserTransaction");
                try {

                        SessionFactory factory = HibernateUtil.getSessionFactory();
                        tx.begin();
                        session = factory.openSession();
```

```
                        session.saveOrUpdate(book);
                        session.flush();
                        tx.commit();

                }catch (RuntimeException e) {

                        try
                        {
                                tx.rollback();
                        }catch(RuntimeException ex)
                        {
                                System.out.println("**** RuntimeException in BookDaoImpl ");
                        }
                        throw e;

                }finally
                {
                        session.close();
                }
        }
```

Note that you explicitly call `session.flush()`. You need to do an explicit flush because Hibernate's default implementation doesn't flush the session. You can, however, override the default implementation by configuring the `hibernate.transaction.flush_before_completion` property. You also configure the `hibernate.transaction.auto_close_session` property to avoid calling `session.close()` explicitly in every method. The Hibernate configuration file is as follows:

```xml
<session-factory name="book">
        <property name="hibernate.connection.datasource">local_derby</property>
    <property
name="hibernate.transaction.factory_class">org.hibernate.transaction.JTATransactionFactory</property>
    <property
name="hibernate.transaction.manager_lookup_class">org.hibernate.transaction.WeblogicTransactionManagerLookup</property>
        <property name="hibernate.transaction.flush_before_completion">true</property>
        <property name="hibernate.transaction.auto_close_session">true</property>
        <property name="hibernate.dialect">org.hibernate.dialect.DerbyDialect</property>
        <property name="hibernate.show_sql">true</property>
        <property name="hibernate.cache.use_second_level_cache">false</property>

        <!--<property name="hbm2ddl.auto">create</property>-->

        <mapping resource="book.xml" />

</session-factory>
```

And the code looks a little simpler, as shown here:

```java
Session session = null;
        UserTransaction tx = (UserTransaction)new InitialContext()
```

```
                    .lookup("java:comp/UserTransaction");
                    try {

                            SessionFactory factory = HibernateUtil.getSessionFactory();
                            tx.begin();
                            session = factory.openSession();
                            session.saveOrUpdate(book);
                            tx.commit();

                    }catch (RuntimeException e) {

                            try
                            {
                                    tx.rollback();
                            }catch(RuntimeException ex)
                            {
                                    System.out.println("**** RuntimeException in BookDaoImpl ");
                            }
                            throw e;

                    }
```

In JPA, the implementation is very similar to Hibernate:

```
EntityManager manager = null;
UserTransaction tx = (UserTransaction)new InitialContext()
              .lookup("java:comp/UserTransaction");

try {
        EntityManagerFactory managerFactory = HibernateUtil.getFactory();
            manager = managerFactory.createEntityManager();
         tx.begin();
        manager.persist(book);
        tx.commit();
        }catch (RuntimeException e)
        {
                try
                {
                        if(tx != null)
                        {
                                tx.rollback();
                        }
                }catch(RuntimeException ex)
                {
                        System.out.println ("Cannot rollback transaction");
                }

                throw e;
        } finally {
                manager.close();
        }
```

13.3 Enabling Optimistic Concurrency Control

Problem

Suppose two transactions are trying to update a record in the database. The first transaction updates and commits successfully. The second transaction tries to update and fails. So, the transaction is rolled back. The problem is that the first update is lost. Or, what if the second transaction successfully updates, as illustrated in Table 13-1? The changes made by the first transaction are overwritten.

Table 13-1. Lost Updates: Transaction 1 Updates Are Lost

Time	Transaction Account
T1	Transaction 1 begins.
T2	Transaction 2 begins.
T3	Transaction 1 updates record R1.
T4	Transaction 2 updates record R1.
T5	Transaction 1 commits.
T6	Transaction 2 commits.

How do you handle such cases of lost updates? And how do you enable versioning in Hibernate?

Solution

You need to understand isolation levels in order to choose a concurrency control mechanism. Access to database records is classified as reads and writes. The concurrency control mechanisms define the rules that dictate when to allow reads and writes.

A *dirty read* occurs when one transaction reads changes made by another transaction that haven't yet been committed (see Table 13-2). Basically, a dirty read means reading uncommitted data.

Table 13-2. Dirty Read: A Transaction Reading Uncommitted Data

Time	Transaction Account
T1	Transaction 1 begins.
T2	Transaction 2 begins.
T3	Transaction 1 updates record R1.
T4	Transaction 2 reads uncommitted record R1.
T5	Transaction 1 rolls back its update.
T6	Transaction 2 commits.

An *unrepeatable read* occurs when a transaction reads a record twice and the record state is different between the first and the second read. This happens when another transaction updates the state of the record between the two reads (see Table 13-3).

Table 13-3. Unrepeatable Read: A Transaction Reading a Record Twice

Time	Transaction Account
T1	Transaction 1 begins.
T2	Transaction 1 reads record R1.
T3	Transaction 2 begins.
T4	Transaction 2 updates record R1.
T5	Transaction 2 commits.
T6	Transaction 1 reads record R1 (the record R1 read at time T2 is in a different state than at time T6).
T7	Transaction 1 commits.

A *phantom read* occurs when a transaction executes two identical queries, and the collection of rows returned by the second query is different from the first. This also happens when another transaction inserts records into or deletes records from the table between the two reads.

Table 13-4. Phantom Read: Reading a Range of Data That Changes in Size During a Transaction

Time	Transaction Account
T1	Transaction 1 begins.
T2	Transaction 1 reads a range of records RG1.
T3	Transaction 2 begins.
T4	Transaction 2 inserts records.
T5	Transaction 2 commits.
T6	Transaction 1 reads the range of records RG1 (RG1's size has changed from time T2 to T6).
T7	Transaction 1 commits.

Isolation defines how and when changes made by one transaction are made visible to other transactions. Isolation is one of the ACID properties. For better performance and concurrency control, isolation is divided by the ANSI SQL standard into levels that define the degree of locking when you select data. The four isolation levels are as follows (see also Table 13-5):

- *Serializable:* Transaction are executed serially, one after the other. This isolation level allows a transaction to acquire read locks or write locks for the entire range of data that it affects. The Serializable isolation level prevents dirty reads, unrepeatable reads, and phantom reads, but it can cause scalability issues for an application.

- *Repeatable Read:* Read locks and write locks are acquired. This isolation level doesn't permit dirty reads or unrepeatable reads. It also doesn't a acquire range lock, which means it permits phantom reads. A read lock prevents any write locks from being acquired by other concurrent transaction. This level can still have some scalability issues.

- *Read Committed:* Read locks are acquired and released immediately, and write locks are acquired and released at the end of the transaction. Dirty reads aren't allowed in this isolation level, but unrepeatable reads and phantom reads are permitted. By using the combination of persistent context and versioning, you can achieve the Repeatable Read isolation level.

- *Read Uncommitted:* Changes made by one transaction are made visible to other transactions before they're committed. All types of reads, including dirty reads, are permitted. This isolation level isn't recommended for use. If a transaction's uncommitted changes are rolled back, other concurrent transactions may be seriously affected.

Table 13-5. Summarizing the Reads That Are Permitted for Various Isolation Levels

Isolation level	Dirty Read	Unrepeated Read	Phantom Read
Serializable	-	-	-
Repeatable Read	-	-	Permitted
Read Committed	-	Permitted	Permitted
Read Uncommitted	Permitted	Permitted	Permitted

Every database management system has a default setting for the isolation level. You can change the default isolation level in the DBMS configuration. On JDBC, you can set the isolation level by using a property called `hibernate.connection.isolation`. Hibernate uses the following values to set a particular isolation level:

- 8: Serializable isolation
- 4: Repeatable Read isolation
- 2: Read Committed isolation
- 1: Read Uncommitted isolation

This setting is applicable only when the connection isn't obtained from an application server. In this scenario, you need to change the isolation level in the application server configuration.

Now, let's come back to the case of lost updates described at the beginning of this recipe (also in Table 13-1). You've seen a case where an update made by transaction 1 is lost when transaction 2 commits. Most applications are database connections with Read Committed isolation and use the optimistic concurrency control. One way of implementing optimistic control is to use versioning.

How It Works

Hibernate provides automatic versioning. Each entity can have a version, which can be a number or a timestamp. Hibernate increments the number when the entity is modified. If you're saving with an older version (which is the case for transaction 2 in the lost-update problem), Hibernate compares the versions automatically and throws an exception.

To add a version number to an entity, you add a property called `version` of type `int` or `Integer`:

```
public class BookCh2 {
        private long isbn;
        private String name;
        private Date publishDate;
        private int price;
        private int version;
}
```

In the `book.xml` configuration file, you add the `version` element. Note that the `version` element must be placed immediately after the `id` element:

```
<hibernate-mapping package="com.hibernaterecipes.chapter2" auto-import="false" >
        <import class="BookCh2" rename="bkch2"/>
        <class name="BookCh2" table="BOOK" dynamic-insert="true" dynamic-update="true"
schema="BOOK">
                <id name="isbn"  column="isbn" type="long">
                        <generator class="hilo">
                        </generator>
                </id>
                <version name="version" access="field" column="version"></version>
                <property name="name" type="string" column="BOOK_NAME" />
                <property name="publishDate" type="date" column="PUBLISH_DATE" />
                <property name="price" type="int" column="PRICE" />
        </class>
</hibernate-mapping>
```

A new column called `version` is created in the `BOOK` table. Using JPA, you add the `version` variable to the `Book` class and annotate it with the `Version` element:

```
@Entity (name="bkch2")
@org.hibernate.annotations.Entity(dynamicInsert = true, dynamicUpdate = true)
@Table        (name="BOOK")
public class BookCh2 {

        @Id
        @GeneratedValue (strategy=GenerationType.TABLE)
        @Column (name="ISBN")
        private long isbn;

        @Version
        @Column (name="version")
        private Integer version;

        @Column (name="book_Name")
        private String bookName;

        /*@Column (name="publisher_code")
        String publisherCode;*/

        @Column (name="publish_date")
        private Date publishDate;

        @Column (name="price")
        private Long price;
        // getters and setters
}
```

You can also use timestamps to version by adding a variable of type `Date`:

```
public class BookCh2 implements Serializable{
        private long isbn;
        private String name;
        private Date publishDate;
        private int price;
        private Date timestamp;
        // getters and setters
}
```

The XML mapping file has a `timestamp` element as shown here:

```
<hibernate-mapping package="com.hibernaterecipes.chapter2" auto-import="false" >
        <import class="BookCh2" rename="bkch2"/>
        <class name="BookCh2" table="BOOK" dynamic-insert="true" dynamic-update="true"
schema="BOOK">
                <id name="isbn"  column="isbn" type="long">
                        <generator class="hilo">
                        </generator>
                </id>
                <timestamp name="timestamp" access="field" column="timestamp"></timestamp>
                <property name="name" type="string" column="BOOK_NAME" />
                <property name="publishDate" type="date" column="PUBLISH_DATE" />
                <property name="price" type="int" column="PRICE" />
        </class>
</hibernate-mapping>
```

You can also implement versioning without a version or timestamp by using the attribute `optimistic-lock` on the class mapping. It works when the entity is retrieved and modified in the same session. It doesn't work with detached objects. If you need to use optimistic concurrency control with detached objects, you must use a version or timestamp:

```
<hibernate-mapping package="com.hibernaterecipes.chapter2" auto-import="false" >
        <import class="BookCh2" rename="bkch2"/>
        <class name="BookCh2" table="BOOK" dynamic-insert="true" dynamic-update="true"
schema="BOOK" optimistic-lock="all">
                <id name="isbn"  column="isbn" type="long">
                        <generator class="hilo">
                        </generator>
                </id>
                <property name="name" type="string" column="BOOK_NAME" />
                <property name="publishDate" type="date" column="PUBLISH_DATE" />
                <property name="price" type="int" column="PRICE" />
        </class>
</hibernate-mapping>
```

This isn't a popular option because it's slower and is complex to implement. In addition, JPA does not standardize this technique. So, if you need to use optimistic locking in JPA, you must use Hibernate's annotations, as shown here:

```
@Entity (name="bkch2")
@org.hibernate.annotations.Entity
```

```
(dynamicInsert = true, dynamicUpdate = true,
                optimisticLock=org.hibernate.annotations.OptimisticLockType.ALL)
@Table        (name="BOOK")
public class BookCh2 {

        @Id
        @GeneratedValue (strategy=GenerationType.TABLE)
        @Column (name="ISBN")
        private long isbn;

        @Version
        @Column (name="version")
        private Integer version;

        @Column (name="book_Name")
        private String bookName;

        /*@Column (name="publisher_code")
        String publisherCode;*/

        @Column (name="publish_date")
        private Date publishDate;

        @Column (name="price")
        private Long price;
        // getters and setters
}
```

13.4 Using Pessimistic Concurrency Control

Problem

How do you implement pessimistic concurrency control in your application to save the **book** entity?

Solution

Most applications have Read Committed as the isolation level. This isolation level permits unrepeatable reads, which isn't desirable. One way to avoid unrepeatable reads is to implement versioning in the application. This upgrading of the isolation level from Read Committed to Repeatable Read comes with scalability issues. So, as an application developer, you may not want to make an application-wide upgrade to versioning—you may just want to upgrade the isolation level on a per-unit basis. To do so, Hibernate provides the lock() method in the Hibernate **session** object.

How It Works

The following code demonstrates how an unrepeatable read can happen. You first get the book using `session.get()`, and then you use a query to read the name of the book. If an update happens between these two calls to the book's record in the database by a concurrent transaction, you have a case of unrepeatable reads:

```
Session session = getSession();
Transaction tx = null;
tx = session.beginTransaction();
BookCh2 book = (BookCh2)session.get(BookCh2.class, new Long(32769));
String name = (String) session.createQuery("select b.name from bkch2 b where b.isbn =
:isbn")
                .setParameter("isbn", book.getIsbn()).uniqueResult();
System.out.println("BOOk's Name- "+name);
tx.commit();
session.close();
```

You can use `session.lock` to upgrade the isolation level. The previous code is updated as follows:

```
Session session = getSession();
Transaction tx = null;
tx = session.beginTransaction();
BookCh2 book = (BookCh2)session.get(BookCh2.class, new Long(32769));
session.lock(book, LockMode.UPGRADE);
String name = (String) session.createQuery("select b.name from bkch2 b where b.isbn =
:isbn")
                .setParameter("isbn", book.getIsbn()).uniqueResult();
System.out.println("BOOk's Name- "+name);
tx.commit();
session.close();
```

Or you can directly call

```
BookCh2 book = (BookCh2)session.get(BookCh2.class, new Long(32769),LockMode.UPGRADE);
```

`LockMode.UPGRADE` creates a lock on the specific book record in the database. Now, other concurrent transactions can't modify the book record.

Hibernate supports the following lock modes:

- `LockMode.NONE`: This is the default lock mode. If an object is requested with this lock mode, a `READ` lock is obtained if it's necessary to read the state from the database, rather than pull it from a cache.

- `LockMode.READ`: In this lock mode, an object is read from the database. The object's version is checked, just as in memory.

- `LockMode.UPGRADE`: Objects loaded in this lock mode are materialized using an SQL `select ... for update`. It's equivalent to `LockModeType.READ` in Java Persistence.

- `LockMode.UPGRADE_NOWAIT`: This lock mode attempts to obtain an upgrade lock using an Oracle-style `select for update nowait`. The semantics of this lock mode, once obtained, are the same as `UPGRADE`.

- `LockMode.FORCE`: This lock mode results in a forced version increment. It's equivalent to `LockModeType.Write` in Java Persistence

- `LockMode.WRITE`: A `WRITE` lock is obtained when an object is updated or inserted. This lock mode is for internal use only and isn't a valid mode for `load()` or `lock()`.

Summary

In this chapter, you've seen how to manage transactions programmatically. You've learned to use the Hibernate Transaction API and the Java Transaction API for transaction demarcation.

Optimistic concurrency control and pessimistic concurrency control are the two approaches used to achieve concurrency control. Optimistic concurrency control involves using either a version or a timestamp to maintain the version as a database column. Pessimistic control is used on a per-transaction basis and is achieved by using `session.lock()` with a lock mode of `UPGRADE` or `UPGRADE_NOWAIT`.

CHAPTER 14

■ ■ ■

Web Applications

Software engineers use layering to break down complex applications or systems. *Layering* is the organization of code into separate functional components that interact in some sequential and hierarchical way. Each layer sits on top of another layer and usually interacts only with the layers that are immediately above and below it. Each layer can be considered a single coherent component that can be used to provide many high-level services. You can work on each layer without knowing the details of other layers. By keeping the dependency between layers at a minimum, it's easy to refractor or replace single layer without affecting all the other layers. Adding too many layers can have an impact on performance.

Patterns are used to create layers and add structure to each layer. Popular patterns include the Model-View-Controller (MVC) pattern, Singleton pattern, Factory pattern, Observer pattern, and Decorator pattern, among many others. MVC is without doubt the most popular pattern used to create layered web applications. MVC splits code into three distinct components: data-access code, business-logic code, and presentation code (see Figure 14-1). By classifying code into these three layers, you achieve decoupling between the layers. Decoupling makes it easier to maintain one layer without requiring you to change other layers. The direction of dependencies is very important: the model doesn't depend on view/presentation or controller. If you're working in the model, you're unaware of the view.

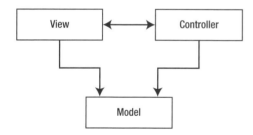

Figure 14-1. The Model-View-Controller pattern splits code into three distinct roles

This chapter demonstrates how to build a web application with this model in mind.

14.1 Creating a Controller for the Bookshop Web Application

Problem

How do you create a simple web application that uses a database as the persistent store?

Solution

To access a web application, you need to deploy it. Web applications are deployed on an application server. Common application servers include WebLogic, WebSphere, JBoss, and Tomcat. In this recipe, you install and deploy on a Tomcat server.

How It Works

Tomcat is an open source application server for running J2EE web applications. You can go to `http://tomcat.apache.org/` and download Tomcat 5.5. Install it into a folder called `C:\Tomcat`. Note that during the installation, you need to specify the Java Development Kit (JDK) installation path, not the Java Runtime Environment (JRE).

Creating a Dynamic Web Project

To develop a web application, you first create a dynamic web project `BookShopWeb` in Eclipse Web Tools Platform (WTP). To do so, select File ▶ New ▶ Dynamic Web Project as shown in Figure 14-2.

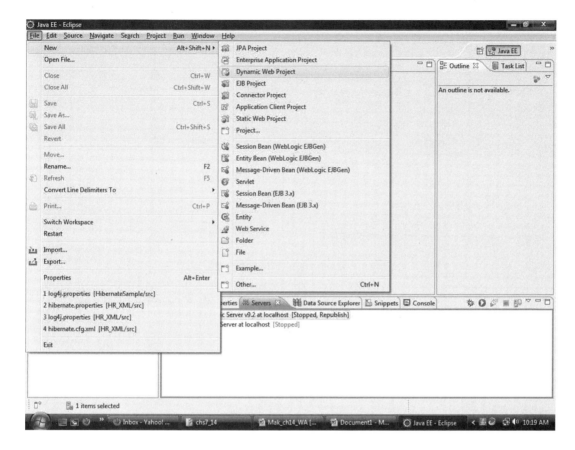

Figure 14-2. Create a dynamic web project in the Eclipse IDE

A wizard opens, in which you create your dynamic web project. For the project name, enter **BookShopWeb**. Use the default project directory, and choose Apache Tomcat as the target runtime (see Figure 14-3). Click the Finish button.

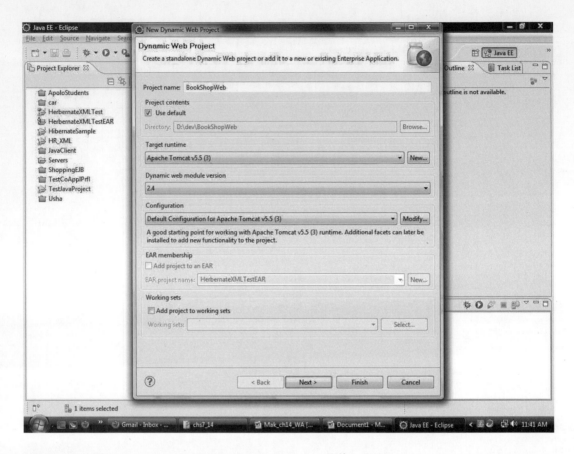

Figure 14-3. *The New Dynamic Web Project wizard in the Eclipse IDE*

You need to configure an Apache Tomcat v5.5 runtime environment for this application. After you finish the wizard, copy the following jars to the `WebContent/WEB-INF/lib` directory. They're added to your project's `CLASSPATH` automatically:

```
${Hibernate_Install_Dir}/hibernate3.jar
${Hibernate_Install_Dir}/lib/antlr.jar
${Hibernate_Install_Dir}/lib/asm.jar
${Hibernate_Install_Dir}/lib/asm-attrs.jars
${Hibernate_Install_Dir}/lib/cglib.jar
${Hibernate_Install_Dir}/lib/commons-collections.jar
${Hibernate_Install_Dir}/lib/commons-logging.jar
${Hibernate_Install_Dir}/lib/dom4j.jar
${Hibernate_Install_Dir}/lib/ehcache.jar
${Hibernate_Install_Dir}/lib/jta.jar
${Hibernate_Install_Dir}/lib/log4j.jar
${Hsqldb_Install_Dir}/lib/hsqldb.jar
${Tomcat_Install_Dir}/common/lib/servlet-api.jar
```

```
${Tomcat_Install_Dir}/webapps/jsp-examples/WEB-INF/lib/standard.jar
${Tomcat_Install_Dir}/webapps/jsp-examples/WEB-INF/lib/jstl.jar
```

The web application you develop in this chapter only deals with the Book, Publisher, and Chapter persistent classes. Copy these three classes and the related mappings to your new project. Don't forget to copy the hibernate.cfg.xml, log4j.properties, and ehcache.xml files as well.

Configuring the Connection Pool

In previous recipes, you established a database connection each time a session was created and closed it at the end of the session. Because creating a physical database connection is very time consuming, you should use a connection pool to reuse your connections, especially for a multiuser environment.

As a web application server, Tomcat supports connection pooling. To configure a connection pool in Tomcat, you need to first copy the following JDBC driver to the ${Tomcat_Install_Dir}/common/lib directory:

```
${Hsqldb_Install_Dir}/lib/hsqldb.jar
```

After the first launch of Tomcat from WTP, a new project called Servers is created. You can modify the settings there for your Tomcat runtime. Open the server.xml configuration file, and locate the context BookShopWeb. You create a connection pool for this context by adding the following resource definition inside the <Context> node:

```
<Resource name="jdbc/BookShopDB"
type="javax.sql.DataSource"
driverClassName="org.hsqldb.jdbcDriver"
url="jdbc:hsqldb:hsql://localhost/BookShopDB"
username="sa"
password=""
maxActive="5"
maxIdle="2" />
```

Now the connection pool is ready to be used. You modify the hibernate.cfg.xml file to use this connection pool instead of creating a database connection each time. For the connection.datasource property, you provide the Java Naming and Directory Interface (JNDI) name of the connection pool configured with Tomcat. Also notice that you need to add the namespace java:/comp/env/ to the JNDI name:

```
<hibernate-configuration>
<session-factory>
<property name="connection.driver_class">org.hsqldb.jdbcDriver</property>
<property name="connection.url">jdbc:hsqldb:hsql://localhost/BookShopDB</property>
<property name="connection.username">sa</property>
<property name="connection.password"></property>
<property name="connection.datasource">java:/comp/env/jdbc/BookShopDB</property>
<property name="dialect">org.hibernate.dialect.HSQLDialect</property>
...
</session-factory>
</hibernate-configuration>
```

Developing an Online Bookshop

In this section, you implement the web-based online bookshop application using the typical MVC pattern. The purpose of this application is to demonstrate how to use Hibernate in a web environment, so it doesn't use any web frameworks such as Struts, Spring, and Tapestry. You implement it with JSPs, servlets, and taglibs, which is the standard way of developing J2EE web applications.

Creating a Global Session Factory

For an application using Hibernate as an object/relational mapping (ORM) framework, you create a global session factory and access it through a particular interface. Here, you use a static variable to store the session factory. It's initialized in a **static** block when this class is loaded for the first time:

```
public class HibernateUtil {

  private static final SessionFactory sessionFactory;

  static {
    try {
    Configuration configuration = new Configuration().configure();
    sessionFactory = configuration.buildSessionFactory();
    } catch (Throwable e) {
      e.printStackTrace();
    throw new ExceptionInInitializerError(e);
    }
  }

  public static SessionFactory getSessionFactory() {
    return sessionFactory;
  }
}
```

Listing Persistent Objects

The first function you implement for the online bookshop lists all the books available. You create a servlet **BookListServlet** to act as the controller and forward to the view **booklist.jsp** when you finish querying the books. Note that the list of books you get from the database is set as an attribute on the **request** object with the method **setAttribute()**. JSPs have implicit variables that help simplify code: the available variables are **request**, **response**, **out**, **session**, **application**, **config**, **pageContext**, and **page**. You set the list of books you receive from the database to the **books** attribute. And in the JSP, you read from this attribute:

```
public class BookListServlet extends HttpServlet {

  protected void doGet(HttpServletRequest request, HttpServletResponse response)
      throws ServletException, IOException {
    SessionFactory factory = HibernateUtil.getSessionFactory();
    Session session = factory.openSession();
    try {
```

```
      Query query = session.createQuery("from Book");
      List books = query.list();
      request.setAttribute("books", books);
    } finally {
      session.close();
    }
    RequestDispatcher dispatcher = request.getRequestDispatcher("booklist.jsp");
    dispatcher.forward(request, response);
  }
}
```

The view booklist.jsp is very simple. Its responsibility is to display the books queried by the servlet in a HTML table. At the moment, you only display the simple properties of books. Showing association properties is discussed later:

```
<%@ taglib prefix="c" uri="http://java.sun.com/jstl/core_rt" %>
<html>
<head>
<title>Book List</title>
</head>
<body>
<table border="1">
<th>ISBN</th>
<th>Name</th>
<th>Publish Date</th>
<th>Price</th>
<c:forEach var="book" items="${books}">
<tr>
<td>${book.isbn}</td>
<td>${book.name}</td>
<td>${book.publishDate}</td>
<td>${book.price}</td>
</tr>
</c:forEach>
</table>
</body>
</html>
```

Figure 14-4 shows the list of books in the bookshop.

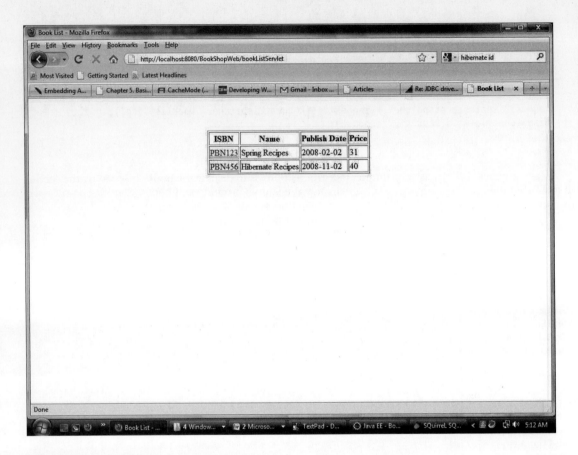

Figure 14-4. List of books in the bookshop

Updating Persistent Objects

Next, you allow administrators to update book details by clicking a hyperlink on a book's ISBN. This triggers another servlet, `BookEditServlet`, to display a form for editing, passing in the identifier of a book:

```
<%@ taglib prefix="c" uri="http://java.sun.com/jstl/core_rt" %>
<html>
<head>
<title>Book List</title>
</head>
<body>
<table border="1">
<th>ISBN</th>
<th>Name</th>
<th>Publish Date</th>
<th>Price</th>
```

```
<c:forEach var="book" items="${books}">
<tr>
<td><a href="BookEditServlet?bookId=${book.id}">${book.isbn}</a></td>
<td>${book.name}</td>
<td>${book.publishDate}</td>
<td>${book.price}</td>
</tr>
</c:forEach>
</table>
</body>
</html>
```

The doGet() method of BookEditServlet is called when the user clicks the hyperlink on the ISBN. You load the book object from database according to the identifier passed in, and then you forward it to the view bookedit.jsp to show the form (see Figure 14-5):

```
public class BookEditServlet extends HttpServlet {

  protected void doGet(HttpServletRequest request, HttpServletResponse response)
      throws ServletException, IOException {
    String bookId= request.getParameter("bookId");
    SessionFactory factory = HibernateUtil.getSessionFactory();
    Session session = factory.openSession();
    try {
      Book book = (Book) session.get(Book.class, Integer.parseInt(bookId));
      request.setAttribute("book", book);
    } finally {
      session.close();
    }
    RequestDispatcher dispatcher = request.getRequestDispatcher("bookedit.jsp");
    dispatcher.forward(request, response);
  }
}
```

The view bookedit.jsp shows a book's details in a series of form fields:

```
<%@ taglib prefix="c" uri="http://java.sun.com/jstl/core_rt" %>
<%@ taglib prefix="fmt" uri="http://java.sun.com/jstl/fmt_rt" %>
<html>
<head>
<title>Book Edit</title>
</head>
<body>
<form method="post">
<table>
<tr>
<td>ISBN</td>
<td><input type="text" name="isbn" value="${book.isbn}"></td>
</tr>
<tr>
<td>Name</td>
```

```html
<td><input type="text" name="name" value="${book.name}"></td>
</tr>
<tr>
<td>Publish Date</td>
<td>
<input type="text" name="publishDate"
value="<fmt:formatDate value="${book.publishDate}" pattern="yyyy/MM/dd"/>">
</td>
</tr>
<tr>
<td>Price</td>
<td><input type="text" name="price" value="${book.price}"></td>
</tr>
<tr>
<td colspan="2">
<input type="hidden" name="bookId" value="${book. id}">
<input type="submit" value="Submit"></td>
</tr>
</table>
</form>
</body>
</html>
```

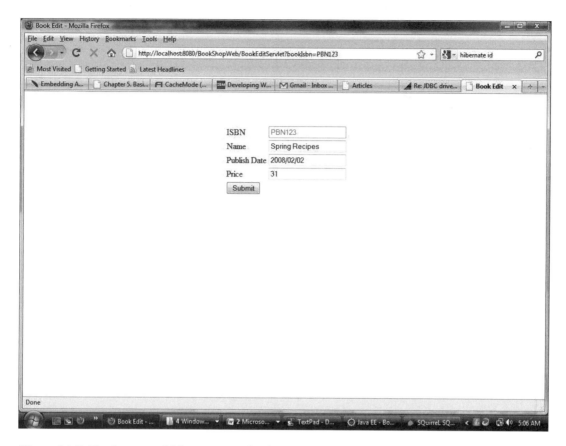

Figure 14-5. The form on which users can edit the properties of a book

When the Submit button is clicked, the `doPost()` method of `BookEditServlet` is called to handle the form submission. You first load the `book` object from the database and then update its properties according to the request parameters. The user is then redirected to the book list page (see Figure 14-6):

```
public class BookEditServlet extends HttpServlet {
  ...
  protected void doPost(HttpServletRequest request, HttpServletResponse response)
     throws ServletException, IOException {

    String bookId = request.getParameter("bookId ");
    String isbn = request.getParameter("isbn");
    String name = request.getParameter("name");
    String publishDate = request.getParameter("publishDate");
    String price = request.getParameter("price");
    SessionFactory factory = HibernateUtil.getSessionFactory();
    Session session = factory.openSession();
    Transaction tx = null;
```

```
    try {
      tx = session.beginTransaction();
      Book book = (Book) session.get(Book.class, bookId);
      book.setIsbn(isbn);
      book.setName(name);
      book.setPublishDate(parseDate(publishDate));
      book.setPrice(Integer.parseInt(price));
      session.update(book);
      tx.commit();

    } catch (HibernateException e) {
      if (tx != null) tx.rollback();
      throw e;
    } finally {
      session.close();
    }

    response.sendRedirect("bookListServlet");
  }

  private Date parseDate(String date) {
    try {
      return new SimpleDateFormat("yyyy/MM/dd").parse(date);
    } catch (ParseException e) {
      return null;
    }
  }
}
```

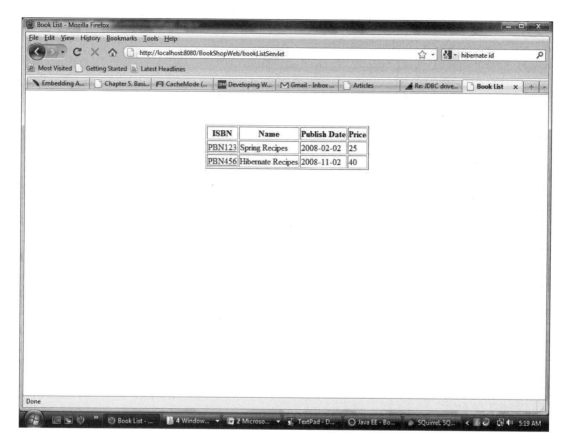

Figure 14-6. The list of books after the price of the book Spring Recipes *has been updated*

Creating Persistent Objects

You should also let users create a new book. You first create a hyperlink on the book list page to add a new book. The target servlet is the same as for updating, but there is no book identifier to pass in:

```
<%@ taglib prefix="c" uri="http://java.sun.com/jstl/core_rt" %>
<html>
<head>
<title>Book List</title>
</head>
<body>
<table border="1">
<th>ISBN</th>
<th>Name</th>
<th>Publish Date</th>
<th>Price</th>
```

```
<c:forEach var="book" items="${books}">
<tr>
<td>${book.isbn}</td>
<td>${book.name}</td>
<td>${book.publishDate}</td>
<td>${book.price}</td>
</tr>
</c:forEach>
<tr ><td colspan="4">
<a href="BookEditServlet">Add Book</a>
</td></tr>
</table>
</body>
</html>
```

The process of adding a new book is very similar to updating an existing book (see Figure 14-7). You can reuse the servlet BookEditServlet by checking whether the book identifier(isbn) is null. If it is, the action should be add; otherwise, it should be update. The generation of an identifier depends on the strategy you pick: you can let Hibernate generate one or have the application generate the identifier itself. The session.saveOrUpdate() method is very helpful for distinguishing the correct action:

```
public class BookEditServlet extends HttpServlet {

  protected void doGet(HttpServletRequest request, HttpServletResponse response)
      throws ServletException, IOException {

    String bookId = request.getParameter("bookId");

    if (bookId != null) {
      SessionFactory factory = HibernateUtil.getSessionFactory();
      Session session = factory.openSession();
      try {
        Book book = (Book) session.get(Book.class, Integer.parseInt(bookId));
        request.setAttribute("book", book);
      } finally {
        session.close();
      }
    }

    RequestDispatcher dispatcher = request.getRequestDispatcher("bookedit.jsp");
    dispatcher.forward(request, response);
  }

  protected void doPost(HttpServletRequest request, HttpServletResponse response)
      throws ServletException, IOException {

    String bookId = request.getParameter("bookId");
    String isbn = request.getParameter("isbn");
    String name = request.getParameter("name");
    String publishDate = request.getParameter("publishDate");
    String price = request.getParameter("price");
```

```java
        SessionFactory factory = HibernateUtil.getSessionFactory();
        Session session = factory.openSession();
        Transaction tx = null;

        try {
          tx = session.beginTransaction();
          Book book = new Book();
          if (bookId!=null && !bookId.equals("")) {
            book = (Book) session.get(Book.class, bookId);
          }
          book.setIsbn(isbn);
          book.setName(name);
          book.setPublishDate(parseDate(publishDate));
          book.setPrice(Integer.parseInt(price));
          session.saveOrUpdate(book);
          tx.commit();
        } catch (HibernateException e) {
          if (tx != null) tx.rollback();
          throw e;
        } finally {
          session.close();
        }

        response.sendRedirect("bookListServlet");
      }
    }
```

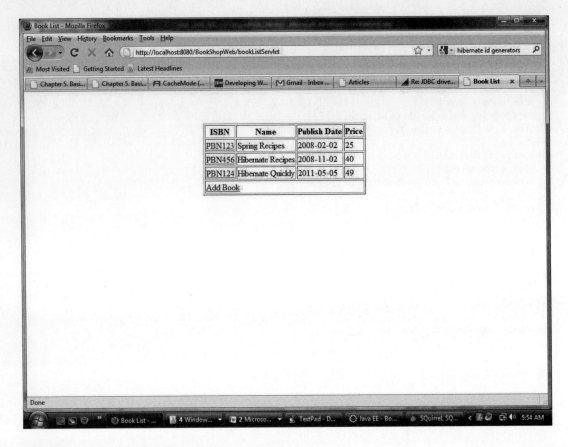

Figure 14-7. The list of books after adding a new book

Deleting Persistent Objects

The last book-management function allows the user to delete a book. You add a hyperlink to the last column of each row:

```
<%@ taglib prefix="c" uri="http://java.sun.com/jstl/core_rt" %>
<html>
<head>
<title>Book List</title>
</head>
<body>
<table border="1">
Page 10 of 10
<th>ISBN</th>
<th>Name</th>
<th>Publish Date</th>
```

```
<th>Price</th>
<c:forEach var="book" items="${books}">
<tr>
<td>${book.isbn}</td>
<td>${book.name}</td>
<td>${book.publishDate}</td>
<td>${book.price}</td>
<td><a href="BookDeleteServlet?bookId=${book.isbn}">Delete</a></td>
</tr>
</c:forEach>
</table>
<a href="BookEditServlet">Add Book</a>
</body>
</html>
```

To delete a book from database, you must load it through the session first. This is because Hibernate needs to handle the cascading of associations. You may worry about the overhead of loading the object prior to deletion. But don't forget that you're caching your book objects in the second-level cache, so there isn't much impact on performance (see Figure 14-8):

```
public class BookDeleteServlet extends HttpServlet {

    protected void doGet(HttpServletRequest request, HttpServletResponse response)
        throws ServletException, IOException {

        String bookId = request.getParameter("bookId");
        SessionFactory factory = HibernateUtil.getSessionFactory();
        Session session = factory.openSession();
        Transaction tx = null;
        try {
            tx = session.beginTransaction();
            Book book = (Book) session.get(Book.class, bookId);
            session.delete(book);
            tx.commit();
        } catch (HibernateException e) {
            if (tx != null) tx.rollback();
            throw e;
        } finally {
            session.close();
        }
        response.sendRedirect("bookListServlet");
    }
}
```

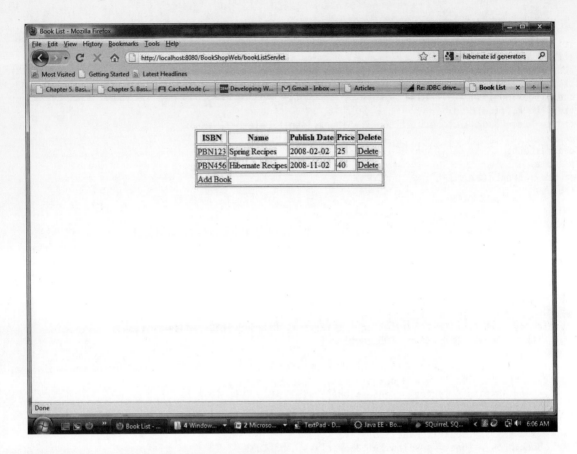

Figure 14-8. The list of books with the Delete link

14.2 Creating a Data-Access Layer

Problem

What is a data-access layer? Why do you need a data-access layer, when the previous recipe appears to work fine? How do you add a data-access layer to the previous recipe?

Solution

A Data Access Object (DAO) layer abstracts the access to data from a persistent store. The persistent store can be a database or a file system. The DAO layer hides this persistent store from the application. A DAO layer may return a reference to objects instead of rows of fields from the database, which allows for a higher level of abstraction. It implements the mechanism to work with a data source. The business layer uses the interfaces provided by the DAO to interact with this data source.

How It Works

Let's see how to create a data-access layer.

Organizing Data Access in Data-Access Objects

Until now, you've put Hibernate-related code inside the servlets. In other words, you've mixed the presentation logic and the data-access logic. This is absolutely not a good practice. In a multitier application, the presentation logic and data-access logic should be separated for better reusability and maintainability. The DAO design pattern encapsulates the data-access logic. It manages the connection to the data source to store, retrieve, and update data. A good practice when using this pattern is to create one DAO for each persistent class and put all the data operations related to this class inside this DAO:

```
public class HibernateBookDao {

  public Book findById(Integer id) {

    SessionFactory factory = HibernateUtil.getSessionFactory();
    Session session = factory.openSession();
    try {
      Book book = (Book) session.get(Book.class, id);
      return book;
    } finally {
      session.close();
    }
  }

  public void saveOrUpdate(Book book) {

    SessionFactory factory = HibernateUtil.getSessionFactory();
    Session session = factory.openSession();
    Transaction tx = null;

    try {
      tx = session.beginTransaction();
      session.saveOrUpdate(book);
      tx.commit();
    } catch (HibernateException e) {
      if (tx != null) tx.rollback();
      throw e;
    } finally {
      session.close();
    }
  }

  public void delete(Book book) {
```

```
    SessionFactory factory = HibernateUtil.getSessionFactory();
    Session session = factory.openSession();
    Transaction tx = null;

    try {
      tx = session.beginTransaction();
      session.delete(book);
      tx.commit();
    } catch (HibernateException e) {
      if (tx != null) tx.rollback();
      throw e;
    } finally {
      session.close();
    }
  }

  public List findAll() {

    SessionFactory factory = HibernateUtil.getSessionFactory();
    Session session = factory.openSession();
    try {
      Query query = session.createQuery("from Book");
      List books = query.list();
      return books;
    } finally {
      session.close();
    }
  }

  public Book findByIsbn(String isbn) {
    ...
  }

  public List findByPriceRange(int fromPrice, int toPrice) {
    ...
  }
}
```

According to object-oriented principles, you should program to the interface rather than to the implementation. So, you extract a BookDao interface and allow implementation other than the Hibernate one. The clients of this DAO should only know about the BookDao interface and needn't be concerned about the implementation:

```
public interface BookDao {

  public Book findById(Long id);
  public void saveOrUpdate(Book book);
  public void delete(Book book);
  public List findAll();
  public Book findByIsbn(String isbn);
```

```
    public List findByPriceRange(int fromPrice, int toPrice);

}

public class HibernateBookDao implements BookDao {
    ...
}
```

Using Generic Data-Access Objects

Because different DAOs share common operations (such as findById, saveOrUpdate, delete, and findAll), you should extract a generic DAO for these operations to avoid code duplication:

```
public interface GenericDao {

    public Object findById(Long id);
    public void saveOrUpdate(Object book);
    public void delete(Object book);
    public List findAll();
}
```

Then, you create an abstract class HibernateGenericDao to implement this interface. You need to generalize the persistent class as a parameter of the constructor. Different subclasses pass in their corresponding persistent classes for concrete DAOs. For the findAll() method, you use a Criteria query because it can accept a class as a query target:

```
public abstract class HibernateGenericDao implements GenericDao {

    private Class persistentClass;

    public HibernateGenericDao(Class persistentClass) {

        this.persistentClass = persistentClass;
    }

    public Object findById(Long id) {

        SessionFactory factory = HibernateUtil.getSessionFactory();
        Session session = factory.openSession();
        try {
            Object object = (Object) session.get(persistentClass, id);
            return object;
        } finally {
            session.close();
        }
    }

    public void saveOrUpdate(Object object) {

        SessionFactory factory = HibernateUtil.getSessionFactory();
```

```
      Session session = factory.openSession();
      Transaction tx = null;
      try {
        tx = session.beginTransaction();
        session.saveOrUpdate(object);
        tx.commit();
      } catch (HibernateException e) {
        if (tx != null) tx.rollback();
        throw e;
      } finally {
        session.close();
      }
    }

    public void delete(Object object) {

      SessionFactory factory = HibernateUtil.getSessionFactory();
      Session session = factory.openSession();
      Transaction tx = null;
      try {
        tx = session.beginTransaction();
        session.delete(object);
        tx.commit();
      } catch (HibernateException e) {
        if (tx != null) tx.rollback();
        throw e;
      } finally {
        session.close();
      }
    }

    public List findAll() {

      SessionFactory factory = HibernateUtil.getSessionFactory();
      Session session = factory.openSession();
      try {
        Criteria criteria = session.createCriteria(persistentClass);
        List objects = criteria.list();
        return objects;
      } finally {
        session.close();
      }
    }
}
```

For the Book persistent class, you can simplify BookDao and HibernateBookDao as follows:

```
public interface BookDao extends GenericDao {

  public Book findByIsbn(String isbn);
  public List findByPriceRange(int fromPrice, int toPrice);
```

```
}

public class HibernateBookDao extends HibernateGenericDao implements BookDao {

  public HibernateBookDao() {
    super(Book.class);
  }

  public Book findByIsbn(String isbn) {
    ...
  }

  public List findByPriceRange(int fromPrice, int toPrice) {
    ...
  }
}
```

Using a Factory to Centralize DAO Retrieval

Another problem when you use DAOs concerns their retrieval. Keep in mind that the creation of DAOs should be centralized for ease of implementation switching. Here, you apply an object-oriented design pattern called Abstract Factory to create a DaoFactory for the central point of DAO creation:

```
public abstract class DaoFactory {

  private static DaoFactory instance = new HibernateDaoFactory();

  public static DaoFactory getInstance() {
    return instance;
  }

  public abstract BookDao getBookDao();
}

public class HibernateDaoFactory extends DaoFactory {

  public BookDao getBookDao() {
    return new HibernateBookDao();
  }
}
```

Now that the DAOs and factory are ready, you can simplify your servlets as follows. Note that there is no longer any Hibernate-related code in the servlets:

```
public class BookListServlet extends HttpServlet {

  protected void doGet(HttpServletRequest request, HttpServletResponse response)
      throws ServletException, IOException {
    BookDao dao = DaoFactory.getInstance().getBookDao();
```

```
      List books = dao.findAll();
      request.setAttribute("books", books);
      RequestDispatcher dispatcher = request.getRequestDispatcher("booklist.jsp");
      dispatcher.forward(request, response);
  }
}

public class BookEditServlet extends HttpServlet {

  protected void doGet(HttpServletRequest request, HttpServletResponse response)
      throws ServletException, IOException {
    String bookId = request.getParameter("bookId");
    if (bookId != null) {
      BookDao dao = DaoFactory.getInstance().getBookDao();
      Book book = (Book) dao.findById(Long.parseLong(bookId));
      request.setAttribute("book", book);
    }
    RequestDispatcher dispatcher = request.getRequestDispatcher("bookedit.jsp");
    dispatcher.forward(request, response);
  }

  protected void doPost(HttpServletRequest request, HttpServletResponse response)
      throws ServletException, IOException {

    String bookId = request.getParameter("bookId");
    String isbn = request.getParameter("isbn");
    String name = request.getParameter("name");
    String publishDate = request.getParameter("publishDate");
    String price = request.getParameter("price");
    BookDao dao = DaoFactory.getInstance().getBookDao();
    Book book = new Book();
    if (!bookId.equals("")) {
      book = (Book) dao.findById(Long.parseLong(bookId));
    }
    book.setIsbn(isbn);
    book.setName(name);
    book.setPublishDate(parseDate(publishDate));
    book.setPrice(Integer.parseInt(price));
    dao.saveOrUpdate(book);
    response.sendRedirect("bookListServlet");
  }
}

public class BookDeleteServlet extends HttpServlet {

  protected void doGet(HttpServletRequest request, HttpServletResponse response)
      throws ServletException, IOException {

    String bookId = request.getParameter("bookId");
    BookDao dao = DaoFactory.getInstance().getBookDao();
    Book book = (Book) dao.findById(Long.parseLong(bookId));
```

```
        dao.delete(book);
        response.sendRedirect("bookListServlet");
    }
}
```

Navigating Lazy Associations

Suppose you want to include the publisher and chapter information on the book-editing page, but for viewing only:

```
<%@ taglib prefix="c" uri="http://java.sun.com/jstl/core_rt" %>
<%@ taglib prefix="fmt" uri="http://java.sun.com/jstl/fmt_rt" %>
<html>
<head>
<title>Book Edit</title>
</head>
<body>
<form method="post">
<table>
...
<tr>
<td>Publisher</td>
<td>${book.publisher.name}</td>
</tr>
<tr>
<td>Chapters</td>
<td>
<c:forEach var="chapter" items="${book.chapters}">${chapter.title}<br></c:forEach>
</td>
</tr>
...
</table>
<input type="hidden" name="bookId" value="${book.id}">
</form>
</body>
</html>
```

Because the two associations are lazy, you get a lazy initialization exception when accessing this page. To avoid this exception, you need to initialize the associations explicitly. To do so, create a new findById() method to distinguish the new association from the original one:

```
public interface BookDao extends GenericDao {
    ...
    public Book findWithPublisherAndChaptersById(Long id);
}

public class HibernateBookDao extends HibernateGenericDao implements BookDao {
    ...
    public Book findWithPublisherAndChaptersById(Long id) {
```

```
    SessionFactory factory = HibernateUtil.getSessionFactory();
    Session session = factory.openSession();
    try {
      Book book = (Book) session.get(Book.class, id);
      Hibernate.initialize(book.getPublisher());
      Hibernate.initialize(book.getChapters());
      return book;
    } finally {
      session.close();
    }
  }
}

public class BookEditServlet extends HttpServlet {
  ...
  protected void doGet(HttpServletRequest request, HttpServletResponse response)
      throws ServletException, IOException {
    String bookId = request.getParameter("bookId");
    if (bookId != null) {
      BookDao dao = DaoFactory.getInstance().getBookDao();
      Book book = (Book)dao.findWithPublisherAndChaptersById(Long.parseLong(bookId));
      request.setAttribute("book", book);
    }
    RequestDispatcher dispatcher = request.getRequestDispatcher("bookedit.jsp");
    dispatcher.forward(request, response);
  }
}
```

Using the Open Session in View Pattern

Is it much trouble to initialize lazy associations explicitly? How can you ask the associations to be initialized on demand—when they're accessed for the first time?

The root cause of the lazy initialization exception is that the session is closed before the lazy association is first accessed during the rendering of the JSP. If you can keep the session open for the entire request-handling process, including servlet processing and JSP rendering, the exception should be able to resolve. To implement this idea, you can use a *filter* in a J2EE web application.

A filter is code that is invoked before the user request reaches the servlet or JSP. You can attach a filter to one or more servlets or JSPs; it looks at the **request** object and validates the request before letting the request pass to the servlet or JSP. You open and close the Hibernate session in a filter such that it's accessible for the entire request-handling process. This is called the Open Session in View pattern.

Hibernate provides the **factory.getCurrentSession()** method to retrieve the current session. A new session is opened the first time you call this method and closed when the transaction is finished, regardless of whether it's committed or rolled back. But what does *current session* mean? You need to tell Hibernate that this is the session bound with the current thread:

```
<hibernate-configuration>
<session-factory>
...
<property name="current_session_context_class">thread</property>
...
```

```
</session-factory>
</hibernate-configuration>

public class HibernateSessionFilter implements Filter {
  ...
  public void doFilter(ServletRequest request, ServletResponse response, FilterChain chain)
      throws IOException, ServletException {

    SessionFactory factory = HibernateUtil.getSessionFactory();
    Session session = factory.getCurrentSession();
    try {
      session.beginTransaction();
      chain.doFilter(request, response);
      session.getTransaction().commit();
    } catch (Throwable e) {
      if (session.getTransaction().isActive()) {
        session.getTransaction().rollback();
      }
      throw new ServletException(e);
    }
  }
}
```

To apply this filter to your application, modify `web.xml` to add the following filter definition and mapping:

```
<filter>
<filter-name>HibernateSessionFilter</filter-name>
<filter-class>com.metaarchit.bookshop.HibernateSessionFilter</filter-class>
</filter>
<filter-mapping>
<filter-name>HibernateSessionFilter</filter-name>
<url-pattern>/*</url-pattern>
</filter-mapping>
```

An arbitrary object can access the current session through the `factory.getCurrentSession()` method. This returns the session bound with the current thread. Note that you can omit the transaction-management code because the transaction is committed by the filter if no exception is thrown:

```
public abstract class HibernateGenericDao implements GenericDao {
  ...
  public Object findById(Long id) {
    SessionFactory factory = HibernateUtil.getSessionFactory();
    Session session = factory.getCurrentSession();
    Object object = (Object) session.get(persistentClass, id);
    return object;
  }

  public void saveOrUpdate(Object object) {
    SessionFactory factory = HibernateUtil.getSessionFactory();
    Session session = factory.getCurrentSession();
```

```
        session.saveOrUpdate(object);
    }

    public void delete(Object object) {
        SessionFactory factory = HibernateUtil.getSessionFactory();
        Session session = factory.getCurrentSession();
        session.delete(object);
    }

    public List findAll() {
        SessionFactory factory = HibernateUtil.getSessionFactory();
        Session session = factory.getCurrentSession();
        Criteria criteria = session.createCriteria(persistentClass);
        List objects = criteria.list();
        return objects;
    }
}
```

Summary

In this chapter, you've learned how to create a web application. You can now see your book list, add books to that list from a web browser, and update book information from the browser. You've also learned the importance of creating multilayered applications and maintaining loose coupling between layers.

Index

■ Special Characters

${Tomcat_Install_Dir}/common/lib directory, 241

% character, 170

■ A

abstract property, 80

ACID (atomic, consistent, isolated, and durable), 219

acquire_increment parameter, 221

Add Library button, 13

addClass( ) method, 14

addEntity( ) method, 198

addjoin( ) method, 198

addResource( ) method, 14

Address class, 95, 104–108, 110, 112

Address entity, 95, 107

Address mapping file, 105

address object, 112

Address property, Customer class, 105, 107–108

ADDRESS table, 105, 109, 111

AddressId foreign key column, 95

addScalar( ) method, 199

aggregate functions, 175–176

aggregation functions, 165–166

and operator, 157

annotation.cfg.xml file, 22

AnnotationConfiguration, 22

annotations, JPA, 52–54

Antlr-2.7.6.jar library, 4

ANYWHERE value, MatchMode class, 171

Apache Tomcat runtime, 239

application variable, 242

applications. *See* web applications

ApplicationServer, 15

areaCode property, 81

areaCode-telNo column, 81

<array> element, 124–125

ArrayList collection, 118, 122

arrays, mapping, 124–125

as keyword, 156, 162

asc property, 132

Assemble method, 82

associations

    caching, 212–213

    fetching, 165

    lazy, navigating, 261

    many-to-one

        problems with, 95–96

solutions for, 96

using lazy initializations on, 95–98, 102–103

using with join tables, 99–102

many-valued. *See* many-valued associations

one-to-one

creating using foreign key, 107–108

creating using join tables, 109–113

primary key, sharing, 104–106

using criteria in, 172–174

atomic, consistent, isolated, and durable (ACID), 219

Atomicity, 219

AUDIO_DISC_3 table, 80

AudioDisc class, 9, 71–73, 76, 79

Auditable class, 190–191

auto-import option, 45–46

AVG aggregate function, 175

avg( ) function, 161, 165

■ B

bag collection, 118

bag type, 118

<bag> element, 61, 115, 118

bags, mapping, 118–121

Base attribute, 123

batch processing

overview, 193

performing batch inserts, 194–195

performing batch updates and deletes, 195–197

begin( ) method, 223

beginPoint property, 158

between method, 170

big_decimal type mapping, 69

big_integer type mapping, 69

binary type mapping, 69

bindings, parameter, 158–160

Book class, 13, 115, 122, 124, 147, 151, 188, 190, 213, 241

Book entity, 5, 99, 102–103

Book mapping class, 189

Book objects, 9, 11, 13–14, 16–17, 25, 27, 97

Book property, 144

BOOK table, 9, 21, 23, 99, 102, 116, 120–121, 140, 175, 198

Book XML file, 149

BOOK_CHAPTER table, 116, 120–121, 146, 150

Book_Id column, 99, 101–102, 140, 146

BOOK_ID foreign key, 144

BOOK_PUBLISHER table, 101–102

BookCh2.java class, 36

BookDAO class, 47

BookDao interface, 256, 258

bookedit.jsp view, 245

BookEditServlet, 244–245, 247, 250

book.getChapters( ) method, 134

book.getPublisher( ) method, 103

Book.hbm.xml file, 13

bookIsbn field, 161

Book.java file, 19

booklist.jsp view, 242–243

bookName field, 161

books attribute, 242

book.setChapters(chapters) method, 139

bookshop application, creating controllers in

configuring connection pools, 241

creating dynamic web projects, 238–241

creating global session factories, 242

creating persistent objects, 249–250

deleting persistent objects, 252–253

developing online bookshops, 242

listing persistent objects, 242–243

updating persistent objects, 244–247

BookShopDB database, 18, 190

BookShopInterceptor class, 191

BookShopWeb project, 238

BookSummary class, 161

Book.xml file, 36–37, 44, 46, 232

boolean type mapping, 69

build.xml file, 29

byte type mapping, 69

■ C

c3p0-0.9.1.jar file, 221

C3P0ConnectionProvider class, 221

<cache> element, 206–207

CacheMode class, 211

CacheMode.GET option, 211

CacheMode.IGNORE option, 211

CacheMode.IGNORE property, 196

CacheMode.NORMAL option, 211

CacheMode.PUT option, 212

CacheMode.REFRESH option, 212

cache.use_query_cache setting, 216

cache.use_second_level_cache attribute, 193

caching, second-level

cache providers, 205–207

cache regions, 207

caching associations, 212–213

caching collections, 213–215

caching queries, 215–217

caching query results, 207

concurrency strategies, 205

configuring, 209–211

overview, 204

using first-level caches, 207–208

calendar type mapping, 69

calendar_date type mapping, 69

cascade option, 104, 107–108, 140–141

cascade="save-update" attribute, 98

<![CDATA[...]]> block, 160

Chapter class, 9, 138, 142–144, 149–152, 213

CHAPTER table, 9, 140

Chapter XML file, 149

CHAPTER_ID column, 146

chapters collection, 140, 144

chapters property, Book class, 116, 118, 122, 124–126, 129

character type mapping, 69

C:\hibernate directory, 13

class hierarchy, mapping entities with tables per, 70–74

class type mapping, 69

<class> tag, 24

clauses

from, 156

select, 161–162

where, 157

clear( ) method, 193–195

close( ) method, 222–223

Cluster scope, 204

collection mapping

arrays, 124–125

bags, 118–121

lists, 122–123

maps, 126–128

sets, 115–121

sorting collections

in databases, 132–133

overview, 128

using natural order, 129

writing comparators, 130–131

using lazy initialization, 133–135

CollectionId annotation, 120–121

CollectionOfElements annotation, 118

collections, caching, 213–215

Column annotation, 118

column attribute, 33

com.metaarchit.bookshop.Book class, 210

com.metaarchit.bookshop.Book.chapters region, 214

com.metaarchit.bookshop.Chapter region, 213

com.metaarchit.bookshop.Publisher region, 213

commit( ) method, 183, 185, 222–223

Commons-collections-3.1.jar library, 4

commons-lang-2.1.jar library, 41

comparators, writing, 130–131

compare( ) method, 130

compareTo( ) method, 129

component class, 67

component element, 49

component mapping, 49–67

adding references in components, 58–60

implementing value types as components

overview, 49

using Hibernate XML mapping, 50–52

using JPA annotations, 52–54

mapping collection of components, 61–64

nesting components, 55–57

using components as keys to maps, 66–67

components

adding references in, 58–60

implementing value types as, 49–54

using Hibernate XML mapping, 50–52

using JPA annotations, 52–54

mapping collection of, 61–64

maps, 66–67

nesting, 55–57

composite keys, creating in Hibernate, 38–42

composite-element tag, 49, 61–62

<composite-id> element, 39

<composite-map-key> tag, 66

CompositeUserType mappings, 87–94

concrete class, mapping entities with table per, 78–80

concurrency

enabling optimistic controls, 228–233

overview, 219

strategies, 205

using pessimistic controls, 234–236

using programmatic transactions in standalone Java applications, 220–223

using programmatic transactions with JTA, 223–227

condition attribute, 109

config subdirectory, 16

config variable, 242

Configuration class, 14

Configuration( ) method, 16

configure( ) methods, 16, 22

connection pools, configuring, 241

connection.datasource property, 241

connection.provider_class parameter, 221

constrained property, 105

Contact class, 51–52, 54, 60, 62

Contact object, 52

Contact table, 64

<Context> node, 241

controllers, creating in bookshop application
    configuring connection pools, 241

    creating dynamic web projects, 238–241

    creating global session factories, 242

    creating persistent objects, 249–250

    deleting persistent objects, 252–253

    developing online bookshops, 242

    listing persistent objects, 242–243

    updating persistent objects, 244–247

controls
    optimistic concurrency, enabling, 228–233

    pessimistic concurrency, 234–236

count( ) function, 161, 165

countryCode business key, 42

countryCode property, 39–40

create method, 23

Create, Read, Update, and Delete (CRUD), 7, 44

CREATE statement, 49

CREATE TABLE query, 120–121, 124, 128

createAlias( ) method, 172–173

createCriteria( ) method, 172–173

createDate property, 190–191

createEntityManagerFactory( ) method, 183

createSQLQuery( ) method, 197

Criteria
    in associations, 172–174

    overview, 168

Criteria API, 168, 170, 172

Criteria class, 168

Criteria interface, 177

Criteria query, 168–169

Criteria statement, 171

Criterion interface, 169

CRUD (Create, Read, Update, and Delete), 7, 44

currency field, 172

currency type mapping, 69

CurrentSessionContext class, 192

custom mapping
    CompositeUserType mappings, 87–94

    mapping entities with table per class hierarchy, 70–74

    mapping entities with table per concrete class, 78–80

    mapping entities with table per subclass, 74–78

    overview, 69

    problems with, 81

    solutions for, 81

Customer class, 39–40, 42, 95, 104–105, 107–108, 110

Customer entity, 95, 107

Customer object, 40–41

customer property, Address class, 106–107, 111–112

CUSTOMER table, 39, 105, 109, 112

Customer type attribute, 95, 112

CUSTOMERADDRESS table, 109, 111

CustomerId object, 41

■ D

DaoFactory class, 259

Data Access Object (DAO)
    organizing in, 255–256

    using factories to centralize retrieval, 259

Data Definition Language (DDL), 5, 78

data filters, 187–190

Data Manipulation Language (DML), 5

data-access layers, creating
    navigating lazy associations, 261

    organizing in data access objects, 255–256

overview, 254

using factories to centralize DAO retrieval, 259

using generic objects, 257–258

using open session in view patterns, 262–264

database management systems (DBMS), 2

Database Name property, 224

database sequences, 35

databases, sorting in, 132–133

Date data type, 232

date type mapping, 69

DB2Dialect, 18

DBMS (database management systems), 2

DDL (Data Definition Language), 5, 78

deepCopy method, 82

DEFAULT FetchMode option, 173

Delete link, 254

delete( ) method, 141, 181, 185

delete operation, 257

DELETE query, 196–197

DELETE statement, 12

delete-orphan option, 141

deleting

batches, 195–197

persistent objects, 185, 252–253

derbyclient.jar file, 7

derbyClient.jar file, 224

Derbyclient.jar library, 4

derby.jar file, 7–8

Derby.jar library, 4

derbynet.jar file, 7

Derbynet.jar library, 4

Derbytools library, 4

derbytools.jar file, 7

desc property, 132

detached objects

merging, 186–187

overview, 180–181

reattaching, 186

dialect property, 18, 30

disableFilter(String filterName) method, 189

Disassemble method, 82

Disc class, 9–10, 71–76, 79–80

Disc_3 class, 79–80

Disc_4 class, 80

DISC_ID primary key, 76

DISC_TYPE column, 73

Discriminator annotation, 73

DiscriminatorColumn annotation, 73

discriminator-value attribute, 73

disjunction( ) method, 171

distinct keyword, 161

DML (Data Manipulation Language), 5

doGet( ) method, 245

Dom4j-1.6.1.jar library, 4

doPost( ) method, 247

.dot operator, 157, 163

Double data type, 129

double type mapping, 69

dynamic SQL generation, in Hibernate, 43–45

dynamic web projects, creating, 238–241

dynamic-insert property, 44–45

dynamic-update property, 44–45

■ E

EAGER FetchMode option, 173

EHCache, 205–206

ehcache.xml file, 205, 209, 241

EJB (Enterprise JavaBeans), 3, 9

Ejb3-persistence.jar library, 4

<element> tag, 139

Embeddable property, 52

EMF (EntityManagerFactory), 24

empty key word, 157

EmptyInterceptor class, 190–191

enableFilter( ) method, 189

END value, MatchMode class, 171

EnhancedUserType extension, 81

Enterprise JavaBeans (EJB), 3, 9

entities

    mapping with tables per class hierarchy, 70–74

    mapping with tables per concrete class, 78–80

    mapping with tables per subclass, 74–78

    naming in Hibernate, 45–48

Entity annotation, 69, 80

Entity class type, 49

EntityManager class, 21, 23–24, 223

EntityManager.createQuery( ) method, 155

EntityManagerFactory (EMF), 24

EntityManagerFactory class, 23, 183

Entity-relationship (ER), 1

equals( ) method, 39, 41, 62, 67, 82, 146, 169

EqualsBuilder class, 41

ER (Entity-relationship), 1

evictCollection( ) method, 215

EXACT value, 171

example, querying by, 176–177

exampleSQLInjection( ) method, 158–159

explicit joins, 163

extends keyword, 71

Extensible Markup Language (XML), Hibernate mapping, 34–37, 50–52

■ F

factories

    global session, creating, 242

    using to centralize DAO retrieval, 259

factory.getCurrentSession( ) method, 262–263

features, pagination, 157–158

fetch attribute, 107

fetch keyword, 102

fetching associations, 165

FetchMode API, 173

FetchMode options, 173

FetchMode.JOIN option, 173–174

FetchMode.SELECT option, 174

filter definition, 187

<filter> element, 189

<filter-def> element, 187–188

<filter-param> element, 188

finally block, 223

find( ) method, 184

findAll( ) method, 257

findById( ) method, 257, 261

first-level caches, 207–208

float type mapping, 69

flush( ) method, 193–195

forClass( ) method, 168

foreign keys

    creating one-to-one associations using, 107–108

    mapping one-to-many associations with, 137–141

    mapping one-to-many bidirectional associations using, 142–144

from clause, 164, 172, 196

FrontBaseDialect, 18

■ G

ge method, 169

GeneratedValue annotation, 38

generator attribute, 33

generators

hilo, 37

increment, 36–37

native, 35–36

generic objects, 257–258

GenericGenerator annotation, 121

get( ) method, 16, 180, 184, 186–187

getCurrentSession( ) method, 16

getEnabledFilter(String filterName) method, 189

getExecutableCriteria( ) method, 168

getFilterDefinition( ) method, 190

getPropertyNames method, 91

getPropertyValue method, 91

getReference( ) method, 184

getTransaction( ) method, 223

global session factories, creating, 242

group by clause, 165–166, 175

groupings, 175–176

gt method, 169

■ H

hashCode( ) method, 39, 41, 62, 67, 82, 146

HashCodeBuilder class, 41

HashSet data type, 129

HashSet property, 115–116

Hashtable cache, 206

having clause, 165–166

hbm files, 14

hbm2ddl.auto option, 109

Hibernate library, 13

Hibernate Query Language (HQL)

creating report queries, 165–166

joins

explicit, 163

fetching associations, 165

implicit, 164

matching text, 164

outer, 164

overview, 155

using query objects

from clauses, 156

creating, 156

named queries, 160

overview, 155

pagination feature, 157–158

parameter binding, 158–160

where clause, 157

using select clause, 161–162

Hibernate XML mapping, 50–52

hibernate_unique_key table, 37

Hibernate3.jar library, 4

HibernateAnnotation package, 17

Hibernate-annotations.jar library, 4

hibernate-annotations.jar library, 18

HibernateBookDao class, 258

hibernate.cache.use_minimal_puts setting, 212

hibernate.cfg.xml file, 14–15, 18, 22–24, 30, 182–183, 209

Hibernate-commons-annotations.jar library, 4

Hibernate.connection.datasource property, 224

hibernate.connection.isolation property, 231

Hibernate-entitymanager.jar library, 4

hibernate.generate_statistics property, 28

HibernateGenericDao class, 257

Hibernate.initialize( ) method, 103

Hibernate.initialize(book.getChapters( )) method, 133

hibernate-mapping element, 45, 187

hibernate.properties file, 14, 16

hibernate.transaction_factory property, 183

hibernate.transaction.auto_close_session property, 226

hibernate.transaction.factory_class property, 221, 224

hibernate.transaction.flush_before_completion property, 226

hibernate.transaction.manager_lookup property, 224

hibernate.transaction.manager_lookup_property, 37

hilo generators, 37

Host Name property, 224

HQL. *See* Hibernate Query Language (HQL)

HSQLDB (Hyper Structured Query Language Database), 35

HSQLDialect, 18

Hyper Structured Query Language Database (HSQLDB), 35

■ I

id element, 33, 36, 232

id property, 96

idbag association, 121

idbag element, 118, 120

<idbag> tag, 61, 115

idCardNo business key, 42

idCardNo property, 39–40

Identifier type, 36–37

identifier(isbn) property, Book class, 250

identifiers, using JPA to generate, 38

idEq method, 170

idle_test_period parameter, 221

IDs, for persistence

Hibernate XML mapping, 34–37

overview, 33

using hilo generators, 37

using increment generators, 36–37

using JPA to generate identifiers, 38

using native generators, 35–36

ignoreCase( ) method, 169

ilike method, 170

implicit joins, 164

import element, 45–46

in method, 170

include attribute, <cache> element, 207

increment generators, 36–37

index element, 122

IndexColumn property, 123

InformixDialect, 18

IngresDialect, 18

inheritance

CompositeUserType mappings, 87–94

custom mappings, 81–87

mapping entities with table per class hierarchy, 70–74

mapping entities with table per concrete class, 78–80

mapping entities with table per subclass, 74–78

overview, 69

Inheritance annotation, 73, 76, 80

inner join fetch query, 165

inner query, 171

inner select, 171

INSERT operation, 45

INSERT statement, 12, 43

inserting, batches, 194–195

int data type, 231

Integer data type, 66, 129, 231

integer type mapping, 69

InterbaseDialect, 18

interceptors, 190–192

inverse attribute, 143–144, 147

inverseJoinColumns attribute, 102

ISBN property, 11, 36

isbn type, 43

isbn variable, 21

isEmpty method, 170

isMutable method, 82

isNotEmpty method, 170

isNotNull method, 170

isNull method, 170

■ J

Java applications, using programmatic transactions in, 220–223

Java Database Connectivity (JDBC), 3, 7, 183

Java Development Kit (JDK), 238

Java Naming and Directory Interface (JNDI), 15, 241

Java Persistence API (JPA)

    annotations, 52–54

    using to generate identifiers, 38

Java Runtime Environment (JRE), 238

Java Transaction API (JTA), using programmatic transactions with, 223–227

Java virtual machine (JVM), 128

java:/comp/env/ namespace, 241

java.io.Serializable interface, 40

java.lang.Comparable interface, 129

java.lang.Integer class, 43

java.lang.Long class, 43

java.lang.String class, 69

java.sql.Types class, 82

Javassist-3.9.0.GA.jar library, 4

java.util.Collection property, 115, 118

java.util.Comparator interface, 130

java.util.Date class, 69

java.util.HashSet property, 115

java.util.List property, 118, 122, 124

java.util.Map property, 126

java.util.Map type, 66

java.util.Set class, 61–62

java.util.Set collection, 115

java.util.Set interface, 115

java.util.Set property, 115–116

javax.persistence.Persistence class, 183

javax.persistence.Query interface, 155

JBoss Cache, 205–206

JDBC (Java Database Connectivity), 3, 7, 183

jdbc.batch_size attribute, 193

JDBCTransactionFactory class, 221, 224

JDK (Java Development Kit), 238

JNDI (Java Naming and Directory Interface), 15, 241

JNDI Name property, 224

join element, 111–112

join fetch query, 165

JOIN FetchMode option, 173

join keyword, 157, 163–164

join query, 165

join tables

    creating many-to-many bidirectional associations with, 150–153

    creating one-to-one associations using, 109–113

    mapping many-to-many unidirectional associations with, 148–150

    mapping one-to-many bidirectional associations using, 145–148

    using many-to-one associations with, 99–102

<join> element, 100–101

JoinColumn annotation, 108

joinColumns attribute, 102

joined-subclass class, 76

joined-subclass element, 76

joins

    explicit, 163

    fetching associations, 165

    implicit, 164

    matching text, 164

    outer, 164

JoinTable annotation, 101, 112, 118

JPA (Java Persistence API). *See* Java Persistence API (JPA)

JPA query language

    creating report queries, 165–166

    joins

        explicit, 163

        fetching associations, 165

        implicit, 164

        matching text, 164

        outer, 164

    using query objects

        from clauses, 156

        creating, 156

        named queries, 160

        overview, 155

        pagination feature, 157–158

        parameter binding, 158–160

        where clause, 157

    using select clause, 161–162

JRE (Java Runtime Environment), 238

JTA (Java Transaction API), using programmatic transactions with, 223–227

JTA transaction type, 24

Jta-1.1.jar library, 4

JTATransactionFactory class, 223–224

JVM (Java virtual machine), 128

■ K

key element, 76, 116, 122

<key> mapping, 109

<key-many-to-one> mappings, 39

<key-property> property mappings, 39

keys, composite, 38–42

■ L

Launch class, 34

lazy associations, navigating, 261

lazy attribute, 107

lazy fetching attribute level, 207

LAZY FetchMode option, 174

lazy initializations

    overview, 133–135

    using on many-to-one associations, 102–103

lazy keyword, 102

lazy option, FetchMode API, 174

lazy property, 133

LazyInitializationException, 133

le method, 170

left join fetch query, 164–165

left outer join, 164

lib/ejb3-persistence.jar library, 18

lib/hibernate-comons-annotations.jar library, 18

Libraries tab, Eclipse, 13

list element, 73

List mapping annotation, 125

list( ) method, 180

List property, 125, 127

list type, 122

<list> element, 61, 122, 124, 126

listing, persistent objects, 242–243

lists, mapping, 122–123

load( ) method, 16, 40, 180, 184, 236

locale type mapping, 69

lock( ) method, 234, 236

LockMode.FORCE option, 235

LockMode.NONE option, 235

LockMode.READ option, 235

LockModeType.READ option, 235

LockModeType.Write option, 235

LockMode.UPGRADE option, 235

LockMode.UPGRADE_NOWAIT option, 235

log4j.jar file, 28

log4j.properties file, 28, 241

LoggableUserType extension, 81

logging, enabling in Hibernate, 27–28

long data type, 43

long type mapping, 69

lost updates, 228

lt method, 169

■ M

main( ) method, 158

many-to-many bidirectional associations, creating with join tables, 150–153

many-to-many unidirectional associations, mapping with join tables, 148–150

<many-to-many> element, 145–146

many-to-one associations

    problems with, 95–96

    solutions for, 96

    using lazy initializations on, 95–103

    using with join tables, 99–102

many-to-one element, 73, 111

many-valued associations

    creating many-to-many bidirectional with join tables, 150–153

    mapping many-to-many unidirectional with join tables, 148–150

    mapping one-to-many associations with foreign keys, 137–141

    mapping one-to-many bidirectional using foreign keys, 142–144

    mapping one-to-many bidirectional using join tables, 145–148

Map property, 126

<map> element, 61, 126–128

MapKey annotation, 127

<map-key> element, 127

mappedBy attribute, 108, 144

mappedby attribute, 146

mappedBy attribute, 147

MappedSuperClass annotation, 69

mapping

    arrays, 124–125

    bags, 118–121

    collection, of components, 61–64

    CompositeUserType, 87–94

    creating composite keys in Hibernate, 38–42

    creating one-to-one association using join tables, 109–113

    creating one-to-one associations using foreign key, 107–108

    custom. See custom mapping

    definitions, creating, 13–14

    dynamic SQL generation in Hibernate, 43–45

lists, 122–123

many-to-many unidirectional associations with join tables, 148–150

maps, 126–128

naming entities in Hibernate, 45–48

one-to-many associations with foreign keys, 137–141

one-to-many bidirectional associations using foreign keys, 142–144

one-to-many bidirectional associations using join tables, 145–148

providing IDs for persistence

    Hibernate XML mapping, 34–37

    problems with, 33

    solutions for, 33

    using hilo generators, 37

    using increment generators, 36–37

    using JPA to generate identifiers, 38

    using native generators, 35–36

SaveOrUpdate in Hibernate, 42–43

sets, 115–121

sharing primary key associations, 104–106

using lazy initializations on many-to-one associations, 102–103

using many-to-one association with join tables, 99–102

using many-to-one associations, 95–98

XML Hibernate, 34–37

maps

    mapping, 126–128

    using components as keys to, 66–67

MatchMode class, 171

MAX aggregate function, 175

max( ) function, 161, 165

max_lo option, 37

max_size parameter, 221

max_statements parameter, 221

merge( ) method, 186–187

merging, detached objects, 186–187

META-INF folder, 156, 183

MIN aggregate function, 175

min( ) function, 161, 165

min_size parameter, 221

Model-View-Controller (MVC), 237

modifying, persistent objects, 185

Multiversion concurrency control, 220

MVC (Model-View-Controller), 237

MySQLDialect, 18

■ N

name attribute, 21, 160

name component, 49

name property, 156

named queries, 160, 199–201

NamedQuery.hbm.xml file, 160

native generators, 35–36

native SQL

    named SQL queries, 199–201

    using, 197–199

natural order, 129

navigating lazy associations, 261

<nested-composite-element> tag, 62

nesting components, 55–57

new keyword, 183

new operator, 179–180

next_hi column, 37

not operator, 157

nullSafeGet method, 82, 91

nullSafeSet method, 82, 91

■ O

object identity
    creating composite keys in Hibernate, 38–42
    dynamic SQL generation in Hibernate, 43–45
    naming entities in Hibernate, 45–48
    providing IDs for persistence
        Hibernate XML mapping, 34–37
        problems with, 33
        solutions for, 33
        using hilo generators, 37
        using increment generators, 36–37
        using JPA to generate identifiers, 38
        using native generators, 35–36
    SaveOrUpdate in Hibernate, 42–43
object model, 1
Object[] array, 166
Object[] elements, 161, 163
object/relational mapping (ORM), 2, 9, 95, 242
objects
    data access, organizing in, 255–256
    detached
        merging, 186–187
        reattaching, 186
    generic, 257–258
    graphs of
        persisting, 11–12
        retrieving, 10–11
    identifying states of
        detached objects, 180–181
        persistent objects, 180
        removed objects, 181
        transient objects, 179

persistent
    creating, 182–184, 249–250
    deleting, 185, 252–253
    listing, 242–243
    modifying, 185
    retrieving, 184
    updating, 244–247
query
    from clauses, 156
    creating, 156
    named queries, 160
    overview, 155
    pagination feature, 157–158
    parameter binding, 158–160
    where clause, 157
    retrieving, 16–17
    using data filters, 187–190
    using interceptors, 190–192
one-to-many associations, mapping with foreign keys, 137–141
one-to-many bidirectional associations
    mapping using foreign keys, 142–144
    mapping using join tables, 145–148
one-to-one associations
    creating using foreign key, 107–108
    creating using join tables, 109–113
one-to-one element, 73, 104–105
online bookshops, developing, 242
onSave( ) method, 190–191
open sessions, using in view patterns, 262–264
optimistic concurrency controls, enabling, 228–233
optimistic-lock attribute, 233
optional property, 101

or operator, 157

order by clause, 132, 166

Order class, 172

OrderBy annotation, 133

order-by attribute, 128, 132

order-by clause, 128

order-by condition, 128, 132

Order.price.unitPrice property, 172

Orders class, 50–52, 54, 63, 66

ORDERS table, 49

Orders XML file, 60

ORDERS_CONTACT table, 64

Orders.xml file, 56

org.hibernate.annotations.Type annotation, 86

org.hibernate.cache.CacheProvider class, 206

org.hibernate.cache.EHCacheProvider class, 206

org.hibernate.cache.HashtableCacheProvider class, 206

org.hibernate.cache.JBossCacheProvider class, 206

org.hibernate.cache.OSCacheProvider class, 206

org.hibernate.cache.QueryCache region, 216

org.hibernate.cache.SwarmCacheProvider class, 206

org.hibernate.criterion package, 169

org.hibernate.dialect.DerbyDialect property, 18

org.hibernate.dialect.Oracle9Dialect property, 18

org.hibernate.LazyInitializationException, 184

org.hibernate.ObjectNotFoundException, 16, 184

org.hibernate.Query interface, 155, 207

org.hibernate.Session objects, 15

org.hibernate.transaction.WeblogicTransaction ManagerLookup class, 224

org.hibernate.type package, 69

org.hibernate.type.Type package, 69

org.hibernate.userType package, 69–70, 81

original parameter, 82

ORM (object/relational mapping), 2, 9, 95, 242

OSCache, 205–206

out variable, 242

outer joins, 164

OutOfMemory error, 193

■ P

Package attribute, 45

package option, 45

page variable, 242

pageContext variable, 242

pagination feature, 157–158

parameter binding, 158–160

ParameterizedType extension, 81

parent class, 71

<parent> tag, 58

Password property, 224

patterns, using open session in, 262–264

Period class, 66

persist( ) method, 183–184

persistence context cache, 204

persistence, providing IDs for
    Hibernate XML mapping, 34–37
    problems with, 33
    solutions for, 33
    using hilo generators, 37
    using increment generators, 36–37
    using JPA to generate identifiers, 38
    using native generators, 35–36

Persistence.createEntityManagerFactory method, 25

persistence-unit tag, persistence.xml file, 25

<persistence-unit> tag, 24

persistence.xml file, 24–25, 156, 183

persistent objects

creating, 182–184, 249–250

deleting, 185, 252–253

listing, 242–243

modifying, 185

overview, 180–181

retrieving, 184

updating, 244–247

pessimistic concurrency controls, 219, 234–236

phone class, 81

phone object, 81

phone property, 51, 56

Phone type, 56

PhoneUserType, 86

Plain Old Java Objects (POJOs), 9

PointbaseDialect, 18

POJOs (Plain Old Java Objects), 9

POM (project object model), 4

POM.XML file, 4

pools, configuring, 241

Port property, 224

PostgreSQLDialect, 18

PreparedStatement, 12

price property, 43

PrimaryKeyJoinColumn annotation, 77, 105

Process scope, cached data, 204

programmatic configuration, 14–15

programmatic transactions

using in standalone Java applications, 220–223

using with JTA, 223–227

ProgressDialect, 18

project object model (POM), 4

projections, 165–166, 174–176

Projections class, 175

projects

dynamic web, creating, 238–241

Eclipse, creating, 7

JAP, configuring, 17–23

.properties file, 14

<properties> tag, 42

property element, 73, 81

property_ref attribute, 107

<provider> tag, 24

providers, of caches, 205–207

Publisher class, 96, 98, 213, 241

Publisher entity, 5, 99, 101–102

Publisher mapping definition, 198

publisher object, 11, 97

Publisher property, 97, 173

PUBLISHER table, 99, 102, 198

Publisher type, 97

Publisher_Id column, 99, 101–102

publisherId field, 172

publisherName field, 161

publisher.name property, 173

■ Q

QBE (Query by Example), 3, 176–177

queries

caching, 215–217

named SQL, 199–201

report, creating, 165–166

query attribute, 160

Query by Example (QBE), 3, 176–177

query objects

from clauses, 156

creating, 156

named queries, 160

overview, 155

pagination feature, 157–158

parameter binding, 158–160

where clause, 157

query results, caching, 207

querying

overview, 167

Query by Example (QBE), 176–177

using Criteria, 168, 172–174

using projections, 174–176

using restrictions, 169–171

query.list( ) method, 196

Query.setCacheable(true) method, 216

■ **R**

Read Committed isolation level, 230–231

READ lock, 235

Read Uncommitted isolation level, 230–231

readAll method, 23

read-only cache usage, 210

read-write cache usage, 211

reattaching, detached objects, 186

recipes.cfg.xml file, 16

recipient property, 51

references, adding in components, 58–60

region attribute, <cache> element, 207

regions, of caches, 207

relational models, 1, 5

remove( ) method, 181, 185

removed objects, 181

Repeatable Read isolation level, 230–231

replace method, 82

report queries, creating, 165–166

request variable, 242

Reservation class, 72

RESOURCE_LOCAL transaction type, 24

response variable, 242

restrictions, 169–171

Restrictions class, 169, 171

ResultSet colection, 12, 196

ResultSet collection, 196

retrieving, persistent objects, 184

<return> element, 199–200

returnedClass method, 82

<return-join> element, 199–200

<return-scalar> element, 200

rollback method, 222

RuntimeExceptions, 222

■ **S**

save( ) method, 180, 183

SaveOrUpdate, in Hibernate, 42–43

saveOrUpdate( ) method, 98, 180, 257

schema attribute, 111

SchemaExport, generating database schema using, 30

schemaexport task, 30

schemaupdate task, 30

SchemaUpdate, updating database schema using, 30

second-level caches

cache providers, 205–207

cache regions, 207

caching associations, 212–213

caching collections, 213–215

caching queries, 215–217

caching query results, 207

concurrency strategies, 205

configuring, 209–211

overview, 204

using first-level caches, 207–208

select clause, 156, 161–162, 165

SELECT clause, 198, 200–201

select count(...) subquery, 157

SELECT FetchMode option, 174

select for update nowait query, 235

select ... for update query, 235

SELECT query, 171, 174

SELECT statement, 12

select-before-update property, 186

SequenceHiLoGenerator class, 37

sequences, database, 35

serializability property, 220

Serializable interface, 39

Serializable isolation level, 230–231

Serializable property, 21

serializable type mapping, 69

Serialization mechanism, 220

Servers project, 241

server.xml file, 241

Session API, 194

session factories, global, 242

Session interface, 182

Session object, 16, 22

Session transaction, 37

session variable, 242

session.beginTransaction( ) method, 222

session.clear( ) method, 196

session.close( ) method, 226

session.createQuery("from AudioDisc").list( )
query, 74

session.createQuery("from Disc").list( ) query,
74

SessionFactory class, 22–23, 183, 190, 204, 209,
225

sessionFactory.getCurrentSession( ) method,
192

sessionFactory.openSession( ) method, 222

session.flush( ) method, 196, 226

session.get( ) method, 234

session.getNamedQuery( ) method, 160

session.lock method, 235

sessions

closing, 16

opening, 16, 22–23

using in view patterns, 262–264

session.save statement, 140

session.save(book) method, 139–140

session.save(chapter) method, 139–140

session.saveOrUpdate( ) method, 141, 250

session.saveUpdate statement, 140

session.setCacheMode (CacheMode.IGNORE)
method, 193–194

<set> element, 61–62, 115–116, 128, 149–150

<set> mapping, 115

setAttribute( ) method, 242

setCacheable( ) method, 207

setFirstResult(int beginPoint) method, 158

setMaxResult(int size) method, 158

setPropertyValue method, 91

sets, mapping, 115–121

short type mapping, 69

show_sql property, 28

Simple Logging Facade for Java (SLF4J), 27

SINGLE_TABLE type, 73

size( ) function, 157

size property, 157

SLF4J (Simple Logging Facade for Java), 27

Slf4j-api-1.5.8.jar library, 4

slf4j-api.jar file, 28

slf4j-log4j12.jar file, 28

Slf4j-simple1.5.8.jar library, 4

sort annotation, 129

sort attribute, 129–130

SQL (Structured Query Language)

    dynamic generation, in Hibernate, 43–45

    native

        using, 197–199

        using named SQL queries, 199–201

        statements issued by Hibernate, inspecting, 28

SQL injection, 158

SQLQuery interface, 197

<sql-query> element, 200

sqlTypes method, 82

sqlTypes( ) method, 87

standalone Java applications, using programmatic transactions in, 220–223

START value, MatchMode class, 171

states, of objects

    detached objects, 180–181

    persistent objects, 180

    removed objects, 181

    transient objects, 179

static block, 242

static method, 225

statistics, live, 28–29

strategy type, 76

strategy value, 38

Strict two-phase locking mechanism, 220

string attribute, 173

String type, 56, 66, 129

String type mapping, 69

String[] property, 124–125

String-type property, 39

Structured Query Language. *See* SQL

subclass, mapping entities with table per, 74–78

subqueries, writing, 171

sum( ) function, 161, 165, 175

superclass, 71

SwarmCache, 205–206

SybaseDialect, 18

■ T

Table annotation, 21

table attribute, 76, 101

TABLE_PER_CLASS inheritance type strategy, 80

tables

    creating, 5

    join

        creating one-to-one associations using, 109–113

        using many-to-one associations with, 99–102

    mapping entities with

        per class hierarchy, 70–74

        per concrete class, 78–80

        per subclass, 74–78

telNo property, phone object, 81

text, matching, 164

text type mapping, 69

time type mapping, 69

timeout parameter, 221

timestamp element, 233

timestamp type mapping, 69

Time-stamp-based control, 220

timeToIdleSeconds parameter, 209

timeToLiveSeconds parameter, 209

timezone type mapping, 69

TOP_SELLING_BOOK view, 198

transaction boundaries, 219

transaction demarcation, 219

transaction schedule, 220

Transaction scope, 204

TransactionManagerLookup class, 37

transactions

    enabling optimistic concurrency controls, 228–233

    overview, 219

    programmatic

        using in standalone Java applications, 220–223

        using with JTA, 223–227

    using pessimistic concurrency controls, 234–236

transient objects, 179

TreeMap data type, 129

TreeSet data type, 129

true_false type mapping, 69

try block, 103

try/catch block, 222

Two-phase locking mechanism, 220

type attribute, 33

■ U

union-subclass element, 78, 80

unique attribute, 111, 146

unique constraint property, 107

uniqueResult( ) method, 17, 159, 169

unitPrice field, 172

unrepeatable read, 229

update( ) method, 181, 186

UPDATE query, 196–197

UPDATE statement, 12, 43

updating

    batches, 195–197

persistent objects, 244–247

UPGRADE option, 235

usage attribute, 207

User property, 224

UserCollectionType extension, 81

UserRank class, 187–188

UserRank mapping file, 188

UserTransaction interface, 223

userType extension, 70, 87

UserType interface, 82, 86–87

UserType mapping, 81

UserVersionType extension, 81

■ V

validate( ) method, 190

Value class type, 49

value object type, 49

value type instances, 81, 115, 126

value type object, 49

value types, implementing as components

    problems with, 49

    solutions for, 49

        using Hibernate XML mapping, 50–52

        using JPA annotations, 52–54

VARCHAR, 69

version column, 232

Version element, 232

version property, 231

version variable, 232

VideoDisc class, 9, 71–74, 79

view patterns, using open session in, 262–264

■ W

web applications

  bookshop, creating controller for

    configuring connection pools, 241

    creating dynamic web projects, 238–241

    creating global session factories, 242

    creating persistent objects, 249–250

    deleting persistent objects, 252–253

    developing online bookshops, 242

    listing persistent objects, 242–243

    updating persistent objects, 244–247

  creating data-access layers

    navigating lazy associations, 261

    organizing in data access objects, 255–256

    overview, 254

    using factories to centralize DAO retrieval, 259

    using generic objects, 257–258

    using open sessions in view patterns, 262–264

  overview, 237

Web Tools Platform (WTP), 238

WebContent/WEB-INF/lib directory, 240

web.xml file, 263

where clause, 157, 168–169, 172, 195

writing comparators, 130–131

writing subqueries, 171

WTP (Web Tools Platform), 238

■ X

XML (Extensible Markup Language), 34–37, 50–52

■ Y

yes_no type mapping, 69

You Need the Companion eBook

Your purchase of this book entitles you to buy the companion PDF-version eBook for only $10. Take the weightless companion with you anywhere.

We believe this Apress title will prove so indispensable that you'll want to carry it with you everywhere, which is why we are offering the companion eBook (in PDF format) for $10 to customers who purchase this book now. Convenient and fully searchable, the PDF version of any content-rich, page-heavy Apress book makes a valuable addition to your programming library. You can easily find and copy code—or perform examples by quickly toggling between instructions and the application. Even simultaneously tackling a donut, diet soda, and complex code becomes simplified with hands-free eBooks!

Once you purchase your book, getting the $10 companion eBook is simple:

❶ Visit **www.apress.com/promo/tendollars/**.

❷ Complete a basic registration form to receive a randomly generated question about this title.

❸ Answer the question correctly in 60 seconds, and you will receive a promotional code to redeem for the $10.00 eBook.

THE EXPERT'S VOICE™

233 Spring Street, New York, NY 10013

Offer valid through 11/10.